"Probably the most comprehensive book in the field today, Stone's narrative allows the reader to go inside a building's life, connecting architectural theory with contemporary art and environmental science to interrogate its layers of history and changes over time."

Markus Berger, Associate Professor and Graduate Program Director, Department of Interior Architecture, Rhode Island School of Design

"An invaluable reference book, *Undoing Buildings* illuminates the myriad attitudes and strategies brought to existing buildings and their accumulated meanings in the manner of preparatory literature for a studio or workshop, in which precedents and their attendant histories and thought are exposed to both enlighten and empower the participant."

Mark Pimlott, TU Delft, Netherlands, author of *Without and Within*, and *The Public Interior as Idea and Project*

"The 21st century is the era of the circular economy. This book is an authoritative and compelling guide to understanding the ideas and values of these approaches to the built environment. It is an essential read for those who want a comprehensive introduction to the fundamental thinking behind building reuse and the formation of the architectured and designed interior."

Professor Graeme Brooker, Chair of Interior Design, Royal College of Art, London

"Sally Stone's book is an important contribution to the emerging discipline of adaptive reuse and its growing theoretical framework. Her attractive discourse considers the built environment as a palimpsest not frozen in the past, but as a possibility for future programs."

Prof. Koenraad Van Cleempoel, Faculty of Architecture & Arts, Hasselt University

"This book provides, aside from an intelligent and inspirational state of the art of an interiorist's approach towards existing buildings, a provocative expansion of the existing body of theory on adaptive reuse. Stone's coherent and captious picture will greatly help students and academics interested in the past and future of our built environment."

Inge Somers, Faculty of Design Sciences, Interior Architecture Program, University of Antwerp

"Buildings witness change over time made visible through physical renovations. These changes are initiated by historical events unrecorded but evident in the appearance of architecture. Sally Stone draws together these narratives of the tangible and intangible to give voice to the latent stories embedded in the history of buildings."

**Lois Weinthal, Chair and Professor,
School of Interior Design, Ryerson University**

UNDOING BUILDINGS

UnDoing Buildings: Adaptive Reuse and Cultural Memory discusses one of the greatest challenges for twenty-first-century society: what is to be done with the huge stock of existing buildings that have outlived the function for which they were built? Their worth is well recognised and the importance of retaining them has been long debated, but if they are to be saved, what is to be done with these redundant buildings?

This book argues that remodelling is a healthy and environmentally friendly approach. Issues of heritage, conservation, sustainability and smartness are at the forefront of many discussions about architecture today and adaptive reuse offers the opportunity to reinforce the particular character of an area using up-to-date digital and construction techniques for a contemporary population. Issues of collective memory and identity combined with ideas of tradition, history and culture mean that it is possible to retain a sense of continuity with the past as a way of creating the future.

UnDoing Buildings: Adaptive Reuse and Cultural Memory has an international perspective and will be of interest to upper level students and professionals working on the fields of Interior Design, Interior Architecture, Architecture, Conservation, Urban Design and Development.

Sally Stone lives in the north of England. She has been designing, formulating ideas and writing about building reuse for 30 years. Sally is a Reader at the Manchester School of Architecture where she leads the Master of Architecture programme.

UNDOING BUILDINGS

Adaptive Reuse and Cultural Memory

Sally Stone

Routledge
Taylor & Francis Group

NEW YORK AND LONDON

First published 2020
by Routledge
52 Vanderbilt Avenue, New York, NY 10017

and by Routledge
2 Park Square, Milton Park, Abingdon, Oxon, OX14 4RN

Routledge is an imprint of the Taylor & Francis Group, an informa business

© 2020 Taylor & Francis

Library of Congress Cataloging-in-Publication Data
Names: Stone, Sally, author.
Title: UnDoing buildings : adaptive reuse and cultural memory / Sally Stone.
Description: New York : Routledge, 2019. |
Includes bibliographical references and index.
Identifiers: LCCN 2019008478 | ISBN 9781138226616 (hardback) |
ISBN 9781138226630 (pbk.) | ISBN 9781315397221 (e-book)
Subjects: LCSH: Architecture–Conservation and restoration. |
Buildings–Remodeling for other use. | Architecture and society.
Classification: LCC NA105 .S75 2019 | DDC 720.1/03–dc23
LC record available at https://lccn.loc.gov/2019008478

ISBN: 9781138226616 (hbk)
ISBN: 9781138226630 (pbk)
ISBN: 9781315397221 (ebk)

Typeset in Bembo
by Newgen Publishing UK

For My Father
Peter William Stone

CONTENTS

x   Contents

ACKNOWLEDGEMENTS

I would like to thank the Manchester School of Architecture for its support while writing this book, especially to the Head of School Tom Jefferies for always saying yes to every barmy suggestion that I might make. Graeme Brooker has been a great friend and writing partner over many projects, indeed a couple of these chapters were once, in much much earlier incarnations, developed together. Katie Hickson conducted valuable research about Corn Exchange in Winchester discussed in Chapter 1. Inge Somers has proved to be a great inspiration and confidant, Bie Plevoets and Koenraad van Cleempoel have provided encouragement and friendship, Ed Hollis has very generously written the foreword, while Eamonn Canniffe, John Lee and Laura Sanderson have always indulged me. As always, I would like to thank Reuben, Ivan and Agnes for their constant interruptions, and of course Dominic for his unwavering support.

MOTIVATION

I embarked upon the Masters in Interior Design course at the old Manchester Polytechnic in the 1980s, studying under Les Maden, Mike Gittoes and Neil Verow. They all encouraged an intellectual and analytical approach to design. The theory of Post-modernism was just becoming an important and influential idea, and the course encouraged the all-encompassing, both/and method which epitomised those early years. Education at that time actively encouraged cross-disciplinary interaction, academics had time to indulge students and so it was common for Joe Jessop and Dave Ellis from the school of architecture to attend reviews of the interior design students' work, and so I was privileged to witness long debates about the position of interior architecture within the world, within Manchester and within the theories of contextualism; and I was introduced to the Nolli plan. I can still vividly remember at a moment of great revelation, Gittoes taking Joe's head in his hands, then kissing his forehead.

The architectural culture of Manchester in the 1980s was receptive to this contextual approach. Forced by the lack of opportunities for newbuild, architects and designers were developing the city from the inside out. This led to a particularly creative approach, one which could not have existed anywhere else. The massive brick Victorian warehouses, many of which still occupied prominent positions within the city, were remodelled, reshaped, re-ordered. Their importance to the history and culture of the city was never in question, and so the development of ideas about their regeneration was part of local architectural life. The grandeur of this industrial legacy created a sort of humility, a realisation that within the cities of the industrial revolution a new form of spatial production was needed. Something that would invest decaying fabric with meaning and use, and in an attempt to claim the space of the warehouse and the factory, the understanding that old rules of Modernism were no longer appropriate and function could follow form.

Another great influence was the Manchester based architect, Roger Stephenson, for whom I worked after leaving university. The practice was years ahead of its time; it didn't distinguish between architecture and interiors. Everyone seemed to be practising both, there was no hierarchy and certainly no snobbery about the quality and worth of the projects. The interests lay within the urban grain of the city, and the importance of appreciating how to directly interact with it, and we were encouraged to take an encompassing approach to the design of everything; nothing was left to chance, nothing un-detailed.

I started life as an academic on the highly influential Interior Architecture course in Cardiff. Mike Fleetwood and Patrick Hannay had created an extraordinary organisation dedicated to the intellectual pursuit of Interior Design. They saw the subject as akin to or even greater than architecture – the purposeful manipulation of space within a realistic urban context rather than as stage dressing. I probably learnt more from them than I ever managed to impart to the students. Their status was such that many important visitors travelled across the land to speak to our students. It was one of the first courses to be called Interior Architecture, and the relationship between place and space became on enduring theme. We observed the introduction of an eclectic, questing approach, something particular to design courses, which was not bound to the orthodoxies and professional conventions of the architecture schools. In Cardiff we mined the history of architecture and industrial design to create a new approach through which the space as product, collided with built fabric, interpreted as a receptacle of memory and history.

The 1980s and 1990s were an extraordinary time; due to the post-modern ideas of such thinkers and architects as Rowe and Koetter, Rossi, Derrida, Machado and Stirling. Contextualism was beginning to be seen as a force, while ideas of heritage, history, memory and appropriation were at the forefront of urban development. Post-modernism helped, it created an architectural approach to ephemeral commercial and retail spaces that was driven by irony and memory, combined with an understanding that the architecture of consumerism could display a lightness of touch and responsiveness to fashion. Architects and designers started to question their pre-eminence in the design process and started to learn and accept approaches to the reconfiguration and refreshment of tired space. Hans Hollein epitomised this duality. He explored a frivolous, almost whimsical approach to the design of shops and offices. These spaces which had once contained a serious and dependable hierarchical intent were invigorated with an amusing and playful determination. And the act of interpretation and remembering in Scarpa's work allowed us to create narratives in relation to existing buildings, stories about our place within a rich continuity of forms and spaces.

In the mid-1990s I moved to the Manchester School of Architecture to work with Dominic Roberts, and together we built the college of Continuity in Architecture. This is a studio for the design of new buildings and public spaces within the historic city and interventions within existing buildings. The college believes in the importance of place and that the design of architecture could be influenced by the experience and analysis of particular situations. The act of interpretation and remembering allowed us to create narratives in relation to existing buildings, stories about our place within a rich continuity of forms and spaces. As well as this we saw the possibilities of sustainability before the term was fully coined; building reuse, passive methods of environmental control, up-cycling and interventions within the urban environment are all ecologically sound approaches to architecture and design.

And so, as the twenty-first century advances, Continuity in Architecture is a thriving and fundamental element of the school and hundreds of students have been encouraged and instructed. They leave the university with a modest and creative attitude towards design and architecture, with an understanding of how to think and how to take a sensitive and appropriate approach to the development of the built environment. Lecturers Laura Sanderson and John Lee, with Eamonn Canniffe, have become energetic advocates of this contextual method of thinking. We expose our students to diverse settlements across Europe and the north of England in combination with technical and programmatic challenge, and thus, Continuity in Architecture has overseen a rich array of urban, architectural and detail solutions for the contemporary city. We have created a motto to encourage this way of thinking, something that can guide every project, in every situation: Remember, Reveal, Construct.

It was at the beginning of the twenty-first century that Graeme Brooker and I began our writing partnership: nine books and at least as many papers and presentations, all of which aim to forward the theoretical thinking about building adaptation and progress ideas about the importance of the interior and its relationship with the wider context. These ideas are not based whimsy, but upon the genuine pursuit of viable solutions to the twin global problems of population growth and urbanisation. Remodelling structures so that they are fit for the contemporary occupation has to be a progressive approach to such challenges.

And so the ideas discussed here have been part of my life for many years and thus this book is an accumulation and synthesis of this developed position. It is an opportunity to relate stories, concepts, beliefs and opinions. Some reaffirm or confirm already thought opinion, others are more radical, but all have integrity and are relevant.

FOREWORD

There's nothing new about reusing buildings – there wouldn't be, would there? People have been reusing buildings for centuries: certainly since God stopped work on site at the tower of Babel, and as this book notes: 'because their structure tends to outlive their function, buildings have continuously been adapted to new uses – a fact which has enabled generation after generation to derive a sense of continuity and stability from their physical surroundings' (P2).

The Ancients built their temples on the foundations of archaic shrines, and the barbarians who ruined them took the marble fragments as Spolia – spoils – to build buildings of their own. In the modern era, institutions from city halls to hospitals to airports have grown incrementally, forming patchwork palimpsests of structures, often without coherence or unity. It's true in the domestic sphere, too: rare it is to find an old home that has escaped a new repainting, a new bathroom, or a house extension on the back, occasioned by changes in the social makeup of the family, technology, or taste.

But, for most of their history, these practices, ubiquitous as they are, have passed largely unnoticed. Not so today: REUSE, the thing itself, and the desire to theorise it, are, to misquote Viollet le Duc, entirely contemporary, as witnessed by a plethora of recent publications including some by the author of this book herself.

This book situates the phenomenon in its own history: from Viollet's restoration of the Chateau de Pierrefonds to the charter of Athens; from Carlo Scarpa's work in the 1960s and 70s to the *grand projets* of reuse of more recent decades, from the Tate Modern to Duisberg Nord.

Nothing new in that, perhaps; but it situates that practice in a developing discourse: from Viollet to Morris, Ruskin to Riegl, Benjamin to Eco, and Arendt to Deleuze. In doing so, this book makes a particularly comprehensive philosophical case for adaptive building reuse.

Nothing new in that, either? Walter Benjamin saw reused buildings – particularly those in ruins – as concrete allegories of historical change: in which case, this book is a history of histories, a reuse of reuses: resolutely, and doubly, backward looking.

But this book isn't called *Reusing Buildings*, rather, the operative word is 'UnDoing'.

It's a word with multiple meanings.

It can involve reversing things which have been done: and conversely, it can mean doing something so awful to someone that it cannot be undone: 'I am undone!' are the last words on the lips of many a tragic hero or heroine; and in both of those usages we find allegories of building reuse, from restoration to ruination, the ethics and aesthetics of both of which are addressed in chapters in this book.

But to undo something – if it were a button, for example – is also to unfasten it, to loosen it, and to let it go: to set it free from servitude as Louis Kahn observes:

> A building being built is not yet in servitude. It is so anxious to be that no grass can grow under its feet, so high is the spirit of wanting to be. When in service and finished, the building wants to say, "look, I want to tell you about the way I was made". Nobody listens. Everybody is busy going from room to room. But when the building is a ruin and free from servitude, the spirit emerges telling of the marvel that a building was made.

It's a phenomenon that the human geographer Tim Edensor has famously observed in his account of the British Industrial Ruin; and it is something that the author of this book relates to Umberto Eco's concept of the 'open work' that 'gains its aesthetic validity in proportion to the number of different perspectives from which it can be viewed and understood.'

Buildings are not, this book would argue, machines for doing things, as Le Corbusier might have wanted them to be, but, over time, machines for *undoing* – for outliving, decoding, resisting, and subverting the imposition of single meanings, functions and occupations upon their bricks and mortar.

Just like the process of undoing a building, this book, then, pulls our idea of the building apart: particularly the idea of a building as a *thing* – an identifiable, unitary, stable structure.

In this book, buildings are no longer the *immeuble* dwelling, but *meuble* itinerant *doings*. Made of curtains (Semper's *wand* – the woven wall) they can be folded up and carried around. At the same time, they anticipate and choreograph movement within them, that, in its turn, carves and smears traces in and on their walls and floors. They form mirrors, nodes, and windows in potentially infinite networks: the author describes a particularly poignant meeting between dimensions of the contemporary real in her chapter on the 'smart' building:

> Recently I was talking to my son, when this disconnected voice wished me a good evening. I bent over towards the computer to greet the best friend, whose image occupied the whole screen. Behind him was a mirror

and reflected in the mirror was obviously his back and the computer, and on his screen was an image of me; and for a fleeting moment I could see myself reflected in the mirror of a bedroom some fifty miles away from where I was standing … intellectually I knew that it was merely a reflected image, and yet this whole process proved that physical distance was no longer an obstacle in the way of real-time visual and aural relationships … The children had embraced the technology for their own purposes: they had no reservations or qualms about using it, and neither did they respect its limitations.

And in that vein, a chapter on spatial agency explores how buildings can act as triggers for public participation and protest, and their undoers – the (re)architect and the occupant – as, in the words of Dan Hill: 'Community Enabler, Contractual Innovator, Educator of Excess, Double Agent, Strategic Designer.'

But why read this book now?

Firstly, a growing body of practice and theory relating to building reuse has brought what was once a peripheral practice into the heart of the doing of buildings: this book provides a comprehensive digest of the state of the art on the discipline.

Secondly, this recent growth in the prestige of the reused building – particularly of the beautifully crafted, historically informed, sensitive Scarpian variety – has also been accompanied by an ironic and unforeseen consequence. The author of this book asks whether our society can support any more museums; and at the Venice Biennale of 2010, Rem Koolhaas observed that everywhere, conservation was 'increasing its empire' – but had no idea what to do with it.

This book extends the vocabulary from reuse to undoing, and in doing so, addresses fields that can only expand the repertoire of inspiration, from installation art to digital media, ballet, literary translation and historiography.

The third reason is perhaps the most crucial and the most pragmatic. Even while writing this short foreword, the environmental crisis has become a great deal more urgent than it was, and, in no small part, that is due to the way we do building. In industrialised countries the building sector – through the construction and operation of buildings – accounts for about 50% of total CO_2 emissions, 20% of which stems from the production and transportation of materials. (Richarz et al. 2007: 3). And that's before we start talking about the ever-increasing proportion of the surface area of the globe that is disappearing under concrete every year. Quite simply, if we want to save energy, cut emissions, and maintain a habitable environment we shouldn't be doing buildings: we should be challenging the 'business as usual' cycle of the construction and demolition of new buildings, and, instead, exploring new ways of undoing old ones.

There's nothing new about re-using buildings – but at no time since the deluge and the aborted construction of the Tower of Babel (what did they convert it into?) is it more important to revisit our buildings, to learn how to reuse them, and to undo, as best we can, what we still can of what we have done.

Ed Hollis
October 2018

1

INTRODUCTION

This is a book about existing situations, buildings and places, and how over time these structures and locations can be allowed or even encouraged to evolve, to sustain new uses, and accommodate new users. It is a discussion about the possible strategies for adaptive reuse, strategies that are not applied as a reaction to the prevailing condition, but in anticipation of it. The idea that building reuse can be a positive and beneficial approach to the development of the built environment is no longer a radical idea; it is not something that is considered when other options are not available. However, adaptive interventions can be expected and encouraged within any situation, which suggests a positive and definite concern for the future.

Building reuse is not a new phenomenon, the act of remodelling and adaptation is almost as old as the idea of buildings themselves, but it has attained a new position at the heart of the building and construction industry. Issues of climate change and heritage have ensured that adaptation, instead of occupying the periphery of architectural concern, is now placed within the central ground of architectural practice. The sheer scale of environmental change has started to produce subtle alterations within a familiar landscape. Progressive adaptation, that is the idea that a thoughtful, rather than passive or reactive response to the situation, is possible. We are continually being told of the need to conserve our valuable resources, to reuse, recycle, upcycle, reinvent: progressive reuse is guided not by that sense of anxiety that this creates, but it can produce an effect that is considerably more careful and considered. Issues of memory and anticipation, discovery and recognition, the current need to belong, combined with advancing technology and digital futures means that the opportunities for adaptation of the existing condition is a positive and progressive attitude, it means that alternative futures are possible in physical form within a tangibly altered world.

Construction is a very diverse industry that includes activities that range from immense infrastructure projects to intimate conservation projects. It makes a massive contribution to the GDP of any country; indeed at the end of the second decade of the twenty-first century in the UK, it is worth about £110 billion a year – 60% of this is new build; therefore about £45 billion is spent annually on refurbishment works. These include basic maintenance and repair work, but even so, it is a considerable investment (1).

The world faces two substantial challenges: climate change and urbanisation. Given that already more than half of the global population lives in urban environments, and by 2050, it is projected that over 70% of us will live in cities, all societies need to be able to accommodate growth while at the same time, reducing consumption. The Kyoto Protocol is an international agreement linked to the United Nations Framework Convention on Climate Change, which commits its Parties by setting internationally binding emission reduction targets. And certainly, the British government is committed to reducing greenhouse gas emissions by 80% (compared with 1990 levels). This situation is complicated by the fact that about 85% of the UK building stock that will be in existence in 2025 has already be constructed (2). Thus, the existing building stock will need to become both more efficient and more resilient. Building reuse, refurbishment and restoration work all contribute towards the development of the existing situation, making it useful and appropriate for an expanding and changing population, whose needs and attitudes are also rapidly evolving.

Palimpsest

'Because their structure tends to outlive their function, buildings have continuously been adapted to new uses – a fact which has enabled generation after generation to derive a sense of continuity and stability from their physical surroundings' (3).

The reuse of existing buildings can create environments that are rich and complex. They are often fallible, imperfect and flawed, and yet they are also joyous, multifaceted and individual. The pre-existing is complex because it contains the preconceptions and prejudices of the society that created it. Existing structures contain character and worth, but they also contain complicated and involved histories. These can provide a multi-layered and intricate background or setting to layer the new collection of needs and meaning upon.

This is often referred to as an architectural palimpsest, and a key proponent of such a theoretical approach is Rodolfo Machado, who refers to the alteration of old buildings as a form of rewriting on the same 'canvas', where the previous old 'story' of a building can be seen through the writing of the new 'plot' on top (4). 'The past provides the already written, the marked "canvas" on which each successive remodelling will find its own place. Thus the past becomes a "package of sense" of built up meaning to be accepted (maintained), transformed or suppressed (refused)' (5). The architect and designer have the ability to envisage alternative futures for buildings and situations. A building may have a definite starting point; It is of course a solid entity but the architect has the skill to imagine other opportunities and prospects, thus any new alteration to a building cannot help but be in influenced by the past. Vittorio Gregotti describes this well: 'Modification, belonging, context, identity, specificity, are all words that assume a pre-existing reality that should be preserved even while being transformed, that should hold down its memory through traces which themselves are built on earlier evidence' (6).

Most buildings are resilient, they can adapt, change, grow, shrink, evolve as those that occupy them change. While issues of heritage, sustainability and smartness are at the forefront of many discussions about architecture today, adaptation offers the opportunity to reinforce the particular character of an area using up-to-date techniques for a contemporary population. Issues of collective memory and identity combined with ideas of tradition, history and culture mean that it is possible to retain a sense of continuity with the past as a way of creating the future. Discovery and recognition are very much parts of the process. Meaning is closely linked to function and perception. The existing built environment has great significance, it has heritage value while also being critical to the cultural future of the place. Buildings contain persistence, usefulness and meaning, all of which are valuable and healthy commodities. Its value to the collective memory of the society that it belongs to is indefinable and ethereal. 'We know that the characteristic elements which have a primary function in the structure of the cities remain immobile and persist in the urban dynamic. These are, for the most part, monuments' (7).

Each building is distinct and the circumstance of that difference means that each has an individual tale to tell, something that describes the narrative of its existence. Some of these stories are elaborate because the building may have an intricate history and is located within a complex situation, but others are much simpler and more straightforward. Importantly though, all are different and within this particularity lies the charm of adaptation. The existing building is already there; it already exists in a permanent and tangible way. It has an established relationship with the immediate environment around it, whether these are other buildings and structures, or elements of infrastructure or urban features. The existing structure will also have a definite rapport with things further away, such as a landmark, or some other element within the landscape. Ephemeral things that exist within the collective memory of the local area may also have contributed towards that nature of the existing situation. Factors such as the manner in which some definite occasion is celebrated, a particular local product, or the way in which the local society will act in a given situation can contribute towards the distinctiveness of place.

The building, structure or situation was physically present before the process of design began, and will continue to exist, albeit in a different form, when the remodelling process is complete and then beyond that. It is not an ephemeral object that can move, change or disappear; it permanently exists within the continuing evolution of the built environment.

It is this individuality of this particular and exact existing situation that can provide the impetus for the remodelling; it can supply the evidence that the architect or designer can exploit to instigate the design. The clues that the architect may search for may relate to the environment: it could be the position of the sun on a winter's afternoon, the proximity of a busy road or the view from an upstairs window. The tactile quality of the materials present within the structure can be relevant: a raw brick wall, an ornamental doorway or perhaps the horizontal extent of a stone floor. Some buildings have had a complicated past, they have already endured a number of different uses; each manifestation different from the last and yet each a continuum of the last. The building can exhibit its own evolution, it can reveal the changes that have happened and embrace the narrative that exists within those transformations. Of course the three-dimensional qualities of the structural system can impose precise restrictions upon the remodelling possibilities. Whether the new elements are to hang from the existing structure, slide between it or act in an independent manner, the very fact of its existence provides liberating limitations. All of these uncovered factors are to be combined with the needs of the users, many of whom, due to the presentism of their own situation, may not be completely aware of what these requirements are. The uncritical adherence to present-day solutions could mean that unexpected or unforeseen solutions can offer surprise and delight.

Definitions

Remodelling, Reuse and Adaptation are just a few of the plethora of different names and titles given to the process of working with the existing situation. Some are interchangeable, while others are more specific and refer to a distinct process.

Reuse or Adaptive Reuse, for example, implies a change of function, of a building whose previous use is now obsolete and therefore is changed to accommodate a new function, with new occupiers with different needs and priorities. This could be the conversion of a deconsecrated church into apartments, or an industrial warehouse into a museum

Remodelling may refer to new users, but is much more focussed upon the actual building, so it could be that exactly the same people occupy the building, but their requirements have changed. Possibly working practices have evolved, or the place wants to project a different image. The manner in which the office building is occupied has radically changed; even over the last generation, individual cellular space with specific meeting areas is now thought to be counter-productive, while the ideas of different types of space to accommodate different working practices is now the prevailing attitude, thus many office spaces need to be remodelled to accommodate this change in attitude. Adaptation has a similar meaning as does Conversion, Alteration and even Extension, but these don't have the simple mantra like character of beginning with Re-. Reduce Reuse Recycle is a slogan or statement that epitomises the twenty-first century post-industrial society's need for everything to be useful, to have a purpose and be interesting, to be authentic or real; that is, to be solidly different from the digitally fabricated.

Retrofitting is much more exact, and indicates a distinctly sustainable approach with the ambition to reduce operational energy consumption. Reducing energy demand is almost completely a matter of human behaviour, and the architect can support this through the design of buildings that are intrinsically carbon neutral combined with easy and obvious methods of sustainable occupation.

Renovation, Restoration, Repair, Renewal and Refurbishment all approximate to the updating of the existing and making it fit for modern day needs. Radical changes need not be made to make it habitable, possibly the services need modernising, even late twentieth century standards are different from early twenty-first century ones.

Conservation is the most loaded of all of the categories, it carries with it connotations of authenticity and truth. The argument really dates back to the nineteenth century and the debate that raged between the French architect Eugène Viollet-le-Duc – who pursued an approach of radical and complete interpretation while reconstructing a number of important Chateaux – and John Ruskin, who later with William Morris promoted an idea of the preservation of monuments in their found condition so that the patina of time could be seen to embellish the legitimacy of their appearance. Thus preservation generally applies to the technique of keeping a building in very much the original state of repair, but making it sound and safe, while reconstruction is considerably more intrusive.

All of these terms are legitimate in that they all deal with the existing situation; all have an attitude towards the retention of the original structure or collection of buildings as important elements within the built environment. Some expressions refer to the amount and type of work completed, while others relate to a particular attitude or sensibility, but they are all aspects of the process of recollection and anticipation, as architectural heritage plays an important role in the definition of cultural identity and origins. Retention of the character of the existing building enables understanding of the original. The original gives meaning to the new. As Christine Boyer suggests: '…pleasure might be found because these fragments reawaken memories that have long been dormant' (8).

History

Changing attitudes towards conservation and preservation can be observed within the adaptation of the existing structure. It is also possible to understand the culture of any society through the analysis of the buildings created by those people. By looking at the manner in which the structures are adapted can also expose many of the preoccupations of that society. The approach that the architect or designer will take to the design of the adaptation has gradually evolved, from one of simply constructing the new elements in the prevailing style of the day, through direct replication or even pastiche, deliberate contrast, careful revelation of narrative, to the highly contemporary need for a sense of completeness or wholeness within the reused building. Thus the history of remodelling really contains five stages: to add to, to rebuild, to contrast, to construct narrative and to create wholeness

Until the eighteenth century, the prevailing attitude really was to add to any building in the style of the time, thus within many historic buildings an evolution can be traced as the building changed owners or the needs of the users altered. Beyond the immediate past, the alteration and extension of an existing building was a simple process of making these changes in the style of the period, using the most modern techniques and processes. The great explorer Francis Drake, for example, took a house, Buckland Abbey, on the south coast of England, fittingly not far from Plymouth, the port that he set off from for many of his greatest seafaring adventures. Drake, who was the first British person to circumnavigate the globe, secured the property from Sir Richard Grenville, both of whom have acquired heroic and legendry national identities. It was Grenville who oversaw the reworking of the abbey church and its conversion into a dwelling (see Figure 1.1).

The reworking of religious buildings into dwellings was not that unusual at the time, given the collection of administrative and legal procedures that set into effect the dissolution of the monasteries between 1536 and 1541. (Interestingly this was just about the same time as Drake's birth, which is thought to be about 1540.) This conversion is particularly unsympathetic, especially the adaptation of the presbytery, the most sacred part of the abbey, into a menial serving area between the hall and kitchens. This demonstrates an aggressive invasion of the secular into a sacred space, which gives an insight into cultural change, and the emergence and growth of rationalism and sectarianism following the Reformation. Other works included the removal of the transepts, the walls of which were simply filled in,

FIGURE 1.1 Buckland Abbey, Devon, England. The disused abbey was converted into a residential property after it was abandoned in the sixteenth century following the Reformation. The conversion is particularly unsympathetic, an act that reflected the general attitude that the nobility had towards the Catholic Church during this period. Credit: JohnArmagh via Wikimedia Commons

and the shortening of the west end of the nave. This was converted into a great hall with a large fireplace, panelling and decorative plasterwork, and a screened circulation area at the east end in the crossing of the church. This passageway is an extraordinary space with the large-scale elements of the church still in place squashed next to the new wall and staircase; the detritus of an earlier manifestation abandoned next to the new world order. Buckland Abbey is now owned by the National Trust, not in recognition of the quality of the architecture, but because of its illustrious owner (9).

By the nineteenth century, many buildings were being restored in the style of their original construction. This brought into question the authenticity of the work. This act of reproduction was felt to devalue both the original structure and the craftsmanship of the new elements. This dispute was played out in public through the writings and work of Viollet-le-Duc against those of John Ruskin and William Morris. Viollet-le-Duc felt that as an architect he was legitimately positioned to 'fill-in-the-gaps', to reconstruct and remodel existing buildings in an historical style of his choosing, while Ruskin and Morris favoured an approach that preserved the building in the found condition. This dispute eventually led to the formation of the Athens Charters of 1931 and 1933 which advocated the use of modern construction techniques and materials, and a definite contrast between the existing and the new.

The Maison de Verre by Pierre Chareau and Bernard Bijvoet (1931) is considered to be a milestone in both early Modern architectural design, and building reuse. The original building was a typical Parisian courtyard house; a quiet and private place, which was entered through a fairly anonymous door from the busy street. The adaptation used highly contemporary ideas of Utilitarian clean space and healthy light, so the façade of the building was replaced with a strongly contrasting and ultra-clean glass-block wall, and the interior remodelled into light and airy open-plan free-space. However, the project was complicated because the resident in the apartment above did not want to move out, so the architects inserted a steel frame under that unit to support it, the columns of which help to frame the space in the new interior. Thus the glazed wall reaches just halfway up the façade of the building, the dense and solid upper stories floating above this translucent plane. The contrast between the old and new is extreme; the materials used are highly Modern, almost High Tech really, while the organisation of the interior reflected the movement away from cellular rooms into free-formed sliding space (see Figure 1.2).

This approach, one of deliberate and obvious differences between the old and new, was the prevailing attitude for most of the early twentieth century. Carlo Scarpa is commonly credited with moving these ideas forward to develop a type of adaptation that contained narrative, that is, a sense of the chronicled history and exposed context of the situation. He explored an approach that encouraged the building to be appreciated as a canvas upon which the detailed cultural account of the place was drawn. Scarpa believed that the story of the building could be exposed through a duel process of scrapping away any erroneous additions, then carefully adding to the structure with judiciously placed interventions. Scarpa's

FIGURE 1.2 The Maison de Verre by Pierre Chareau and Bernard Bijvoet (1931). One of the first truly Modernist conversions, the new elements radiate an appreciation of clean, smooth lines, combined with the sense of light healthy space.
Credit: via Wikimedia Commons

work has become a fundamental reference point for the careful, selective and story-telling approach to reuse.

The Castelvecchio Museum in Verona, Italy, a project that he worked on for almost 20 years from 1957 to 1974, is generally considered to be his masterpiece. The museum was originally constructed in the fourteenth century as a fortified palace for the della Scala family. Even then it incorporated several existing structures, such as the eighth century church of San Martino and a piece of the twelfth century wall. The castle also had a long bridge across the immediately adjacent Adige River, not for benevolent access for the townsfolk, but to be used in emergencies for the family to escape quickly in times of trouble. The town of Verona has become part of the collective memory of the entire western world, made famous in Shakespeare's Romeo and Juliet. The courtyard-shaped collection of buildings was added to during Napoleon's occupation of the town, when the castle was used to quarter the troops. It was at this point that the immediate connection with the river was lost, when a large barracks building was constructed along the side that had previously been open to the water. Arnaldo Forlati, using a sort of romantic Gothic style, converted the castle to a museum in the 1920s. This work included

FIGURE 1.3 The Castelvecchio Museum in Verona, Italy by Carlo Scarpa (1957–74). This project is generally considered to mark a watershed moment within adaptation and reuse, and is thought of by many as the greatest work of remodelling in the world. Credit: John Lee

the creation of a new façade in front of the Barracks, plus the opening up of the bridge to the general public. This was liberating for the town, but effectively cut the building in half (see Figure 1.3).

Scarpa was asked to design an exhibition in the west wing, and based upon the success of this, then commissioned to complete the whole museum. He was a confirmed Modernist and within the static and somewhat visually stable buildings instilled a sense of movement and promenade. The building is to be seen in motion. The interventions encourage the visitor to move, to turn around, to always deviate from the obvious route and travel in a more circuitous manner; a journey of discovery. Thus the memory of what has been combined with a process of recognition and innovation allows the visitor to enjoy the artefacts within the building, and simultaneously the joy of reading the building as well.

Scarpa proved to be a very great influence, and his careful approach of exposing the narrative of the place became the recognised approach to building reuse and adaptation. However, as the twenty-first century has progressed, another approach has begun to develop; one of completing the building, of making it once again whole. This doesn't mean that narrative had been forgotten, but instead of leading the approach, it has become one of many contributing factors within the remodelling process.

Wholeness is the fusion of new and old into a distinct and single entity. Differentiation between new and old is not particularly important, nor is the need to display the historical strata of the evolution of the building. It is the relationship with the context, the contribution to the urban environment and the importance of the composite whole that are main design drivers.

Kleihues was an architect who managed to successfully combine the contemporary with the historical, and in a series of museum projects he created a distinct dialogue between place, materials and form. These were mostly new buildings, but

FIGURE 1.4 Within the Museum of Pre-History in Frankfurt, Germany, Paul Kleihues creates a dialogue between the existing and the new elements, with historical references to the elements within the wider urban context as well as more direct translations of the original situation.

Credit: Carole Raddato via Wikimedia Commons

the Museum of Pre-History in Frankfurt, Germany, he modestly and calmly reused the ruined Carmelite Church. There are two distinct parts of the adaptation, both of which contribute to the sense of completeness of the project and the conscious intention of recreating a feeling of wholeness (see Figure 1.4).

Kleihues constructed new three-storey structures at the front of the site; this actively reinstated the street line while also creating courtyard spaces behind. These could almost be modern interpretations of the missing cloisters, a possible allusion to the previous function of the building. These long narrow buildings are clad with red and white banded sandstone, a direct reference to the Stock Exchange that had been destroyed during the Second World War. One of the structures is raised on slender stripey legs and is set at a jaunty angle slightly back from the others and so appears to be wandering away from the group, breaking free in a bound of Post-modern irony.

The second intervention was considerably more restrained and understated, yet equally important in the sense of the complete project. The roof of the nave of the church had been badly damaged, and the approach that Kleihues took was to simply reinstate it in exactly the same position. However, instead of replicating the original stone vaults, the architect designed an open, trussed structure made from laser-cut steel. This impossible intervention has the qualities of being very old, in that it contains a recollection of the huge timber roof structures that could span great distances, but the contemporary material could not belong to a previous age. Thus the collection of buildings have been made complete once more; the history, context and culture of the area are all referenced but nothing is prioritized, all have equal weight within the design process. Kleihues described this process as containing a sense of recompense or restoration

'The new museum building, which rather strives to be an extension, restitutes a sense of uniformity to the whole area, which does not only reflect towards the interior, but bestows the necessary constructional calm on the environment' (10).

Connections

It is possible to draw a direct connection between a building and the society that constructed it – this includes the subsequent modifications of the structure. The evolving attitudes of a culture are present within the organisation and programmatic use of a building, thus each change and adaptation reflects the concerns of the residents of that environment. So it can be argued that every act of remodelling can be seen to epitomize, in microcosm, the culture of the place and by extension the culture of the country.

A fine example of this is the Corn Exchange, which was constructed in the mid-1830s in the small city of Winchester, the county town of Hampshire in the south of England. A chronological description of the building shows how the changes that were made to it reflected the concerns of the nation. The Exchange opened at a time when Britian was undergoing rapid transformation, from a pre-industrial society into an industrial one. Huge amounts of food needed to be transported quickly from the provinces to the cities, to accommodate the large number of people who had moved into urban areas to work in the factories and mills, and the subsequent population increase that accompanied this. This was about the same time as the town railway station opened, another symbol of industrialisation. The methods of food production and distribution were radically changing, industrial approaches to farming were being introduced, and advancing systems of marketing and delivery supported this.

Local architect Owen Brown Carter designed the yellow and white neo-classical building. According to Pevsner (11), the portico was inspired by the magnificent façade of St Paul's Church in Covent Garden by Inigo Jones, and it is easy to see why he would make this comparison. The entrance of the Corn Exchange consists of a great pediment with deep overhanging eaves and a centrally placed circular window, all of which is supported by four huge Tuscan columns. However, behind this portico, although the façade does still bear some resemblance, especially within the design of the flanking gatehouses, the Corn Exchange is considerably less restrained than St Paul's. Eight elevated arched windows throw light into the market halls, while a centrally place turret provided extra height. Behind these street-facing rooms was an open circular courtyard, which was used for the cattle (or pitcher) market. The formal neo-classical language of the building was not a simple whim of the architect, but it communicated the importance placed upon the business of agriculture within the community of the city. Interestingly, Carter was probably the only properly qualified architect practising in Winchester at that time, and his biographer, Freeman, claims that: 'most of the correctly detailed buildings of that period are likely to be by him' (12) (see Figure 1.5).

The first alteration to the building was to enclose the open rear courtyard later that century. This made the area suitable for formal society events, such as the county elections and festive gatherings. There is a fantastic image of a huge number of townsfolk crowded into the space to celebrate the Diamond Jubilee of Queen Victoria in 1897. Thus the building had evolved from somewhere dedicated merely to the advancement of commerce to a place for the betterment of society. This was a reflection of the changing attitudes of the nation at large and the wish to develop a better and more liberal country.

At the beginning of the twentieth century the Corn Exchange closed. This was for a combination of reasons including a series of poor harvests, the removal

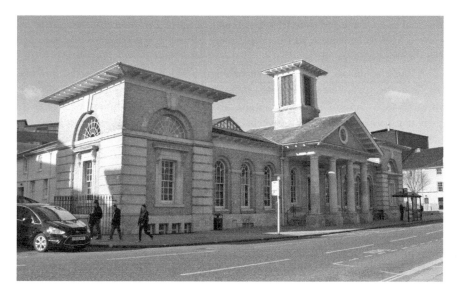

FIGURE 1.5 Owen Brown Carter's designs for the original Winchester Corn Exchange was inspired by the great portico of St. Paul's in Covent Garden.
Credit: Katy Hickson

of the embargo on the import of cheap foreign products and the opening up of the huge wheat prairies of North America. Simultaneously during this period, a national preoccupation with much more benevolent ideas of health and welfare instigated a tangible reduction in working hours, which meant that many ordinary people in Winchester began to have definite leisure time. In an extraordinary act of adaptation, in 1909, the huge now-covered courtyard was converted into a roller-skating rink. The floor was re-laid with maple boards and apparently three sessions were held daily (13). This was a time when it was beginning to be acceptable for women to take part in sporting activities (they were first allowed to partici-pate in the Olympic games in 1900) when the liberation and suffrage of women was becoming a force, and roller-skating was considered to be a fashionable and becoming pursuit for the modern woman.

In 1915 the building was converted to the Regent Theatre, however, after the outbreak of the First World War, and the nearby presence of a military encamp-ment, in 1917, it reopened as the Regent Picture House. The cinema showed silent movies and included a pit for the orchestra, and a restaurant and tearoom. The exchange rooms at the front of the building were remodelled as individual shops. After the war, the building again reflected the 1920s' and 30s' national obsessions, this time it was for dancing and so it was possible for the residents of Winchester to '…Follow the crowd every Saturday night…dancing 8pm to midnight to Drake's Elite Dance Quartette' (14).

By the mid-1930s, self-betterment, education and progress through learning were very high upon the agenda of the government, and thus the next incarnation of the building was as the City Library. For the next 30 years the building generally retained the same organisation, although small changes did reflect national concerns – these included the 1939 construction of concrete air raid shelters underneath the carpark. The post-war baby boom and the beginning of society's preoccupation with children were marked with the 1953 opening of the Junior Library. The 1944 Education Act effectively meant that the government moved responsibility for the education of children from central control to local councils, therefore Winchester City Council was accountable for the schools and libraries within its district. The shops in the north side of the façade were simply converted into a dedicated space for the young. Given the level of austerity that existed at that time, the conversion is somewhat rudimentary; the space and the façade weren't materially altered; the shop sign was merely repainted to reflect the new use.

The apparent optimism of the 1960s is reflected within the next remodelling of the building. The 1964 Public Libraries Act expected improvements to be made to all library buildings, but this was complicated by the Grade 2 conservation listing that was applied to this particular structure, something that reflected the importance of the architecture to the nation. The City Council approached the highly eminent architect and designer Sir Hugh Casson to remodel and update the building. The front of the building was sensitively and carefully restored. It was within the area at the rear, the spaces that had already undergone many different manifestations, that Casson dragged Winchester into the Space Age. All of the rooms were opened-up, thus effectively creating a sense of a Free-Plan, and encouraging interaction between all parts of the library. A false ceiling was installed; a huge orthogonal gridded horizontal plane that stretched across the complete space. This abstract Cartesian grid, reminiscent of the Superstudio utopian ideal, signified the liberation of society from worldly concerns and the tyranny of objects, but also the pursuit of social equality and the egalitarianism of space that this particular era offered. The library was slightly updated in the 1970s, but very much left alone until the beginning of the twenty-first century.

The new millennium and the digital revolution instigated a need not for knowledge or things, but for experiences, and thus the current obsession for real life tangible involvement in actual things that happen is evident within the most recent remodelling of the building: as the Winchester Discovery Centre. The aspiration to shift the focus from an accumulation of knowledge and belongings to the choreography of enacted physical experiences and interactions is one of the most obvious present-day concerns. The future of the city centre is based upon encounter and exchange. Thus experiences such as those that tourism affords are very much the future of any built environment, whether these are aimed at the local population, or visitors, or both.

In 2008 the latest realisation of the building opened as a cultural facility with library attached and all of the accompanying facilities in place. Hampshire County Council Architects (15) completed the remodelling (they are one of the very few publicly funded architects still in existence in the UK). The project included removing most of the previous adaptations, especially the suspended ceiling, recreating the sense of the original building and designing a small extension to the west of the structure. The simple steel and glass language of the new wing contrasts strongly with the classical design of Owen Carter and is set back slightly from the building line to avoid clashing with it. The installation of a dynamic under-lit flying balcony within the huge interactive rear gallery is an echo of the original circular courtyard and the most obvious signal of intent by the architects.

The Corn Exchange has been an important element of the cultural and built environment of Winchester. Over the last two centuries it has undergone a number of transformations; as the priorities of the residents of the city have changed, so the organisation of the building has kept pace with them. The basic resilience of the building has meant that it has the ability to adapt to different circumstances, changing needs and desires within the society that it inhabits, and thus become a continually evolving element within the collective memory of the place.

Interiorist

Contradiction in architecture can be manifested through the difference between the inside of a building and the outside. The modernist ideal demanded continuity between them, indeed the concept of transience or flowing space meant that at times the line between in and out became so blurred that it was impossible to ascertain the actual position of the boundary between the interior and the exterior. The interior became little more than a product of the position of the exterior walls, while the pursuit of transparency dictated that little difference existed between the two. The position of the openings, the ingress of light and the shape of the rooms were completely dictated by the strict requirements of the external envelope. The pursuit of transparency within much of contemporary architecture has taken this reduction in the importance placed upon the integrity of the interior even further. It means that the division between the inside and the outside of the building all but disappeared. The interior is a continuation of the landscape with just the structural columns acting as almost insignificant interruptions. The theoretician, Fred Scott, describes this as the interior having escaped from the building (16).

But an interior can have some independence from the exterior of the building. There are many examples of this, especially in massive public interiors such as shopping centres and airports. A more poetic example is the series of offices created within the confines of factory structures by Robert Stern in the late twentieth century. These were autonomous, self-contained and self-reverential spaces set within the rhythm of the industrial buildings. The language is dis-similar to that of the factory and the organisation was limited only by the organisation of the structure. The identity of these little jewels was intensified by their proximity to the places of production.

The situation is really that interior architecture is much greater than the product of the exterior but part of a symbiotic agreement between the two. Building reuse is in the strange position of being neither in the domain of the architect nor the interior designer. This has meant that Interiorists are repositioning themselves to look at the inside plus the implications that this has for the whole building and its immediate surroundings.

The practice of building reuse has over the last half-century massively increased, and now in western societies, accounts for the majority of all building work. This has much to do with the post-industrial society acknowledgement of the worth tied up within the existing building stock and ideas of cultural memory, combined with a need to belong to somewhere specific and a desire for something tangible in an increasingly more digital and fragmented world. The building and the surrounding conditions are considered as a complete entity, so the architect or designer will deliberate upon all of the existing situation rather than just the shell of the building or the qualities of the inside space alone. This has led to a change in the definition of the subject of Interiors. There has been a distinct rise in the number of Interior Architecture programmes at universities across the world. This reflects the position that building reuse has within the construction industry. And so it has become obvious that the term 'interior' does not simply indicate a category of space, i.e. the inside of the building, but it is also a conceptual term; denoting a radically new approach to the discipline of architecture (17).

The Book

This book contains many chapters, each focussing upon a different aspect of the subject, if indeed it can be called that, rather than lots of bits of other subjects, somewhat like a collage of different material things that when viewed together actually produces a coherent picture. The idea was to start with a sort of overview, then progress through different aspects, some of which do indeed have a slightly tenuous connection with buildings and reuse, but are definitely relevant, and then to end with a sense of intimacy that comes from looking closely at something.

References

1. Designing Buildings Wiki: www.designingbuildings.co.uk/wiki/UK_construction_industry
2. Designing Buildings Wiki: www.designingbuildings.co.uk/wiki/UK_construction_industry
3. Cantacuzino, S. (1975) New Uses for Old Buildings. London: The Architectural Press, p. viii.
4. Machado, R. (1976) "Old Buildings as Palimpsest" from Progressive Architecture. 57 (11) pp. 46–49. Stamford: Reinhold Publishing.
5. Machado, R. (1976) "Old Buildings as Palimpsest" from Progressive Architecture. 57 (11) pp. 46–49. Stamford: Reinhold Publishing.
6. Gregotti, Vittorio (1996) Inside Architecture. Cambridge MA: MIT Press, p. 29.
7. Scott, F. (2007) On Altering Architecture. London: Routledge, p. 192.
8. Boyer, C. (1994) The City of Collective Memory. Its Historical Imagery and Architectural Entertainments. Cambridge MA: MIT Press, p. 19.
9. Buckland Abbey: https://historicengland.org.uk/listing/the-list/list-entry/1018366
10. Kleihues, J. P. (1989) The Museum Projects. New York: Rizzoli, p. 125.
11. Pevsner, N. and Lloyd, D.W. (1967) Hampshire and the Isle of White. New Haven, Conn. London: Yale University Press.
12. Freeman, R. (1991) The Art and Architecture of Owen Brown Carter (1806–1859). Winchester: Hampshire County Council.
13. Hickson, K. (2013) The Corn Exchange: A microcosm of Changing Attitudes to Architectural Conservation. Unpublished.
14. Hickson, K. (2013) The Corn Exchange: A microcosm of Changing Attitudes to Architectural Conservation. Unpublished.
15. Hampshire County Council: www3.hants.gov.uk/propertyservices/design/architectural-design.htm
16. Scott, F. (2009) Unpublished Lecture: 6th Modern Interiors Research Centre Conference, Kingston University. May 2009.
17. Plevoets, B. Berger, M. and Stone, S. (2018) An Interior Approach to Education and Adaptive Reuse. Delivered at Contemporary Positions in Interior Theory. Deutsches Architektur Zentrum DAZ. Berlin. Unpublished Lecture.

2

READING AND RECOGNITION

Landmarks of Memory

Introduction

The fairy tale of Little Red Riding Hood is internationally very well known. It is the story of a little girl in a red cape, who, while wandering through the woods to visit her sick grandmother, encounters a wolf. He is the consummate gentleman; he chats to the little girl, then wishes her a safe journey before licking his lips and racing to the grandmother's house himself. Little Red Riding Hood dallies in the woods innocently picking flowers and singing, so that by the time she reaches her grandmother's house it is the wolf that is in her grandmother's bed not the old lady. The grandmother is … well it depends upon who is telling the tale, she could be in the wolf's belly or in the cupboard, and whether she is alive or dead is also open to interpretation. The story continues, again there are variations, but they all include an encounter between the wolf, now in the bed and dressed in the grandmother's nightclothes, and the guileless Red Riding Hood:

> "Oh what big ears you have Grandmother"
> "All the better to hear you with my dear"
> "Oh what big eyes you have Grandmother"
> "All the better to see you with my dear"
> "Oh what big teeth you have Grandmother"
> "All the better to eat you with my dear"

This is a story that has lived in the western collective memory for hundreds of years. It has been written down innumerable times during history, it has been changed, remodelled, modified, but the basic story still survives. I have read versions told by Little Red Riding Hood in her new wolf-skin coat, versions where a woodcutter saves both the girl and grandmother and of course versions in which the wolf staggers away, his stomach straining and bulging dangerously with the weight of the two people he has eaten.

Why is it so important to retain this and other fairy or folk stories? Of course, to show the social and cultural development of a society, especially in small communities where not very much writing occurred. These were stories that provided moral guidance for children; that helped define what was and wasn't acceptable and identified the rules and laws by which society developed. Although Charles Perrault produced the first written version of this folk story in the seventeenth century, it is thought to date back over two and a half thousand years.

Fairy tales can vary in shape and style according to the period and culture in which they are found. Many details may change – even the ending may be either happy or unhappy. Yet with all the changes, the vision remains constant. The important point that emerges for a modern sympathetic understanding of an activity with such ancient roots is the mixture of stability and variations both in stories and in the circumstances of their telling.

The folk tale can also be described as a mnemonic, a device to aid the memory. The basic story is set in stone, it is well known and well remembered, and however many deviations come from the path of the tale, the narrative is always guided by the original version. Digressions, such as a discussion about the length and colour of Little Red Riding Hood's hair, the exact size of the wolf's teeth, the type of flowers available in the woods and even the actual fate of the little heroine, can easily be accommodated as both the narrator and the audience are familiar with the account of the story.

The fable also changes depending upon who is telling the story and to whom. The narrator impresses their own attitude and style upon their particular account, retelling and modifying the story to accommodate the particular audience. The specific tales retain certain general patterns and an underlying structure; they possess an internal logic that the storyteller can manipulate, adapt and interpret. The surface meanings are clear, but all have further depths of meaning and many valid interpretations.

The same argument can be applied to buildings. Throughout history, places, buildings and situations have been reused and adapted; they can survive as cultures and civilisations change. The already built provides a direct link with the past; it is a connection with the very building bricks of our society. The existing tells the tale or story of how a particular culture evolved. A simple building may depict a certain moment in time; it may relate the particular sensibility of a specific era. A more complex structure may have a much more elaborate story to tell. Jorge Silvetti describes this direct link with the past as part of our 'fundamental urban condition'. He links the physical survival of particular elements of the city with the spiritual survival of our civilisation, and it is this visibility and durability of the physical man-made environment that are testimonies to the societies that produced them.

> At the risk of sounding too partisan and biased, I would say that even in historic times documents were not always available, and buildings (monuments,

vernacular constructions, and public works) are themselves important texts, often providing the first and most lasting impression of a culture.

1

It is through a thorough knowledge and understanding of the existing condition that the architect or designer can uncover the meaning within a place, activate and therefore use it to instigate and liberate a new future. Just as the tale of Red Riding Hood can be simple, straightforward and innocuous, it equally can be complicated and woven through with intrigue, daring, double-crossing and surprise. So the existing building has a story or narrative that the architect or designer can decipher, interpret and elucidate upon.

Adaptation

The reuse of an architectural site creates a direct connection with the past. It is a strategy that establishes an explicit relationship with history, not just of the building and its immediate surroundings, but also with the society that constructed it. The reading of a building or site can uncover a layered and stratified narrative. The understanding of the inherent qualities and conditions of building or site can provide clues to the redesign of the place. It is through a thorough knowledge and understanding of the existing condition that the architect or designer can uncover the meaning within a place. This knowledge can be used to activate, liberate and instigate a new future for the building. And so the architect or designer who is to modify, transform or change the building to accommodate a new use has to adhere not just to the agenda of the new users, but also the intentions of the original building. This act of modification is part of the evolution of the building, it as another layer in the archaeology of the site.

Scarpa pursued this approach at the Castelvecchio, sometimes bringing a layer of history to the fore to be consciously observed, whilst at other times allowing elements to recede almost into non-existence. Gordon Matta-Clarke described the manner in which he cut up existing structures as undoing buildings. Robert Irwin when describing his site-conditioned or site-determined artworks explained that the sculptural response drew all its cues or reasons for being from its surroundings, and Herzog and de Meuron described their approach to the Tate Modern project as a kind of Aikido strategy, 'where you use your enemy's strategy for your own purposes. Instead of fighting it, you take all the energy and shape it in an unexpected and new way' (2) (see Figures 2.1 and 2.2 Tate).

Gregotti describes this search for meaning in a specific site as a discovery and examination of the truth, that is the narrative that is embodied within the existing. The process of adaptation is a revelation of the underlying condition and therefore an expose of the truth: 'Modification tells us that each specific situation offers a specific truth, to be sought, and revealed as the truth of both the site and the geography embodies that site's particular history' (3).

Unlike many of the arts, architecture belongs to a specific location; it is inextricably intertwined with the experience of that particular place. A really good building

FIGURE 2.1 The language that the architects Herzog and de Meuron use within the conversion of disused power station into the Tate Modern in London, England is as robust and uncompromising as the original building.

Credit: Sally Stone

can only inhabit that exact position; it cannot be moved, copied, transported or relocated without losing its intrinsic link with the place that it inhabits. It was designed to act in response to a precise set of circumstances, to occupy and act with or against the character and qualities of the site.

A building occupies a distinct place; it has a direct relationship with the immediate area surrounding it, such as other buildings, street patterns and the surrounding urban environment, as well as a relationship with things further away, such as landmarks and monuments. Every area has its own dialect or specific language; equally, it has evolved a vernacular style of architecture. A certain and specific set of conditions have driven a particular style of building to develop. Vernacular architecture grew from its place of existence. Early structures were made from locally available materials, wood, stone, reeds. Those who constructed them were acutely aware of the climatic conditions that they had to endure, and so were designed to protect the user from the worst of the weather, while allowing warmth, water, food and fuel to be easily collected. The construction of settlements became more sophisticated, but the understanding of place and situation wasn't lost. The vernacular offers many clues into the realisation of what is possible.

There is a tradition in Spain of taking a walk after dinner. When the heat of the day has passed and work is complete, then the residents of a town will indulge in

FIGURE 2.2 The great hall of the Tate Modern by Herzog and de Meuron, which once held the huge machinery necessary for the generation of massive amounts of power, retains those qualities of industrial production.

Credit: Sally Stone

a little 'el paseo'. It is the dividing line of the day, and is a gesture towards the time of indulgence or leisure. This stroll or perambulation is not choreographed, but also not accidental; it is a social occasion and an opportunity to meet and greet friends and family. During the el paseo (which does literally translate as 'the stroll'), the entire community can be seen walking slowly through the streets. They do not make formal appointments to see each other, but as everyone is heading for the same place, all are confident that they will bump into someone they know. This important custom acknowledges a climate that is just too hot to spend too much time outside during the day, and so as the cool of the evening descends, as a light breeze blows softly across the town, it is the moment that the residents find for social interaction.

Teruel is a small town just to the north of Valencia in the Aragon region of Spain. The terrace of the Paseo del Ovalo is the historic promenade; it was constructed on the site of the city walls, and is perfectly position for the 'el paseo'. The walkway is elevated above the fertile floodplains of the river Turia, much of which have now been incorporated into the city, and marks the point where the old city ends and the new one begins. This wide esplanade separates the magnificent six- or seven-storey townhouses from the city walls and breath-taking view across the valley. The railway station is situated in the lower city, just below the Paseo del Ovalo, and a monumental staircase, the Escalinta, links it with the upper town. The Escalinta, or the Staircase of Teruel, was constructed in the early 1920s by the local engineer José Torán de la Rad as an act of liberation for the town; the previous route was by all accounts both difficult and treacherous. It is highly ornamented and is constructed from brick with ceramic and iron decoration. The staircase could be described as Neo-Mudejar; in that it is geometric, elaborate and is influenced by both Christian and Moorish cultures.

David Chipperfield Architects with b720 Architects were appointed to supplement the magnificent staircase with a route that would make it easier for residents and holidaymakers who have to carry their own heavy luggage from the low level station to the historic town above. The architects have created a second connection, an elevator, which offers an alternative path to the Paseo del Ovalo. The project also included works to the public space that separated the station form the city walls. The first move was to present the traveller with a choice of two diverging white paths; the first having perhaps the better claim to the existing and well worn staircase, the other gently sloping down leads to a new opening in the city wall. This weathered steel lined portal leads to a top-lit underground cavern and the almost insignificant lift. The magnitude of the space accentuates the weight of the historic city walls above. The elevator leads directly to the great balcony above and opens immediately onto the spectacular view. The orthogonal glass-block protective box is deliberately austere against the highly decorated local architecture, but does acknowledge the tradition of the 'mirador', or viewing platform. A large rectangular opening encourages the wanderer to linger slightly and admire the view before turning towards the old town and setting forth across the great open urban lounge of the Paseo del Ovalo (see Figures 2.3, 2.4, 2.5 and 2.6).

Analysis and Exploration

Every situation has a relationship with the topography, the geology and the climate. Many buildings were originally constructed to take advantage of the prevailing weather conditions; to shade the worst of the hot summer sun, while also allowing the long warmth of the winter light to enter. They may be designed to provide shelter from the worst of the wind and rain while actively using these properties to cool the building.

An existing building or situation always contains a history. This may be relatively simple, it may previously have had just one type of occupant, who had specific needs, so the building was fitted out to accommodate their particular function. It could have endured a turbulent past, have contained many different and conflicting events. All of these will have marked the building in some way. Alterations may have been necessary to facilitate different functions, or perhaps violent incidents have actually left physical scars. Walter Benjamin summed this up in his well-known aphorism: To live is to leave traces.

The manner in which a building is constructed can be much more than just a prosaic organisational system. The structure can provide rhythm, it can inform

FIGURE 2.3 Paseo del Ovalo by David Chipperfield Architects with b720 Architects, Teruel, Spain. The wide promenade is elevated upon the old city walls and affords a marvellous view across the flood planes of the River Turia.

Credit: Hisao Suzuki

patterns and balance. The materials that it is built from may be found locally or may have been brought from distance. The mass and form of the building can respond to the immediate environment and the manner in which the building is constructed can provide many clues to the society that constructed it.

The architectural heritage offers a direct link with the evolution of a society. It is a connection to both the past and an opening to the future. The conscious sense of

FIGURE 2.4 Paseo del Ovalo by David Chipperfield Architects with b720 Architects, Teruel, Spain. Upon leaving the station, the traveller is presented with a choice of routes: the highly decorated staircase that leads straight to the old town, or the sunken, more secretive path, towards the elevator.

Credit: Hisao Suzuki

continuity with the past can offer many possibilities and indicators to future development. This is not about replication or pastiche, but the use of the advanced technical
and conceptual ideas of the twenty-first century in a sensitive and appropriate manner.

Giancarlo de Carlo regarded the historic environment first and foremost as a
place of human activity, not a fount of nostalgic inspiration for visiting architects.
He considered that one of the greatest threats to the future of the historic city was
the erosion of urban memory. That is, if urban forms lose their old associations
and at the same time did not invite new uses and stimulate new associations, then
the built environment was in danger of becoming little more than a cultural curiosity, a scarified object for tourist consumption and architectural contemplation.
Importantly he felt that the memory of a piece of architecture is never lost; even
when it seems to have been mislaid, it carries on, and instead of being in the fore-
ground of human consciousness it acts at a subliminal level. He was one of the
founding members of Team X, a group of architects that challenged the modernist
doctrines set out by CIAM and was also a key figure in the discourse on participation in architecture.

FIGURE 2.5 Paseo del Ovalo by David Chipperfield Architects with b720 Architects, Teruel, Spain. The architects have established a direct relationship between the heavy lower level and bright promenade above.

Credit: Hisao Suzuki

He posed two fundamental questions: First, can an old form retain its significance when the activities of the city itself have radically changed? And second, can a modern architectural form be successfully woven into the old architectural fabric (4)? For new uses to be imposed upon existing structures, de Carlo felt that the spaces of the past, which in a way record that place's fundamental culture, must be detached from the system of meanings to which they originally corresponded through the use of sensitive and subtle interventions. The forms that are most capable of undergoing adaptation are those with sufficient force of character to retain their integrity. These can then play a stimulating role within the built context that is a new and different purpose from the one for which they were originally designed. This would endow them with contemporary systems of meanings, based upon the culture of those that constructed the building overlaid with the culture of those who newly occupied it. The existing structures would otherwise remain silent and unexperienced because they could not be understood (5).

Much of de Carlo's built work is located in Urbino, a small Italian hill town for which between 1958–64 he created a master plan. This project was slowly implemented over the following 40 years, and thus he will always be associated with

FIGURE 2.6 Paseo del Ovalo by David Chipperfield Architects with b720 Architects, Teruel, Spain. The language of the new elements is as spare as the original is decorated. Credit: Hisao Suzuki

the place. De Carlo also oversaw restorations, designed new buildings and proposed renovations, all of which were carefully inserted into the built fabric. But before the project could commence, he analysed the existing city, he looked at both the tangible and intangible aspects by carrying out detailed surveys of the infrastructure, the fabric of the buildings and the public areas, and also paid close attention to the social life of the town, commissioning statistical analysis of the population, geography and economies of use. He also compiled reports on sanitary conditions, ownership and the uses of buildings. His study mapped out landmarks, views, paths, entrances, green spaces and road surfaces. It described the gradient of Urbino's streets, the architectural quality of the buildings and their condition. De Carlo likened the process of site analysis to Patrick Geddes' notion of 'reading', something that Geddes referred to as 'Urban Surgery'. He felt that the architect must have a sense of the site's formal parameters of complexity.

Probably the most famous building is Il Magistero, the School of Education, built for the University of Urbino in the mid-1970s. The brick building with glass roofs is placed directly into the undulating topography of the town and provides educational and public facilities including a library, teaching rooms for seminars and a congress hall. Il Magistero does not 'reconstruct' a past at all, but it refers to the city's many transformations; from the fifteenth century, when Renaissance geometries were overlaid on the medieval town, to the twentieth, when Catholic churches were replaced by more contemporary centres of urban culture. The organisation of the building reflects the tight pedestrian nature of the town itself, thus the interventions are very much a microcosm of the existing context. The design embraced the fabric of the city and the lives of the locals:

> For the architecture of the new Magistero to become embodied and accepted, it has to be embedded and layered with the existing stories; allude to and reverberate with them – not excluding those of the transitory young students, often from a different culture, perhaps having left home in southern Italy for the first time.
>
> 6

Giancarlo de Carlo created another collection of interventions within a complex of structures at the Benedictine Monastery of Catania, a building that has had a turbulent history. A Cassinese congregation founded it in the mid-1500s, and although the expected evolution of such buildings means that work is still occurring today, two massive natural calamities – the eruption of Mount Etna in 1669 and the catastrophic earthquake of 1693 – substantially affected the collection of buildings.

On 8 March 1669 the Volcano Etna exploded. Lava started to flow from two deep fissures in the side of the mountain towards the city. By the end of April, the lava flow had reached the city walls, and posed great danger to the Benedictine Monastery. The city walls and the dykes constructed next to them provided some protection, but the monks supplemented this with their own fortifications constructed around the monastery and then relied upon the power of hard prayer. The monastery was saved, but not the Church attached to it, which was completely destroyed by the lava. The area surrounding the Benedictine Monastery changed completely. Lava, up to 12 metres high in places had destroyed the cultivated estates around the buildings, leaving behind an extraordinary barren landscape of hard dense black stone. Just 18 years later, the earthquake caused further damage; the basement and part of the first floor of the Monastery were saved, but only 14 columns of the cloister were still standing, the others were destroyed. The changes to the landscape were such that over the next few centuries as the Monastery underwent reconstruction, and many of the new structures and buildings were not placed upon the original foundations, but actually three or four storeys higher resting upon the new floor of tremendously hard lava.

By the time that the new Italian state confiscated the Monastery in 1866, it had grown to one of the largest in Europe, second only to the Benedictine Monastery of Mafra in Portugal. The buildings then had various fuctions including a barracks, a school and a place of storage. It was in a sorry state when in 1977, as part of a project to regenerate the historic centre of the town, the city council donated it to the University of Catania for their Faculty of Letters and Philosophy.

Giancarlo de Carlo was invited to oversee the restoration. The architect had already garnered a reputation for the sympathetic interpretation of historic structures in the work that he had completed in Urbino, where his concern for the social and political implications of the remodelling combined with great contextual sensitivity and interpretation of the modern had revitalised the town and in particular the university.

The majority of the work in Catania was based within the conservation of the existing structures; however, two highly interpretive interventions elevate the project above simple restoration. According to de Carlo:

> There is no separation between conservation and planning. It is necessary to wander between tradition and innovation so that stimulus, comparisons, suggestions, interpretations can develop continuously, avoiding that the interest in tradition leads to imitation, and that the interest in innovation leads to superficiality. The project value depends on its capacity to change in order to penetrate the various existing architectonic layers to become a layer itself modifying the meaning of the others.
>
> 7

The Monastery stable block was converted into an open–plan study area. An unassuming steel and timber platform was strung across the space, thus creating two floors linked by a simple utilitarian staircase. Students occupy the room in a creative and carefree manner, sitting wherever they feel comfortable; at the communal desks, at the individual workstations or at the modest tables slotted into the window openings. The large study room is quiet and industrious, and retains the unpretentious functional and practical qualities of its original use (see Figure 2.7).

The second intervention is much more flamboyant. The original kitchen was converted into a small museum. It is an octagonal room with the remains of an extraordinary four-sided classical cooking range in the centre of the space. This was serviced by a communal fire, which was fed from the floor below. Years of neglect combined with the inherent unpredictability of the lava meant that the floor was structurally unsound, so Giancarlo de Carlo designed an expressive red painted steel structure to support it. This lightweight structure is attached to the walls of the cellar, so no structural loading is placed upon the thick lava floor. A steel ring-beam is situated directly under the communal stove opening and from this are tangentially stretched beams, which rise and fall as they cross the ceiling thus echoing the very fire that they replace; an expression of flames licking the underside of the kitchen floor. This dramatic statement reflects the frantic activity

FIGURE 2.7 Benedictine Monastery of Catania by Giancarlo de Carlo 1980. The study spaces use an austere language that echoes the somewhat severe quality of the stables that originally occupied the building.

Credit: Afshin Khalife

that had once occupied the place combined with the innate danger of the flaming hot lava. It is invisible from the kitchen, but the visitor stumbles upon it while walking through the undulating landscape of the lava floor of the basement. There is an immediate recognition of the relationships between the force of the fire in the basement and the warmth of the kitchen above, thus creating a direct and emotional connection between the past and the present, between the order of the contemporary world and the perilous uncertainty of the history of the place (see Figures 2.8 and 2.9).

Conclusions

The designer and the architect have the opportunity to reflect upon the contingency, usefulness and emotional resonance of particular places and structures through the reuse of existing buildings. This process of analysis and understanding promotes a certain kind of sensibility, an acceptance of what is already on or off-site, and the willingness to accentuate any of those found elements or narratives. The shadow of the past can influence the present and indeed the future and an investigation of the archaeology of the original can reveal previously hidden or obsolete characteristics that contain the possibility of being exploited.

FIGURE 2.8 Benedictine Monastery of Catania by Giancarlo de Carlo 1980. The extraordinary ceiling in the cellar, which supports the reconstructed floor of the original kitchen above, suggests heat and intensity.
Credit: Afshin Khalife

The architect and the designer regard the existing building not as a blank canvas, but as multi-layered structure, which they have the opportunity to activate. The discovery and recognition of the embodied meaning of a place can be interpreted through building. And it is through the understanding of the pre-existing that the remodelled building can become endowed with a new and greater meaning. The place can be activated.

Aldo van Eyke describes this duel process as 'Memory and Anticipation' while Dominic Roberts in his Continuity in Architecture blog uses the expression 'Remember Reveal Construct'. And so, the study of the citiy, or the built landscape, can provide clues not only into the manner in which we once lived, but also provide

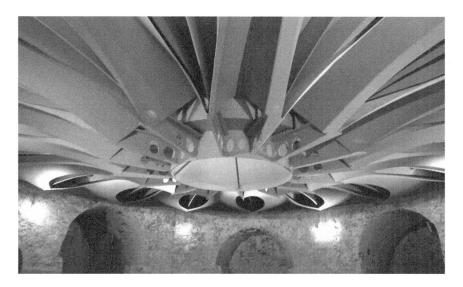

FIGURE 2.9 Benedictine Monastery of Catania by Giancarlo de Carlo 1980. The ceiling structure is a moment of high colour (red) within the relatively subdued monastery scheme.

Credit: Afshin Khalife

clues, inspiration and guidance into the manner in which we ought to strive to live. Sébastien Marot, in his discussion about the importance of memory and place, suggests that the urban environments that we inhabit already have imbued within them the power to evoke a remembrance of the collective consciousness of the previous occupants and that these are the important elements in the future development of the place: '...thus one can picture the built reality of the city's antiquity being continually rebuilt, recomposed in the imagination of their inhabitants and repopulated with symbolic figures and landmarks of memory' (8).

References

1. Silvetti, Jorge (1996) "Interactive Realms" from Modernism and History. Alexander von Hoffman (Ed.). Cambridge, MA: Harvard University Press, p. 33.
2. Moore, Rowan and Ryan, Raymund (2000) Building the Tate Modern. Tate Galley Publishing, p. 125.
3. Gregotti, Vittorio (1996) Inside Architecture. Cambridge MA: MIT Press, p. 67.
4. de Carlo, Giancarlo (1992) Benedict Zucchi. Oxford: Butterworth Architecture, p. 46.
5. de Carlo, Giancarlo (2004) "Tortuosity" from Domus. 866, January, pp. 24–25.
6. McKean, John (2003) Space and Society (1 of 2) Architects Journal, 13 February, p. 26.
7. de Carlo, Giancarlo (1980): www.monasterodeibenedettini.it/en/giancarlo-de-carlo-for-the-benedictine-monastery/
8. Marot, Sébastien (2003) Sub-Urbanism and the Art of Memory. AA Publications, p. 85.

3

THE PERCEPTION OF THE PAST

The Task of the Translator

Introduction

The reuse of an architectural site creates a definite connection with a bygone age and it is a strategy that establishes an explicit relationship with context and history, not just of the building and its immediate surroundings, but also with the society that constructed it. The reading of a building or site can uncover a layered and stratified narrative. The understanding of the inherent qualities and conditions of a building or site can provide clues to the redesign of the place. It is through a thorough knowledge and understanding of the existing condition that the architect or designer can uncover the meaning within a place. This knowledge can be used to activate, liberate and instigate a new future for the building. And so the architect or designer who is to modify, transform or change the building to accommodate a new use has to adhere not just to the agenda of the new users, but also the intentions of the original building. This act of modification or translation is part of the evolution of the building; it is another layer in the archaeology of the site.

Walter Benjamin likens the act of translation to that of fragments of a broken vessel which are incorporated into a replica of the original: '…thus making both the original and the translation recognisable as fragments of a greater language…' (1).

Consequently buildings, structures and situations that are reused represent both the culture that originally constructed the building and also the society that remodelled it. O'Donnell + Tuomey Architects explore this approach in much of their work, and describe this process:

> Our buildings have open, permeable edges … They have more complex relationships with ground and air. There is an exchange between place and building, inside and outside, old and new. This phenomenon exists in time as well as place, in spirit as well as fabric.

Perception

It can be argued that our perception of the past is determined by the present. That is, the manner in which the past is perceived is not solely dependent upon the available information about the past, but it is also influenced by the interpretation of that information by the contemporary individual or society. Culture can be been seen to nurture values, and likewise values can best be described within the context of culture. Thus a process of translation occurs when contemporary cultural values are imposed upon remodelled buildings and contemporary value judgements inform the interpretation of the past. This interpretation of the past cultures and societies is often conducted through a system of what historians call 'empathy'. This method encourages the past to be understood through the experiences of those present. However, this empathetic system needs a base or context to frame it; that is a moral or cultural judgement with which it can be compared and rationalized.

Our contemporary society imposes modern values and morals upon any interpretation of a previous culture. So, if we examine a remodelled building, we see both the evidence of the society that constructed the original building and we see evidence of the values of the society that carried out the remodelling. The narrative of the remodelling can tell us as much about the culture and interpretations of the society reusing the building as the original structure does about the original builders/occupants.

History can be regarded as a discourse; it contains facts, interpretations, bias and empathy. It can be argued that inevitably, anyone viewing material from the past, however well informed, will only be able to understand it from their own position. It is obvious that all historical analysis is an act of translation; the historian (whether architectural, cultural, scientific, feminist, amateur or using any other focus) will not be able to view the historical material through any other lens than that of their own culture. Thus any history contains many different readings and interpretations. It is this very act of translation that provides every project with its individual particular focus. Keith Jenkins, in his important book *Re-Thinking History*, argued: '…given that interpretations of the past are constructed in the present, the possibility of the historian being able to slough off his present to reach somebody else's past on their own terms looks remote' (3).

It is obvious that the study of design, interiors, architecture and history is directly related to this examination and interpretation of history. From the past to the present designers and architects have and still do analyse past precedent. They have surveyed, studied, measured, drawn, replicated and more recently filmed, photographed and digitally modelled buildings, not only to study the particular form and structure, but also to understand how and why they were created, which in turn leads to an examination of the society and culture that created the architecture. This study of precedent has a purpose: to allow architects and designers to understand and grasp the issues of the subject building so they may be appropriated and considered for use in their own buildings; so that the architect or designer may, from the perspective of the twenty-first century, understand how past architects and master masons have solved problems and created forms. This information can then be translated into a contemporary context. This form of scrutiny of past precedent through an 'architectural empathy', not unlike the study of history through historical empathy, is open to interpretation rather than being fact. Contemporary architects will look at an architectural past precedent with their own teachings and predisposition in mind, superimposing that over the ideas and concepts behind that of the precedent.

A very direct example of this can be observed in the study of Ancient Greece. It was common for eighteenth century architects, artists and other such scholars to embark upon a 'Grand Tour'. This was effectively to study the ruins of the Roman and Greek classical world, to assimilate their meaning and worth in order to carry this language back to their own homeland. Thousands of years of neglect and decay had rendered these relics an extremely romantic quality. Wind, rain and sun had removed almost every vestige of the colourful paint which had once enveloped these buildings. They possessed an authentically pure and untainted character: the stone was smooth, clean and white; an image that was strikingly different to the original. The architects did not see the tiny remnants of colourful paint that clung to the remains, nor did they want to observe fragments of pigments and tincture in the sheltered corners. They became so fixated by the form that the possibility of it not being true excluded the possibility of anything else. And so, this clean white image of the classical world became the preferred architectural language for a century (see Figure 3.1).

FIGURE 3.1 Phidias Showing the Frieze of the Parthenon to His Friends (1868), Lawrence Alma-Tadema's painting in the Birmingham Museum and Art Gallery imagines how the Parthenon may have originally looked.

Credit: Birmingham Museum and Art Gallery via wikimedia commons

It is hard to imagine the beauty of these pure classical figures tarnished with bright and gaudy colours. For example, the drama of the Parthenon frieze that ran continuously around the centre block of the building would look completely different if painted. The Horsemen preparing for the Panathenaic procession are fine and noble; it could be argued that the simple relief of the carving vastly increases their beauty. The drapery is especially realistic and does appear to flutter away from the marble. If this were painted, it would completely change the relationship between the figures and the background. Instead of appearing as a single entity, difference would be introduced. This would make the figures heavy; they would no longer float just above the architrave, but would stand upon it. The colour would make the figures more human, more life-like and would reduce the distance between the viewer and the sculpture. To the modern audience this contamination would be errant, but of course to the original audience the unpainted frieze would appear to be unfinished. They did not appreciate the stripped-down essence of the sculpture; this reduction of the artefacts to their essential nature would not have been understood. It is difficult for the population of the twenty-first century to appreciate the original highly decorated surface just as it would be impossible for the Ancient Greeks to enjoy the cleansed purity that was achieved after two millennia of weather and inattention (see Figure 3.2).

FIGURE 3.2 Part of the Cavalcade south frieze, X XI, 26–28, at the British Museum in London. The panel is a stripped and clean articulation of form, with no reference to the once highly coloured representation of the characters.

Credit: British Museum via wikimedia commons

Remodelled Buildings

So, within the examination of the remodelled building, it is possible to see both the evidence of the society that constructed the original building and also see evidence of the values of the society that carried out the remodelling. The narrative of the remodelling can tell us as much about the culture and interpretations of the society reusing the building as the original structure does about the original builders and its occupants. Umberto Eco argued that the architect or designer shouldn't offer a fixed way of reading art, instead, 'work gains its aesthetic validity in proportion to the number of different perspectives from which it can be viewed and understood.' By allowing for this openness of interpretation the viewer is activated, encouraging acts of 'conscious freedom' (4). This freedom can be used as a basis for the strategies of adaptation. Openness can mean flexibility of function and future adaptability, but it is openness to interpretation of memory that allows for the act of translation. He argues that more important 'honest' entertainment (architecture) is that which:

> … acknowledges the complexity, the problematic character of the historical circumstances in which we live, because it allows for the possibility of change and serves for a stimulus to reflection and criticism, generates a sense of independence and choice instead of conformism and passivity.
>
> *5*

Benjamin, in his seminal essay, *The Task of the Translator*, argued that translation marked the continuation of a piece of work, because inevitably the translation came after the production of the source. Thus it contains interpretation and therefore can be regarded as containing subjectivity: 'The idea of life and afterlife in works of art should be regarded with an entirely unmetaphorical objectivity. Even in times of narrowly prejudiced thought, there was an inkling that life was not limited to organic corporeality' (6).

He further contests that the task or even the responsibility of the translator is to find the particular intention that is present within the target audience, and echo this within the language of the translation. The translation should contain transparency, it does not obliterate the original, but allows the new and the old to coexist. This does not mean making a literal word-for-word translation, but rather allowing the essence of the text to appear in a new language. This, he argues, will liberate the language imprisoned in a work in his re-creation of that work. This led him to use the fragments of broken vase metaphor:

> Fragments of a vessel that are to be glued together must match one another in the smallest details, although they need not be like one another. In the same way a translation, instead of imitating the sense of the original, must lovingly and in detail incorporate the original's way of meaning, thus making both the original and the translation recognizable as fragments of a greater language, just as fragments are part of a vessel. For this very reason translation must in large measure refrain from wanting to communicate something, from

rendering the sense, and in this the original is important to it only insofar as it has already relieved the translator and his translation of the effort of assembling and expressing what is to be conveyed.

7

Ricardo Bofill remodelled the vast complex of an abandoned concrete factory on the outskirts of Barcelona as a home and office. The cement factory was partly ruinous and the adaptation began with further demolition. This removal of the extraneous accrual and additions stripped back the complex to its bare essentials. A series of distinct and complete spaces were discovered, which were little more than cleaned. Bofill designed a series of small interventions to facilitate the change of use; these had a similarly raw language to the original structure, but were consciously more refined and at a more human scale. The architect did not embark upon the project with a preconceived idea of the final outcome, rather through a process of discovery and recognition; he negotiated the final form of the adaptation. This act of translation or reworking of the collection of structures was a product of this arbitration (see Figures 3.3 and 3.4).

FIGURE 3.3 Ricardo Bofill remodelled an old cement factory on the outskirts of Barcelona as his own home and office. The new elements are certainly more refined than the original, but are no less robust.

Credit: Ricardo Bofill

FIGURE 3.4 The interior of the cement factory by Ricardo Bofill is decorated in a simple and lightweight manner, something that highlights the rough nature of the original building.

Credit: Ricardo Bofill

Sebastian Marot imagines this as a continual process of building and rebuilding. Redirecting the emphasis from programme to site allows the nature and character of the situation to lead the translation. The reading of the condition of the location facilitates the adaptation. The act of interpretation and translation is based upon the architect or designers discerning investigation and analysis of the existing: '…thus one can picture the built reality of the city's antiquity being continually rebuilt, recomposed in the imagination of their inhabitants and repopulated with symbolic figures and landmarks of memory' (8).

Colin Rowe and Fred Koetter describe 'the city as a didactic instrument' (9) (and by extension, the existing building can also be assumed thus) that is, a place in which a desirable discourse can be formulated and it is through these conversations that the evidence for the argument of interpretation is collected. The reading and understanding of the message of the city or of the individual building provides the basis for the discussion. Architecture and design can facilitate the exploration of identity through the examination of the specificity of the context in which it is embedded. The constructed environment is often charged with narrative content, certain elements come to the fore, while others are more modest, more unassuming, but no less important or carefully considered. These mechanisms tell stories, they engage the imagination, they enable, through the construction of space, time and sequence, the development of new forms and places.

Industrial Ruins

An example of this approach is the wholesale remodelling of mill and warehouse buildings. The problem of what to do with redundant industrial buildings is common to all of the western world. The post-industrial society no longer needs these huge edifices, but given their position within the collective memory of the population, does not want to demolish them. These are usually converted into flats or offices, although there are a number of high profile instances of other uses (art galleries in London, Duisburg and Kuala Lumpur, for example). The form and position of these buildings does make them very good vehicles for conversion into domestic dwellings; the internal spaces are big with plenty of natural light, and the structures are generally strong and the constructional system of brick exterior walls with internal cast iron columns means the buildings are relatively easy to convert. When constructed, these kinds of buildings were often deliberately positioned close to the city centre, to be near to the centre of commerce and transport links. This makes them ideal for housing the young childless professionals who want to take advantage of the sort of facilities that urban living has to offer.

Developers are definitely aware of this desire and have benefitted from this attitude. One such company is the Manchester (UK) based, but now nationally active, Urban Splash, which has built a reputation for innovative, yet sensitive conversions. Their publicity shows happy couples enjoying themselves in well-proportioned light and airy homes. These are furnished with the most contemporary furniture, which contrasts sharply with the clean yet rustic bricks and cast iron. This, in a way, contains a certain truth, the buildings were originally bare and sparse. The windows would have been uncovered and exposed boards of the floor; clean and free from fluff. However, this does deny the appalling circumstances that those who worked in the factories had to endure. There are many readily available images that depict the horrendous conditions that existed at the time. There is, understandably, no reference made to this, instead, the romantically wholesome image of decent honest folk who once worked in the mills pervades. The disused mills have become associated with a more simple and idealistic time of great community, comradeship and hard work. This yearning for an industrial society has managed to filter the worst elements of that society thus retaining an idealist image of the mill at the centre of a happy society. The translation of the nature and use of the original building into a desirable place to live is very cleansed; the negative or traumatic connotations connected with the buildings have been negated, while the positive and uplifting qualities have been stressed. The developers actively reinforced this message (as well as the purchasers and the council, etc., of course). Urban Splash innocently used this motto on their homepage: 'In the beginning there were factories. And then they weren't working anymore. But we thought they were beautiful' (10).

We can admire the beauty of the raw brickwork, the benefit of the space and appreciate the sheer enormity of the natural light through the massive windows, because we can select a particular reading of this environment, one that allows us to enjoy the buildings from our contemporary position without the need to fully comprehend its history. This nostalgia is based upon what the artist Abigail Reynolds calls 'a lazy set of emotions in connection with the past' (11). Nostalgia could be described as the melancholy feeling of dispossession. The word became widely used after the upheaval that was urbanisation, industrialisation and political revolution. This altered people's perception of time and produced a paradox, a vague collective longing for a bygone era; despite people cherishing the past and hating the changes, they also believed there was no going back. Thus the act of translation is based not just on the practicalities of the form and position of the buildings, but also the style or language directly connects with a wistfulness within the twenty-first century post-industrial society.

It is interesting to observe that nostalgia always contains a sense of a break with the past, a period of neglect or forgetting. A discontinuity has to occur before reconciliation can be made. This interval of forgetting allows society to rediscover the past. A great example of this need to forget is the now demolished Haçienda Club in Manchester, UK, which was once described as the most famous nightclub in the world. It thrived in the steamy, crazy atmosphere of the late 1990s MaDchester; it epitomised the outlandish image and housed their mad warehouse parties. The nightclub was actually constructed in 1982, at a time when discos were still populated with coloured flashing lights, thick carpets and strict door policies.

Interior designer Ben Kelly created an image for the Haçienda that really reflected the Factory name and the brand that the graphic designer Peter Saville was developing; a club that looked like a warehouse. The building was really once a warehouse (for yachts … in Manchester!), and the interior had the almost cartoon quality of a great workshop; a huge pigeon blue space with black and yellow hazard warning stripes. Above the dance floor was a massive roof-light, not really the sort of element beneficial to a nightclub. The journey from the queue outside to the dance floor was one of different experiences, almost akin to a streetscape. The signing on the exterior was minimal; just a 30-centimetre-long nameplate. The cramped ticket booth and enclosed cloakroom did nothing to prepare the visitor for the enormity of the dance hall with its preposterous roof-light. This did mean though that the building certainly looked better in daylight than it did at night.

This somewhat ironic interior was initially not well received; Anthony H Wilson, the Granada Reports presenter and owner of Factory Records, described it as 'a middleclass conceit, a playing out romanticism about the industrial and post-industrial city' (12), and in the beginning many questioned why they would want to visit a nightclub that looked like the places that they worked in every day. (How little they knew!) The design was too early; it was only after the warehouses had closed, after all the factories had disappeared, that the sense of nostalgia came into effect and the club became a place of pilgrimage. It took eight years for it to find its audience, and by then jobs in manufacturing were rarely available. The generation of club-goers really had had no experience of industrial toil. People who had little knowledge of hard industrial labour flocked to visit an interior that made direct reference to a bygone era. The interior harked back to a time of certainty, jobs for life and a community spirit, and became a destination for who the age of industry was just a romantic vision (see Figures 3.5 and 3.6).

Act of Transition

The remodelled building can act as a point of transition from one culture to another; it can symbolise that change, as it is in reality, has an interest or stake in both establishments. The original building would have been constructed during one regime and then remodelled during a different one. It can act as a symbol of the upheaval, it can represent new by adapting the old. The magnificent Hagia Sophia Mosque in Istanbul, for example, was originally constructed as a Christian Greek Orthodox church. From the sixth century until the fall of the city in the fifteenth century, it served as the seat of the Patriarch of Constantinople. From 9 May 1453 until 1931 the building was an Ottoman mosque, and from then onwards, it has been used as a museum. For a thousand years the building was the largest cathedral in the world, and could be described as the epitome of Byzantine architecture, and as such when the Ottomans conquered the city, the change of religious use would have been symbolic. It immediately became the principle mosque in Istanbul, and thus represented the power of the new occupiers of the city and the authority of their religion (see Figure 3.7).

The Bull Staircase in Prague is a much smaller and less dramatic example of how the remodelling of a structure can represent the change of the ruling regime. Czechoslovakia was a new state created in the aftermath of the First World War, when the country was declared independent from the Austro-Hungarian Empire as part of the Treaty of Saint-Germain-en-Laye. Prague Castle was to be used as the seat of the President of the new republic. This was somewhat ironic, given the regal nature of any castle, and especially this one. It is positioned on an outcrop high above the city and had developed over almost a thousand years into an enormous complex of churches, palaces and government buildings, connected by a series of

FIGURE 3.5 The Haçienda Club in Manchester, England, by Ben Kelly was a theatrical somewhat ambiguous space, as this interpretive model suggests.

Credit: Charlotte Fuller, Simina Ionescu, Christina Lipcheva

courtyards and gardens. At the centre of the castle is the St Vitas Cathedral, which consists of a thirteenth century Gothic chancel with a nineteenth century Gothic revival nave.

The well-recognised local architect Josip Plecnik was instructed to make the new-found democracy visible; to remodel Prague Castle in a style in which the features of egalitarianism would be clearly evident to everybody. Plecnik made a series of changes to the grand courtyards that surrounded the castle buildings. He also remodelled the gardens, the ramparts and the official residence. This all made the castle itself easier to use as a seat of government and less imperial, but did not

FIGURE 3.6 The Haçienda Club in Manchester, England, by Ben Kelly. The language of the interventions reflect a preoccupation with post-industrial graphic techniques.
Credit: Charlotte Fuller, Simina Ionescu, Christina Lipcheva

address the problem of the relationship between the building and the city. Dense high walls protected the castle from the urban area below; they served to keep the citizens out and safeguard the royal family within.

Rather than remove the walls, Plecnik chose to disrupt the monolithic integrity of them. He cut a hole in this colossal barrier – in the far corner of the third courtyard, a barely significant sheltered position just behind the cathedral. However, this inconsequential moment within the castle confines marked the central position within the walls themselves: the fundamental point in the vertical relationship between the town and the castle. From the city below, this also marked the point of

FIGURE 3.7 The Hagia Sophia Mosque in Istanbul has been adapted for a different religion on a number of occasions; the memory of each is still embedded within the structure of the building.

Credit: Sally Stone

greatest royal accumulation, the position where the grandeur of the great cathedral climbs above the wall in the most magnificent manner (see Figures 3.8 and 3.9).

This slice through the walls creates a direct connection between the residents of the town and the place of government. It was a liberating action; the penetrating hole dissolved the great distance between the two and created a direct republican relationship. The Bull Staircase was inserted into this gap, thus completing this revolutionary connection.

The staircase sits completely within the mass of the great walls, with just the projecting balconies hovering over the terrace on the city side, and an extraordinary draped portico marking the position of the connection within the confines of the cathedral courtyard. A Minoan Column is situated at the pivotal or turning point of each flight of steps, which reduces the mass of the insertion and therefore more fully opens up the view. The portico is almost primitive; it is simply four square columns, and upon each stands a magnificent bull. These support two horizontal beams over which is draped a lead awning. This Semperian gesture is both decorative and primeval. It is very much part of Plecnik's quest to find a type of architecture fitted to a new county, but also suggests something much older, perhaps an instinctive connection with a much earlier time. The Bull Staircase is a symbolic

FIGURE 3.8 The insertion of the Bull Staircase in Prague by Josip Plecnik (1931) into the city walls was an act of liberation that created a direct link between the town and the palace.

Credit: Sally Stone

FIGURE 3.9 The language of the Bull Staircase in Prague by Josip Plecnik (1931) is designed in a modern decorative manner, something that reflected that attitude within the new republic.

Credit: Sally Stone

act of translation. The intervention acts as a mediator between the royal and the republic; it recognises both by liberating a future for the building.

An interesting example of the obvious disparity between the intentions of the creator of the original building and those that altered it can be observed within La Cité Frugès, a small housing estate just outside Pessac to the southwest of Bordeaux in Southern France. The estate was designed by Le Corbusier in the early 1920s, and crucially was constructed shortly after the publication of *Vers une Architecture*. This revolutionary book contained seven polemic essays, all but one of which were originally published in the magazine L'Espirit Nouveau. The papers built into a manifesto for a new type of architecture, one that embraced new technologies, suggested simple effective structures and honed construction. Interestingly, although Le Corbusier maintained that the book was aimed at architects and academics, a much wealthier clientele read L'Espirit Nouveau. And it seemingly served its purpose, because after reading the articles the wealthy industrialist Henry Frugès commissioned the architect to design two estates to house the families of those who worked in his sugar refinery business. La Cité Frugès was designed to house the employees of the actual sugar factory; the other, designed with his cousin Pierre Jeanneret, was a much smaller and earlier development situated on the coast to the west of Bordeaux, and was for those who constructed the timber crates to carry the sugar.

La Cité Frugès estate was one of Le Corbusier's first substantial projects and although his Five Points of Architecture were not finally published until 1926, they were obviously being formulated during the gestation of this project. The idea of the horizontal garden city was advanced within this development. As were freestanding façades, horizontal strip windows, roof terraces (some of which are accessed by exterior staircases) and column-grid construction. The principle was to standardise the housing and thus construct low-cost quickly assembled buildings. The 50 units that were actually built followed just seven templates; this allowed builders to reuse the same formwork for pouring concrete, which greatly reduced costs. Le Corbusier also experimented with colour in these houses, using just green, red and blue in an attempt to suppress the sensation of mass and amplify the qualities of areas and planes.

The houses were experimental, and probably far too progressive for the original inhabitants. The estate garnered a reputation as a Modernist failure, as an experimental and elitist utopian project that was totally unsuited to the needs of the population that actually had to live in the buildings.

However, the houses were substantial; the poured concrete was, in places, up to four centimetres thick. And the urban plan was much more like a garden village than a Modernist estate, so the homes were not without all hope and the inhabitants began to deliberately adapt the houses to suit their own style. The simple buildings were sufficiently robust to accept change, while individuality could easily be accommodated within the modesty of the identical concrete boxes.

Some of the open-plan interiors were subdivided to provide separate rooms, the open verandas boxed in to create extra indoor space or even garages, ornamental tubs and planters were placed within the sparse gardens, and the unforgiving raw concrete façades decorated. One particularly creative intervention is the addition of three small hemispherical window boxes below each of the upper floor openings of one property (see Figures 3.10, 3.11, 3.12 and 3.13).

The buildings are resilient. The simple robust concept means that the changes do not undermine the estate's original concept, nor do they destroy the basic nature of the place. Ada Louise Huxtable in her review of the estate for *The New York Times* in the early 1980s expected to see an utterly failing hosing complex, but was delightfully surprised by the way in which the adaptability of the houses allowed the occupants to recognise their own requirements within the solid organisation of the orthogonal buildings. She quotes the French architect, Philippe Boudon, who documented the process of change within the estate in the book *Lived-in Architecture, Le Corbusier's Pessac Revisited*: 'The Quartiers Modernes Fruges were not an architectural failure' he wrote:

> The modifications carried out by the occupants constitute a positive and not a negative consequence of Le Corbusier's original conception. Pessac not only allowed the occupants sufficient latitude to satisfy their needs, by doing so it also helped them to realise what those needs were.

13

FIGURE 3.10 The original design of La Cité Frugès, Bordeaux, France by Le Corbusier was a progressive attempt to provide an open, clean and healthy environment for the townsfolk.

Credit: Sally Stone

FIGURE 3.11 The utilitarian buildings of La Cité Frugès, Bordeaux, France by Le Corbusier exhibited his experimental ideas of modularity and standardisation. This was not always appreciated by the residents.

Credit: Sally Stone

FIGURE 3.12 After many years of neglect, La Cité Frugès, Bordeaux, France by Le Corbusier is receiving much admiration and respect, and is thus in the process of being revived.

Credit: Sally Stone

Conclusions

The post-modern interpretation of reality is both fragmentary and plural; it therefore allows for multiple points of view. History as the construct of individuals or groups has replaced the Modernist idea of absolute facts or objective truths, which means that discourse cannot escape from its producer, who always approaches the subject from his or her own interest or identity. Objectivity may not even be that desirable, given that research methodology encourages a multitude of alternative voices. History is more than the illustration of a particular moment in time; it is the personal translation of that moment. Those who know history have already carried out an act of interpretation. Which leads to the question of whether something being true or false as possibly not important, but whether the fact or statement is acceptable becomes a priority.

This small selection of examples shows how diverse the interpretations of the existing can be. All evaluations are positional, and the architect or designer is in the position to act as the translator. It is part of the role to understand how the old and the new can work together. Even the language that the designer uses to describe their work reinforces this: conversion, transformation, alteration, remodelling. The redesign of any space is an act of translation. Buildings are mnemonic devices, and

FIGURE 3.13 Many of the original residents of La Cité Frugès, Bordeaux, France by Le Corbusier do not appreciate the austere language of their home, and have remodelled many of the features to accommodate their own ideas of homeliness. The buildings do seem sufficiently robust to accommodate this.

Credit: Sally Stone

by necessity the designer will read the existing space, he or she will examine, analyse and interpret that space before deciding upon the form and nature of the design any new elements. Of course, every architect or designer will interpret a given space differently; this is part of the marvellous qualities of design.

Thus all histories are positional. Designers and architects who work with an existing building will select a version of the past and the very fact of appropriating that particular vision of history will have definite effects. This will inevitably align with some readings, but against others, and this does lead to an ethical question: Does the designer have a responsibility to recognise and respect all of the activities that the building once enclosed, or should we be allowed to forget?

References

1. Benjamin, W. (1996) Selected Writings: Volume 1 1913–1926. M. Bullock and M. W. Jennings (Eds). Cambridge MA: The Belknap Press of Harvard University, p. 260.
2. O'Donnell + Tuomey (2014) Space For Architecture, the Work of O'Donnell + Tuomey. Artifice books on architecture.
3. Jenkins, K. (1991) Re-Thinking History. London: Routledge, p. 40.
4. Eco, U. (1997) The Role of the Reader: Explorations in the Semiotics of Texts. Bloomingdale: Indiana University Press, p. 49.
5. Eco, U. (1989) The Open Work. Introduction by D. Robey. Cambridge, MA: Harvard University Press, p. xvii.
6. Benjamin, W. (1996) Selected Writings: Volume 1 1913–1926. M. Bullock and M.W. Jennings (Eds). Cambridge MA: The Belknap Press of Harvard University, p. 254.
7. Benjamin, W. (1996) Selected Writings: Volume 1 1913–1926. M. Bullock and M.W. Jennings (Eds). Cambridge MA: The Belknap Press of Harvard University, p. 260.
8. Marot, Sébastien (2003) Sub-Urbanism and the Art of Memory. London: AA Publications, p. 85.
9. Rowe, C. and Koetter, F. (1983) Collage City. Cambridge MA: MIT Press, p. 121.
10. Urban Splash: www.urbansplash.co.uk, accessed October 2016.
11. Reynolds, A. Unpublished Conference Presentation: Sinister Dialogues, 25 September 2014.
12. Stone, S. (2014) "The Haçienda: The Manufactured Image of a Post-Industrial City" from Interiors: Design, Architecture, Culture. 5 (1) p. 48.
13. Huxtable, Ada Louise (1981) "Architecture View; Le Corbusier's Housing Project – Flexible Enough to Endure" from The New York Times: www.nytimes.com/1981/03/15/arts/architecture-view-le-corbusier-s-housing-project-flexible-enough-endure-ada.html

4

SITE SPECIFIC ART

Unintentional Monuments

Introduction

James Turrell is an artist who works with artificial and natural light. Not the source of the light, as in the fittings such as the lamps or bulbs, but he actually manipulates the light itself to create environments that are both beautiful and disturbing. Within his early work he controlled and directed pure artificial projected light so that it appeared to hover in front of the gallery wall, rather than merely adhering to the surface of it. These carefully controlled installations generated a sense of wonder within the viewer – at the simplicity of the idea, the cleverness of the application and the serenity of its operation.

Later projects took this idea further with the creation of small environments. Within these contained spaces, such as a room, lobby or specially constructed chamber, the light was manipulated to create a feeling of infinity. It became impossible to see where the space ended, almost as if the gaze of the viewer was into an abyss, looking towards limitless space.

His Skyspace projects have also created the same awareness of the intensity of pure light and space, but using natural, rather than artificial, light. Again within this series of projects, it is the light rather that the construction of the light that is important. Turrell has created a series of individual Skyspace buildings, some are in new constructions, but others are within existing structures. These are spaces for contemplation and revelation. Each installation is a single square room (with a carefully separated entrance) which has a deliberately angled reclining bench fitted all the way around the perimeter and a pure square-shaped aperture in the roof. The visitor reclines upon the seat and contemplates the view through the hole in the ceiling. Again it is the light rather than the fitting that is important, so the window in the roof has no visible frame. The view is not interrupted with such distractions, which would interfere with the deliberation upon the changing sky, the advent of dawn or dusk, the weightlessness of the birds that enter and leave the canvass, or the ephemeral nature of the clouds.

In 2007, James Turrell created a Skyspace at the Yorkshire Sculpture Park, in the north east of England. (The YSP is an independent charitable trust that was founded in 1977, it was the first sculpture park in the UK, and is the largest in the Europe (1).) It is within an existing building in the picturesque 500 acre estate grounds of the eighteenth century Bretton Hall. The Grade II Listed building that Turrell chose for his installation was originally designed as a somewhat quaint shelter for the deer that wandered through the grounds, but had been used as a storage space for many years (see Figures 4.1 and 4.2).

The unassuming square chamber has no environmental control, and is simply open to the elements. The hole in the roof has no covering; that would be a distraction from the perfect view. The opening is carefully detailed to ensure that only the lip of the space is seen, while the frame and the drainage are hidden on the exterior of the roof. The only non-natural intrusion is the very fine artificial light inserted immediately behind the continuous bench. This is faint enough to be unnoticed during the day, but sufficiently ambient to just adequately illuminate the space after dark. So the experience is of the brightness of the sky during the hours of daylight, and the denseness of the sky at night. The experience is most magical when

FIGURE 4.1 Skyspace at the Yorkshire Sculpture Park by James Turrell (2007); a site specific installation within an existing building.

Credit: Sally Stone

FIGURE 4.2 The interior space at the Skyspace at the Yorkshire Sculpture Park by James Turrell serves no purpose other than for the visitor to look at and appreciate the sky.

Credit: Sally Stone

this condition changes at dusk or dawn. The work does not alter the landscape or manipulate the site in any way; it just accentuates and heightens the vision of the sky and the connection between the viewer and the changing light of the Yorkshire heavens.

Art and Architecture

Unsurprisingly, Turrell's work is extremely influential. Architects and designers seek to appropriate the inventive manipulation of light and form to create buildings and spaces that are imbued with the same atmosphere. The architects Herzog and de Meuron converted the Bankside Power Station in London into the Tate Modern gallery in the early twenty-first century. Their approach was to enhance the monumental and industrial character of the building without significantly detracting from its form. Light is used almost as a construction material in a number of significant ways.

The first is an enormous artificial light beam, which appears to hover above the gallery spaces along the whole length of the exterior of the top of the building – as a sort of horizontal illuminated foil to the immediately adjacent dense brick vertical chimney. This artificial insertion is echoed with a huge natural roof-light above the massive entrance or Turbine Hall. This hole in the ceiling is necessarily large to balance the scale of this enormous interior public space. The architects also created a series of lightboxes that hover over this great entrance hall. The boxes are uncorrupted and pure; they are simply illuminated three-dimensional rectangular containers that glow with latent energy. Turrell's influence can definitely be seen within the design of these elements; the fittings are not visible, there is no sense of the construction of the installations, of the position of the light fittings, of where the energy is inputted and where it is plugged into the mains. They are just glowing boxes of coloured light (see Figure 4.3).

The architect Steven Holl creates buildings that glow, that often appear as a collection of luminous structures that float gently above the ground rather than having a heavy connection with it. The Maggies Centre at St Bartholomew's

FIGURE 4.3 The glazed bays at the Tate Modern by Herzog and de Meuron appear to make a direct reference to the artificial light installations by James Turrell.

Credit: Sally Stone

Hospital in London is one such structure. It is a vertical volume of floating coloured light attached to the heavy masonry walls of James Gibbs' eighteenth century building. The extension is constructed from matt white, internally illuminated glass, into the surface of which are embedded small fragments of coloured glass. The façade is organised as a series of horizontal strips in imitation of the rhythm of the distinctive façade of the adjacent building. The collection of rooms and spaces contained within this glowing box is a peaceful and demure addition to the series of substantial hospital buildings (see Figures 4.4 and 4.5).

Installation art can act as a significant influence upon interior architecture and design. Artists such as Marcel Duchamp, Robert Irwin, Gordon Matta-Clarke, Kurt Schwitters, Daniel Buren, Roger Hiorns, Doris Salcedo, Alison Turnbull, Richard Wilson and Rachel Whiteread are often cited as inspirational. Within their work these artists strive to activate a place. Using a process of investigation and recognition, they utilise the properties of the existing to stimulate and provoke a transformation or translation. Their work engages directly with the spaces of the city, with the existing situation, and they all strive to comment upon the relationship between the built structure, the environment that it is contained within and the culture of those who view it.

The notion of removing art and cultural events from the rarefied atmosphere of the art gallery or institution, and relocating them into the open situation of the publicly accessible building, is not new. The removal offers greater possibilities of interpretation, and certainly larger and more culturally varied audiences. Artists who interrupt the recognisable and comfortable pattern of the current situation can provoke reaction. Artists who work with the prevailing condition, who create art that is situated outside of the setting of the gallery and within the public domain are deliberately activating a familiar setting with an unusual or unexpected object. This may be a freestanding sculpture placed in a public position or a series of interventions that deliberately interact with an existing situation, building or structure.

Complexity

The existing building can be considered as an object that has been taken out of context and understood from an unexpected viewpoint; this is a process that will disrupt the familiar and rational structure of a given everyday. This is a strategic act of interruption, which effectively promotes the de-familiarisation of the everyday environment and habitual scenario. The ephemerality of this manoeuvre can suggest alternative situations and different possibilities, and thus the familiar becomes strange and the unfamiliar recognisable. The everyday context also not only blurs the distinction between the different disciplines that contribute to the project, but also ensures that the work is more accessible. Audience members may have encountered the site previously and therefore have a different memory of the space, or have varied perspectives of the site informed by their knowledge or lack of knowledge of the surroundings. The artist Gordon Matta-Clark described this as 'a kind of complexity which comes from taking an otherwise completely normal,

FIGURE 4.4 The Maggies Centre at St Bartholomew's Hospital in London is a white glazed form with colourful inserted panels.

Credit: Sally Stone

conventional, albeit anonymous situation and defining it, translating it into overlapping into multiple readings of conditions past and present' (2).

The process of understanding, analysis and interpretation that informs site specific installation art enables the artist to speak beguilingly of performance, space

FIGURE 4.5 Steven Holl's transluscent Maggies Centre at St Bartholomew's Hospital in London is in strong contrast to the robust masonry construction of the original building.

Credit: Sally Stone

and interpretation. A complex series of investigations inform the approach of the artist. Often the clues are already in the place; it is the process of discovery and recognition that allows the interpretation of this information and the production of a viable proposal to enhance or stimulate the environment, context, situation or place. Thus site specific installation can sometimes be little more than a process of recognition, understanding and heightening of the qualities of the existing situation, while at other times they are outrageous interpretations.

The eminent architect Louis Kahn once said: 'What will be has always been' (3). He implies that what already exists is only apparent when it can be seen, when the individual parts can be distinguished and how they contribute to the whole appreciated, when the relationships with each other can be perceived and their individual strengths visualised, and when the complex connections and associations can be comprehended and sense made within the meaning of the place. The artist strives to discover what currently exists, to enhance, justify, interpret or adapt what is already present then desires to see, to experience and to uncover that presence.

The influential artist Robert Irwin (born 1928) explained his own work: 'There is no there there, until you see there there' (4). It is the lack of clarity that characterises the familiar; the well known or commonplace is something that is so recognisable that it is impossible to acknowledge its independent existence. Certain aspects of our day-to-day existence are taken for granted and perhaps only when these artefacts, statements, images, events and things are highlighted do they become apparent. Thus the artist will mentally remove an element from its given context to emphasise the qualities of it as an individual.

Robert Irwin works with places or environments. He creates minimal site specific and site adjusted interventions, which validate the importance of sensory perception of the viewer when looking or seeing what a space is made up of. From this he developed a theory of aesthetic perception, which was based upon the idea that the level of integration between a work of art and its immediate context could be measured and quantified. He proposed four categories of art, which ranged from absolutely no amalgamation to the other extreme where the art and the context are so completely combined that they formed a new whole.

Site Dominant discussed works of art conceived and constructed in the studio with absolutely no thought or idea of the final position of the piece. Site Adjusted is the classification for artwork that contains a certain amount of compensation for its eventual location. Works of art that are intended to occupy a specific position and are designed to occupy that space and no other are in the Site Specific category, and the most extreme group is the Site Conditioned or Determined. This is art that is totally integrated with its site. Here the sculptural response draws all its cues (reasons for being) from its surroundings. This requires the process to begin with an intimate, hands-on reading of the site to identify the particular characteristics (5) (see Figure 4.6).

Irwin believes that it is impossible to divorce the understanding and the appreciation of an artwork from the place in which it is situated. This perception is twofold in that it encompasses the context: so the space, the orientation, the position, whether inside or out, the scale of the surrounding objects and the type of objects these are. The other factor is the changing environment that the object is viewed in: this includes the fluctuating light, weather, seasons and even the other people who are viewing the piece at the same time. Art is never seen in a vacuum, and it is comprehended differently depending upon the physical circumstances of the exhibition. Appreciation is always an act of translation, depending upon its position, whether inside a national gallery or a provincial gallery, within a municipal park or an urban square, inside someone's home or in a scruffy warehouse, all of which is combined with the personal circumstances of the viewer.

The expression of the inside of a building and the relationship between the particular spaces was explored by Marcel Duchamp, who created an expressive installation that was door hinged precisely in the corner of the room. This allowed it to swing between two door openings, closing one as it opened the other, thus rendering it either useless or symbolic – or perhaps it was a comment upon the barriers that we put up between ourselves. It does, however, bring to mind the very old question: 'When is a door not a door? When it's ajar!'

Gordon Matta-Clark (1943–76) was the son of the artist Roberto Matta, and the Godson of Marcel Duchamp, and so was to some extent, artistic royalty. He created

FIGURE 4.6 Scrim Veil Black Rectangle Natural Light, Whitney Museum of American Art (1977). The artist Robert Irwin has created a series of installations that appear to intensify the sense and clarity of the existing space, often without actually changing very much at all.

Credit: Mduvekot via Wikimedia Commons

a body of work that questioned the lack of capacity inherent within buildings to absorb change. He actually trained as an architect before abandoning this in favour of much more hands-on site specific art. His inter- and trans-disciplinary practice was informed by this qualified knowledge of architecture and was based upon a reaction to the fixed parameters of buildings and the fundamental laws of occupation. He developed a series of projects that examined the nature of existing buildings before conducting activities that introduced disorderly change into the intrinsic nature of the structure. He made use of things that had outlived their usefulness, and these artistic interventions usually involved taking something away from the building. This disturbing event would alter the perception of the place; it would dislocate the equilibrium and encourage the viewed to consider the building from a different and surprising perspective. These acts subsequently raised questions about the ability of buildings and by extension cities to observe, appreciate, withhold and utilise modification, that is, to evolve.

Matta-Clark is best known for his 'building cuts'. These were sculptural transformations of abandoned buildings produced by cutting and dismantling the actual fabric of the structure. 'Splitting' (1974) was an ingenuous idea that produced a striking change and reaction. Using little more than a chainsaw, Matta-Clark simply cut an abandoned family clapboard house in half. He sliced the horizontal boarded, timber framed building in two vertically down the centre of the shortest dimension. Then by carefully removing a horizontal layer of the cinderblock foundations on one side only, that half of the house tilted back slightly to open up a V-shaped space between the two parts. This completely undermined the notion of home, of house, of family and community; it made the habitable inhabitable. The cuts, although made gently and carefully, were perceived as destructive, forceful and violated the notion of home.

Conical Intersect (1975) was greeted with an equally hostile reception. In February 1975 Matta-Clark was invited to participate in the ninth Paris Biennale. This project, on the site of the Plateau Beaubourg, connected two seventeenth century buildings with a spiralling, cone-like cut that was visible from the street. Again these were abandoned buildings, destined to be demolished to make way for the great plaza of the Pompidou Centre. The project illustrated the dichotomy that the search for progress delivers. Two projects happening side-by-side, one which embodied the future – the dynamic new and shockingly High-Tech Centre Pompidou – while the other, which celebrated the rich cultural heritage, was being torn down in the name of progress. (Matta-Clark's first idea was apparently to cut the conical hole in the new building, but it soon became clear that this was not feasible.) The purpose of the hole was to throw light through the unexpected connections that had been created within the building and liberate the interior from its petite bourgeois past. Again the unsympathetic reaction to the installation was based upon the idea that the artist was exploiting the sanctity of the domestic space (6).

Rachael Whiteread (born 1963) also faced great hostility for her Turner Prize winning sculpture: House. She is an artist who works directly with existing objects, including buildings, to reveal the previously hidden and overlooked characteristics. She casts meaningful representations of everyday objects; not of the outside of the object, but the inside. She started with a cast of the inside of a hot water bottle, then a mattress, the underside of chairs and tables, before progressing onto castings of a room, then the highly ambitious production of House in 1993. These castings show the negative space, the stuff inside that is not tangible or solid – it is the space or the air behind the exterior of the walls of the building. But the sculpture also shows all the marks of occupation that had been inscribed upon the interior surface of the room or object. These simulacra deal with such issues as memory, relationships and occupation. House was a cast of the inside of an entire abandoned Edwardian terraced house in East London. The project involved spraying the interior of the house with concrete and then removing the shell of the building itself to leave just a perfect casting of the interior. The sculpture was a positive cast of the previously negative space of the house. 'House' became the centre of a political controversy, instigating a Parliamentary debate about its retention as a monument. Opponents argued that not only was it ugly and a waste of money but also that the sculpture defiled every notion of the 'home' and was disrespectful to those who once lived in the house. The local London authority in which it resided threatened it with removal, and the dispute raged until 11 January 1994 when House was demolished.

FIGURE 4.7 The Judenplatz Holocaust Memorial in Vienna by Rachel Whiteread (2000). This monument is a casting of the rear of hundreds of books; it appears to be an inside-out library.

Credit: Sally Stone

Another highly significant project by Whiteread is the Judenplatz Holocaust Memorial in Vienna. This is a casting of the inside of a library, taken from the extraordinary position of between the walls of the building and the back of the books; thus the monument is of hundreds of unopened books, all lined up one next to another, shelf upon shelf. A metaphor of course to the many lives of the local residents cut short. This memorial is positioned at the edge of an urban square in the former Jewish area of the city, and in reference to the hundreds of people who were forced to leave their homes; it is also known as the Nameless Library (see Figures 4.7, 4.8 and 4.9).

The idea of working with or being inspired by the existing or the already created is something that many artists have explored. Peter Scolzold and Abigail Reynolds both work with images that are already there. They take the original picture, whether this is photograph or even a postcard, and then add to it by weaving or layering into it another image. Reynolds may use a picture of a particular historical scene or happening, possibly something with a sinister edge to it, and then overlay a present-day image of the same place to create a somewhat ambiguous multi-layered image. Scolzold is much more humorous, creating rather ridiculous composite pictures from two quite different events to generate a third image,

FIGURE 4.8 The Judenplatz Holocaust Memorial in Vienna by Rachel Whiteread (2000). Just the backs of the unopenable cast concrete books are visible.

Credit: Sally Stone

FIGURE 4.9 The Judenplatz Holocaust Memorial in Vienna by Rachel Whiteread (2000). The great doors of the library are missing their furniture, thus reinforcing the concept of a lost and impenetrable place.

Credit: Sally Stone

5 FAREWELL, LONDON: VANISHING CITY

FIGURE 4.10 St Paul's 1975/1926 (2013). Abigail Reynolds creates ominous, somewhat unsettling, images that use visual imagery to create a link between the present and the past. The manipulated photographs weave a direct connection through time to create an ambiguous composite image.

Book pages cut and folded, 22.5 (h) x 30 (w) cms (unframed)

something slightly attached to the first two that formed the amalgamated image, but with a completely different meaning. The existing condition inspires these art works, but by combining the new with the old, an underlying meaning hidden within the depths of the images is released (see Figure 4.10).

The simulacra, copy or representation of an earlier work of art is of course not new. Rubens brazenly repainted Caravaggio; not an exact copy, but an interpretation, almost an evolution really of the original paintings. Picasso, who famously said that 'good artists copy, but great artists steal', reproduced Manet's Le Déjeuner sur l'herbe in his own style. Jake and Dinos Chapman have long been obsessed with the work of the nineteenth century artist Goya. The brothers called one of their earliest tributes to the great Spanish painter, printmaker and visionary 'Great Deeds Against the Dead'; within this work they reproduced one of his horrific images of cruelty as a life size tableau. This copy or translation was possibly as shocking a depiction of cruelty as those acts that Goya was effectively illustrating.

Some years later, the Chapman Brothers obtained a complete set of Goya's prints 'the Disasters of War'. This collection of horrific images was actually printed in 1863, about 35 years after the artist's death, and the images are considered to be a modern masterpiece. They are an unrelentingly grim depiction of the cruelty of war. Jake and Dinos Chapman have carefully and systematically defaced every single image. They have drawn over every print, replacing the horrific heads with those of clowns or puppies, added bursts of violet and white colour to the aging prints, and added smiles to the faces of the massacred animals. This act of adaptation generated massive controversy, not because of the depictions of rape and slaughter, after all a modern audience can no longer be shocked by such images, but because of the desecration of the great works of art. This act of vandalism was considered outrageous by a generation that is generally beyond surprise; defacing a great work of art is perhaps the last taboo?

Louis Kahn spoke of the spirit of the building being released when the building is free of servitude, that once the burden of the function has been lifted from it that the true nature of the structure would be revealed. The vital force that characterises a living being as being alive will emerge only once the building has become deserted or derelict, only then the enthusiasm and energy of the living qualities of the form will be disclosed:

> A building being built is not yet in servitude. It is so anxious to be that no grass can grow under its feet, so high is the spirit of wanting to be. When in service and finished, the building wants to say, "look, I want to tell you about the way I was made". Nobody listens. Everybody is busy going from room to room. But when the building is a ruin and free from servitude, the spirit emerges telling of the marvel that a building was made.
>
> 7

But buildings and spaces need not be abandoned or dilapidated for this spirit to be released. Architects and artists who work with existing situations, buildings and structures strive to reveal this hidden spirit; through a process of exposing and exploiting the hidden memories of a situation, they seek to reveal and interpret these meanings and construct a new layer of meaning that will breathe new life and consequence into the place.

The installations of the Dutch artist Sarah Westphal are painfully nostalgic. Within a series of projects she has reflected upon the ideas of the uncanny, the unheimliche and the intimacy of barely remembered memories. She has been described as an 'interiorist pur sang' (8), as her work embodies many of the attributes of the subject; that is, someone whose interests go beyond the interior to also look at the impact that the inside has upon the exterior world (9). The backdrop to her work is the commonplace everyday, the overlooked and the almost forgotten. The series Draperies (2010–11), for example, utilises abandoned soft furnishings to decorate a barely restored home in Ghent, Belgium. The house was still a construction site when Westphal temporarily appropriated it; the walls were bare and still showed the signs of the building work, while the floors were uncovered. She hung a collection of worn and tattered curtains in strategic places within the building. The fabric was old and hardened with dust, but the colours reflected the bygone age from which it came. Westphal then lit the installation with the strong and incessant lights of the building industry. The fittings heated up just sufficiently to encourage the prevailing dust within the building site to circulate, thus creating a wonderful brilliant orange and pitch black space filled with a slowly moving visible atmosphere. From outside, the glowing rooms contained a sort of wistful cosiness. While within the house, the space was uncomfortably beautiful. The space was both familiar and unfamiliar; it contained the attributes of home but also had a strange and slightly unsettling atmosphere. Westphal's installations are disconcerting in that they play with the security of the already known. The expectations of the visitor are tested; the space is disturbed and presented in an unconventional manner, thus encouraging the imme-diately recognisable to be seen differently, for the viewer to reappraise their original preconceptions of the space, and reassess their opinions upon the contingency and usefulness of it (see Figure 4.11).

FIGURE 4.11 Fugitive Piece (2012). Sarah Westphal reflects upon the resonance of lost and forgotten spaces within neglected buildings and abandoned homes.
Fugitive Piece Inkjet print mounted between plexi, 2012, 90 cm x 130 cm

An approach based upon a perceptive and discriminating reading of the existing can produce both dynamic and appropriate results. The unearthing and appreciation of the embodied meaning of a place can be interpreted through building. The architect, designer and artist all have the opportunity to reflect upon the contingency, usefulness and emotional resonance of particular places and structures through the reuse of existing buildings. It is through the understanding of the pre-existing that the remodelled building can become endowed with a new and greater meaning. An investigation of the archaeology of the original can reveal previously hidden or obsolete characteristics. The function of a building, the method in which it is occupied, that is, how it is actually used, can obscure the interpretation of a place. Louis Kahn speaks of the building: only once it becomes a ruin, it is liberated, it is free from servitude. Installation artists, who work within an existing situation, exploit this lack of occupation when creating a new meaning for the space or structure. The intervention will allow a reading and interpretation of a place that is not clouded by issues of function. The actual notion of accommodation can confuse the interpretation process; it is too easy to become embroiled in issues of the relationship between one function and the next, the basic organisation of the spaces and the relationship of the service area to those that they serve.

The legendary Marcel Duchamp, when asked about the difference between art and architecture, is fabled to have replied, 'Drains!'

It is this liberation of not having to consider these service functions that allows the creator of the intervention the freedom of interpretation not always available to the architect. Sebastien Marot, in his Manifesto for Sub-Urbanism, speaks of 'Redirecting emphasis from programme to site' (10); that is, rather than letting the use of the new building dictate the building process by razing everything on a site and starting again, instead allowing the new to be generated by the old.

When the programme is abandoned, then the focus of the project can be concentrated upon the site, the place or the situation. Relationships that exist between the different textures within the condition of the location can be explored, translated and interpreted. And thus the form of the new is influenced not by the function but by the form of the existing, and so it is not that form follows function but form follows form.

Adrien Tirtiaux is an architect-artist. He understands how buildings are put together and uses this knowledge to make systematic changes to them. He has developed a dynamic practice based upon a discerning and sometimes sensitive response to the urgent surroundings of the intervention. Because there is no necessity for the installation to adhere to building regulations, no need to provide environmental control or even have the acceptable safety features such as adequate balustrading, the pieces become emotional responses to the immediate environment. His work, which often includes an element of performance, is always meticulously researched, and thus includes references to history, geography or social structure. Bruggen Bouwen (2013) (which sort of translates from Dutch as 'to Build Bridges') related directly to the immediate proximity that one building had with another in the town of Sint-Niklaas, just to the west of Antwerp in Belgium. Tirtiaux started from

FIGURE 4.12 Bruggen Bowuwen (2013). Adrien Tirtiaux created a suspended timber performative structure that physically connected two adjoining buildings, which although next to each other, by their very nature, had negligible interaction. It was constructed for the exhibition Coup de Ville, Sint-Niklaas, from timber and screws.

Credit: Jasper de Pagie

a fixed point at the top of one building with the construction of a simple timber frame. He then dexterously and dangerously added more lengths of softwood until he had in effect constructed a long projecting cantilever that almost reached the roof of the opposite building. The artist celebrated the final moment of installation with a small leap from the treacherous end point of the almost-bridge onto the safety of the other roof (see Figure 4.12).

Plan de Carrière (2015) was a much simpler proposition, but was equally provocative. This commission was for the public employment service of Flanders in Antwerp. The offices of which were actually situated about 1,500mm above street level, and appeared to rest upon a sort of pedestal of Belgian Blue Stone. Tirtiaux was commissioned to design the new entrance, and so in an act intended to give the impression that the organisation had a substantial basis, he clad the interior of the reception area up to the datum level with the same stone, but this time it was very roughly carved – this gave the impression that the entrance area had been hewn from solid rock. This is a commercial project, a piece of public art, but has the qualities of a conceptual interrogation, a sort of act to liberate a particular factor within the building (see Figure 4.13). The final example of Tirtiaux's work also has this quality: Boven de Muur (2016). The back gardens of a street of houses in Leuven directly surrounded a public park, but the gardens all had high brick walls, which

FIGURE 4.13 Plan de Carrière (2015). Adrien Tirtiaux reinforced the idea of the substantial base of the building by attaching roughly carved stone panels to the bottom of the structure. This is a permanent intervention in a building of the public employment service of Flanders (VDAB Competentiecentrum), Antwerp, made from blue stone.

Credit: Pauline Niks

meant that there was no physical relationship between the two. The residents of the street could not immediately access the park, and so had to take a convoluted route to even visit this outdoor space. Tirtiaux constructed a series of shelters and steps that allowed the inhabitants to enjoy the immediate proximity of the park. The simple timber structures were all different, and based upon in-depth conversations between the artist and the homeowner. Their needs were carefully assessed and the simple softwood structure adapted to each individual dwelling. The facilitating structures were attached to the wall, sometimes as steps, other times as a balcony or even as a little shelter, but each offered a little bit of freedom for the residents (see Figure 4.14).

The nineteenth century Austrian art-historian and philosopher Aloïs Riegl published in 1903, *The Modern Cult of Monuments: Its Essence and Its Development* (Der Moderne Denkmalskultus) (11). (Intriguingly it wasn't until 1982 that this was translated into English.) He was concerned with the manner in which objects of art are a translation or representation of the culture or the epoch that created them. According to Riegl, there exist two kinds of monuments: Intentional, and Unintentional. Intentional monuments have commemorative value, and the aim is to preserve a moment in the consciousness of later generations and thus to a certain extent, control behaviour and expectations. Unintentional monuments are

FIGURE 4.14 Boven de Muur (2016). Adrien Tirtiaux generated links between a public park and the gardens that directly adjoined it with a series of facilitating structures. This was part of the exhibition: Tracing the Future. Made from timber and shrink-wrap plastic.

Credit: Dirk Pauwels

sometimes referred to as historical monuments, and the value of these represents the development of human activity in a particular field. Age-value is contained within all monuments, and it makes explicit the life-cycle of the artefact and thus the culture as a whole. Through these investigations Riegl suggested that historic monuments had a constantly evolving and transformative urban role, and significantly the appreciation of them shifts throughout their lifetime.

Thus the artist who works with existing buildings creates unintentional monuments. Artistic works epitomise the concerns of the culture, often in advance of their own self-knowledge, and focuses the ideas inherent within the population. Artistic interpretations of existing structures, including adaptations, modifications and reuse can all provide valuable and experimental motivation while also enabling a sense of continuum to be established by the incorporation of events, sometimes dramatic or tragic, into the structural evolution of places.

References

1. Yorkshire Sculpture Park (YSP): https://ysp.org.uk/about-ysp
2. Matta-Clark, Gordon (2009) "Statement From Interview with Donald Wall. Arts Magazine, May 1976" reproduced in Situation: Documents of Contemporary Art. Claire Doherty (Ed.). Cambridge MA: MIT Press, Front piece.

3. Kahn, L. (1986) What Will Be Has Always Been. Richard Saul Wurman (Ed.). Rizzoli.

4. Irwin, R. (1996) "Being and Circumstance Notes Towards a Conditional Art" from Theories and Documents of Contemporary Art. Kristine Stiles and Peter Sels (Eds). Berkeley CA: University of California Press, p. 573.

5. Irwin, R. (1996) "Being and Circumstance Notes Towards a Conditional Art" from Theories and Documents of Contemporary Art. Kristine Stiles and Peter Sels (Eds). Berkeley CA: University of California Press, p. 572.

6. Lee, Pamela M. (1999) Objects to be Destroyed: The Work of Gordon Matta-Clarke. Cambridge MA: MIT Press, p. 187.

7. Kahn, L. (1973) "The Room, the Street, and Human Agreement" from A + U. 1 (January), p. 30.

8. Pur sang is a French term for a thoroughbred horse that has evolved to mean something that is beyond doubt.

9. Somers, Inge (2017) An Interiorist Attitude. In the Black Cat Territory: Fictions and Frictions of Inhabited Space. Lut Pil and Sarah Westphal (Eds). Ghent: Luca School of Arts, p. 57.

10. Marot, Sébastien (2003) Sub-Urbanism and the Art of Memory. AA Publications, p. 6.

11. Riegl, Aloïs (1903) Moderne Denkmalkultus: Sein Wesen und Seine Entstehung. Wien: K. K. Zentral-Kommission für Kunst- und Historische Denkmale: Braumüller. Translation first published as Aloïs Riegl, "The Modern Cult of Monuments: Its Character and Its Origin," trans. Kurt W. Forster and Diane Ghirardo, in Oppositions, n. 25 (Fall 1982), 21–51.

5

THE PROBLEM OF OBSOLETE BUILDINGS

A Society Can Only Support So Many Museums

Genk is situated in the heart of Belgium's Kempen coalfield, and is part of an enormous coal deposit that stretches to the Ruhr Valley. The area was exploited at an industrial scale for almost the whole of the twentieth century and over this period Genk grew from an agricultural village to become one of Belgium's most important industrial centres. Winterslag is a suburb of Genk; it was specifically constructed by the mining company to house their workers, and the homes and other buildings were situated around the pit-head. The mine itself extends over a vast area, with shafts up to a kilometre deep. The landscape is littered with the massive accumulated debris of the process of coal extraction; from the great slagheaps that tower over the horizontal countryside, to the forests of specially planted trees, a particular species of pine that groans under excessive compressive load, so warning those underground of imminent collapse. The Winterslag pit closed in 1988; it was the last of the great mines within this important coalfield.

The post-industrial western society has the common problem of what to do with the obsolete landscapes and the buildings of production. The character and identity of each individual industrial development was predicated upon the technical principles necessary for the optimum output and efficiency and so each is different as it contains a direct connection to both the land and the process of production. A palpable anxiety has been created in the wake of the economic void of such massive and whole-scale closures. These post-industrial landscapes contain historical and cultural heritage and if they are to have a sustainable and viable future, and, if their particular character is to be protected and retained, great care must be taken to ensure that their redevelopment is managed in a sympathetic manner.

It is well recognised that the heritage industry is extremely productive, and these almost forgotten areas of production have proved to be a very popular source of entertainment. The C-Mine Cultural Centre by Architects 51N4E is an attempt to replace the obsolete industry of heavy production of the area with the light industry of heritage tourism. This project, which was completed in 2010, reworks the heavy-duty structures into a cultural complex containing: two differently scaled multipurpose auditoria, meeting rooms and spaces for flexible cultural programming; and accommodation for technical support and administration.

The masterplan for the brownfield site sets the series of buildings around a formal square, which is dominated by the pit-head machinery itself. The approach that the designers took was not to fight against, but to work with, the scale and character of the buildings and structures. The former machine hall was adapted to become the cultural hub of the redevelopment. The ground floor is used as the foyer from which to access all other spaces; it acts as a huge field that holds the collection of fragments and detritus of the industrial processes. These are interrupted with a small number of carefully placed interventions which serve to facilitate the needs of the new users, and thus the space has a consciously cluttered feel in which the contrast between the old and the new is deliberately highlighted. The first floor is much more serene and contains a feeling of completeness (or wholeness); the checkerboard terracotta floor which extends all the way across the immense space has been repaired, the obsolete machinery is carefully preserved and fenced-off, and natural light which falls through the vast open-structured glazed roof is allowed to stream across the whole space. It is from this elevated hall that the visitor can access the Mine Experience, the Café and the new roof terrace, with a unique view of the mine's slagheap (see Figures 5.1, 5.2, 5.3 and 5.4).

This situation does beg the question: What is the point of protecting these buildings? They are obsolete, their useful life is finished and the need for these buildings has long past. Why is it important to keep this industrial heritage? Undoubtedly, if it wasn't for the fact that the structures are legally protected they would long ago have been demolished. It could be argued that it has also become clear that it is one thing to cherish heritage and historic buildings, but another to hold value in structures that are in disuse and falling apart. The buildings have become museums to themselves; despite their embodiment of the area's identity they do little more than celebrate their own obsolete past. They are preserved for no other purpose than to exhibit the lost industry of the area. The quality of the conservation is laudable; Viollet-le-Duc would be impressed with the manner in which they have been preserved; to almost a state that is more pristine than could ever have really existed (1). They are too clean, too immaculate, far too sanitised to really show what the working conditions were really like. It is quiet, the air is clean, the buildings are scrubbed and it is empty, devoid of workers and atmosphere. The museum doesn't attempt to conjure the feeling of the time of production, but offers a romantic, presentable, palatable version of the past. There is a nostalgic perception of this history as a golden period of certainty, of full employment and of great social comradeship.

Post-Modern Attitudes towards Obsolete Buildings

One of the fundamental characteristics of our post-modern society is the rise of individualism. Advances in communications, information and transport technologies

FIGURE 5.1 The C-Mine Cultural Centre by Architects 51N4E. The interventions to the industrial buildings are as uncompromisingly robust as the original structure. Note the Gordon Matta Clark inspired vertical slot cut all the way through the building on the right of the image.

Credit: Sally Stone

have facilitated a revolution in the global flow of objects, information and people. This has led to a pluralism of world-view, an expansion of individual choice and a liberation of lifestyle (2). This suggests that the global diffusion of culture and identity is incompatible with the traditional structures of the post-war period, which has inevitably led to a more diverse and separated pattern of sociability. This has prompted a questioning of traditional forms of authority, and conventional ideas of citizenship, social contact and allegiance.

The past has traditionally been seen as highly structured and highly political. A definite hierarchical system existed, one which reinforced conventional patterns of behaviour. J. B. Jackson describes how the present was once a continuation of this

FIGURE 5.2 The C–Mine Cultural Centre by Architects 51N4E. Visitors dine among the detritus of the industrial past.

Credit: Sally Stone

past, that is, the re-enactment of the past modified by intervening events (3). The population of a community would be constantly reminded of its original identity and its ancient pledges. This relationship was given visual form with monuments and temporal form in a series of days of commemoration. The emphasis was on the continuity of history. A traditional monument is a reminder of something

FIGURE 5.3 The C-Mine Cultural Centre by Architects 51N4E. The crisp white tablecloths are a marked contrast to the worn and obsolete machinery.

Credit: Sally Stone

important: a great event, public figure or declaration, while a traditional festival will commemorate a previous event or reinforce a particular attitude. It is a persistent reminder of something specific within the hierarchy of the past. Thus through this dual process of tangible and intangible reminders, a population was continually reminded of their position within the organisation of that community, and so the

FIGURE 5.4 The C–Mine Cultural Centre by Architects 51N4E. The pithead winding gear has been retained as a symbolic reminder of the lost industry.
Credit: Sally Stone

monument had the double function of an aide de memoir, but also a guide to behaviour and attitude in the future, in that its presence determined the actions of forthcoming generations.

Many of these social conventions began to crumble with the fall of Modernism and rise in the significance of the working-man and importantly the working-woman. The established metanarratives were no longer acceptable, and coinciding with the rise in economic prosperity of the beginning of the second half of the twentieth century was the emergence of the individual point of view. The plural-istic reading of society ensured that history was no longer seen from the privileged view of those in power. This meant that the customary frameworks of organisation that presupposed the privileging of various centres were no longer seen as the pri-mary frameworks. These include traditional points of view such as: Anglo-centric, Euro-centric, gender-centric, ethno-centric, etc., and has led to an attitude of gen-eral incredulity that challenges many historical narratives and has led to a new way of celebrating past events.

All histories are now seen as important and all narratives are viable and relevant; the basis of historical existence is no longer seen as a sequence of political events. All history is positional; it is dependent upon the position of the narrator of that history. History can therefore be regarded as a discourse; it contains facts, interpret-ations, bias and empathy. It can be argued that anyone viewing material from the past, however well informed, will only be able to understand it from his or her own position. Historical analysis is an act of translation; the historian (whether architec-tural, cultural, scientific, feminist, activist or any other of a myriad of other focuses) will not be able to view the material through any other lens than that of their own culture. Thus any history contains many different readings and interpretations.

Post-modernism has exacerbated this; society is now post-industrial, post-Marxist, post-western, post… etc. Lyotard's definition of the way that we live now describes this well: 'a social formation where under the impact of secularising, democratising, computerising and consumerising pressures, the maps and status of knowledge are being re-drawn and re-described' (4). Thus the old centres have been almost completely destroyed and so those without power and with little prop-erty are anxious to commemorate their own achievements. This reaction to the traditional hierarchy has had a profound affect upon the character of architecture. It is no coincidence that public buildings have begun to lose their monumental char-acter and a huge number of museums are being created to celebrate many different aspects of society. One of the first examples of this pluralist attitude to the past is the monument to the unknown soldier, which again celebrates a different past, not the past that history books describe, but an acknowledgement of the ordinary person.

Nostalgia

This idea of history as a chronicle of everyday existence describes a vernacular past, a golden age where there are no dates or names, just a sense of the way it used to be. Kerstin Barndt describes how:

> the slippage between the historical saturation of the postindustrial landscape on the one hand and its embeddedness in geological time is highly sug-gestive and speaks of our postmodern condition, in which playful, individual appropriation ostensibly trumps the discarded master narratives of history, the nation, the collective.

This new way of celebrating past events could be described as containing a certain sentimentality for the past or nostalgia. Nostalgia is a longing typically for a period or place with happy personal associations and is derived from the Greek nóstos, meaning homecoming and álgos, meaning pain. It is thought to have been first used to describe the anxieties shown by seventeenth century Swizz mercenaries fighting away from home. It is interesting that is has also come to mean a yearning for a golden age; it could be described as a time which begins precisely where the active memory ends (6). A golden age is an idyllic, often imaginary time in the past; a time of peace, prosperity and happiness, when society had an innocence and a simplicity that has since been lost, and importantly, it is a time without significant events. This sentimentalising over an obscure part of the ill-defined past has created a romantic idea of an industrial society; one which contained certainty, jobs for life and a real sense of community spirit. Whether this time actually existed is irrelevant, it is the yearning for the half-forgotten past that is fuelling the nostalgia.

This period of neglect and discontinuity and the subsequent return of history is of great significance for the post-modern society, as is the need to acknowledge a personal history in a time of individualism. One of the most important things that the ordinary person has to offer in the way of remembering is work. A reflection of this is the extraordinary rise in the number of industrial museums; that is, museums dedicated to the industrial work that once consumed the whole of the western world. These are a contemporary celebration of the past as a remote, ill-defined period or environment when a golden age prevailed.

The official Basel websites describe the city thus: 'With over 40 museums in an area of just 37 km², Basel is a city of art and culture par excellence and a must-see destination for any trip to Switzerland': I counted 43 on the official website for the city: 43 museums! (7) The majority of the museums are situated within existing buildings: the Museum of Paper set within the walls of a 'fascinating mediaeval mill', the Museum of Cartoons – from the caricature to the comic, the Historisches Museum Basel in a converted church, Switzerland's largest collection of musical instruments in the historic Lohnhof building, the Museum of Horse-Power-coaches and sleighs of the nineteenth and twentieth centuries in a converted barn, the Museum for the Traditional House is one of Switzerland's principal museums of domestic life and is situated within the converted home of a Basel silk ribbon manufacturer, the Museum of the Flour Mill in a mill, 2,500 teddy bears in the Spielzeug Welten Museum and another Toy Museum is housed in the seventeenth century Wettsteinhaus, the unique collection of items from funerary objects at the Sammlung Hörnli Museum and even a Shipping Museum (in Basel??).

Basel, a city with a population of barely 160,000, even the wider area of the canton is less than 200,000 people, contains 43 museums. The need of the individual to understand his or her own heritage and to acknowledge that their past has great worth has fuelled a massive tourist industry. Buildings of the nostalgic past are being indiscriminately saved with little thought as to their new programme or those occupiers. A society can only support so many museums and so consideration needs to be made as to what else they can be used for. Is the preservation and restoration movement little more than a means of promoting tourism? Could these buildings have been changed into anything other than a museum?

Ruins-Lust

The concerns of the population of the twenty-first century population are radically different to those of previous ages and a particular concern is the need for everything to be useful; the idea that it is possible for everything to make a contribution to society, for it to be productive. All things are considered to have some worth, and if they are not, then some useful purpose has to be devised. There is a need for nothing to be considered as completely obsolete, it can be adapted, recycled, upcycled. The twenty-first century mantra Reduce, Reuse, Recyle is highly appropriate to the remodelling of outmoded existing buildings.

It is displeasing to observe an empty building, to see a structure that is no longer in use, not so much because it is sad to see that it is obsolete, but because it is no longer making a contribution. It is offering nothing to the society, to culture and to the environment. It is taking up room for no reason and giving nothing back. It requires support to prevent extreme decay and possible damage, but what is it giving in return?

The problem with this approach is that sometimes the most specific buildings, that is, those with the most character, that were designed so specifically for their purpose are almost impossible to transform into anything else. It seems that the only solution to the need to find a productive use for these extremely particular buildings is a museum, but is there another way? Could these building be allowed to just decay? A Modernist building that has become a celebrated ruin is the St Peter's Seminary, designed by the Glasgow practice Gillespie, Kidd & Coia, which was consecrated in 1966 as a training college for Roman Catholic priests. It is a powerfully Modern cast concrete or Béton Brut building set within the wild countryside of southern Scotland. It contains the traditional elements of religious buildings – cloister, chapel, refectory, cells – all of which are organised around an open court. These essential components are reordered over multiple levels in an unexpected manner, alternately engaging with or hiding the user from the surrounding landscape. The long residential block has an extraordinary stepped section, which allows internal balcony corridors to look down upon the continuous space of the refectory and chapel below, and the dramatic cantilever of the classroom block reinforces the expressive character of the building. The beauty and character of building was commended; it won the RIBA royal gold medal for architecture, however just half a century later, the buildings are now registered as one of the World Monuments Fund's most endangered cultural landmarks.

Its construction was somewhat misguided: by the time it was completed the Second Vatican Council had decided to train priests in parishes and small houses among their congregations, rather than in isolated communities, and so even when it was brand new there were insufficient trainee priests to fill the building. In 1980, the Catholic Church closed St Peter's down, and the building was used as a drug rehabilitation centre for a few years. Since 1987 the building has lain empty and has been allowed to become derelict.

The building was very exact; it responded completely to the needs of the users, so acutely that it has proven impossible to convert it into anything else. Most buildings have resilience, in that they are sufficiently robust to allow a remodelling to occur. An uncomplicated building may have a number of distinct lives; it may undergo many quite simple transformations. For example, an English Georgian Townhouse is basically a collection of large rooms, with a front door at ground level and a back door at the rear, and so it can accommodate many different activities; it is often said that almost 90% of all human activity can take place within it.

St Peter's Seminary is far from simple; it is a complex collection of incredibly precise interrelated volumes, which are so specific, so exactly designed for their purpose, that attempts to provide the building with a new use have proven futile. Schemes to convert the buildings include proposals for a hotel and for domestic accommodation, but the inconvenience of the site, the cost of the proposals and the very specificity of the building itself defeated these. It seems that the programme for the seminary was so exact, and the relationship with the site so acute, that it is impossible to convert it into anything else.

But is this a problem? Does the building have to be restored? Is it necessary for it to once again become productive? Could the seminary, in the rich tradition of pastoral landscaping, become a romantic and ruinous folly? Artists have appropriated the building, it is becoming a situation for graffiti and installations, and rock bands have used the evocative environment as a backdrop for their promotional movies. This Brutalist masterpiece is a place of pilgrimage for architects, who stare in wonder at the exposed structure. Louis Kahn once described how a building only reveals its true spirit when it becomes a ruin; when it is being constructed it is too busy with the process of becoming to reveal anything, and when it is being used, it is too busy serving those who occupy it to notice, but when it is empty, when it has fallen into disrepair, when it has nothing but itself to show, then the very nature of the building is exposed and the true character of its existence is revealed (see Figure 5.5).

A ruin could be regarded as an acknowledgement of the force of history, of nature, climate and culture. It is a sign of an obsolete society, a monument to a distant time of different priorities and values. The preservation of a building in a ruinous state recognises this. The seminary has become a memorial to a long lost culture of isolated education, but also, because it has been appropriated by young artists hoping to escape from the restrictive atmosphere of the well ordered city and enjoy the freedom that the shell of the modernist masterpiece can offer, it has become a symbol of the resilience and resourcefulness of a contemporary society. Walter Benjamin takes this idea further when he claimed the connection between the ruin and the allegory, meaning that each concretises historical change. The allegory within art and architecture is conscious (self-conscious really) of the prospect of its own ruination. The intrinsic beauty of the art or the architectural object is always subject to the attrition that time brings, and this is highlighted when it transgresses the limits that history has set for it. Thus the allegory and the ruin communicate the inevitable obsolescence of the present (8).

FIGURE 5.5 St Peter's Seminary, Gillespie, Kidd & Coia, 1966. As the superfluous decorations crumble and fall, then the true structural nature of the abandoned building has become apparent.

Credit: Mad4brutalism via Wikimedia Commons

Ruins are romantic. Throughout history they have been perceived as objective and subjective assemblages, in that a ruin provides a physical connection between man and nature. The mass of the ruin provides a degree of shelter combined with a relative transparency. It allows the viewer to both engage and disengage their imagination though the connection with the ruin and the disconnection with the intact structure. Pallasmaa regards this silent air as vital in generating remembrance: silence focuses our attention, instead of on our own existence, on our fundamental solitude (9). Romanticism of the eighteenth and nineteenth centuries enjoyed ruins-gazing. There was a growing disenchantment with an over-materialist society and the inevitable victory of nature over all things was something to be celebrated. W. G. Sebald recognised this in his description of northern Europe after the Second World War:

> At the end of the war, some of the bomb sites in Cologne had already been transformed by the dense green vegetation growing over them – the roads made their way through this new landscape like 'peaceful country lanes'. In contrast to the effect of the catastrophes insidiously creeping up on us today, nature's ability to regenerate did not seem to have been impaired by the firestorms.

10

Conclusion

Why not let obsolete unused buildings fall into ruin? Let them naturally decay; let nature absorb the very building bricks of their structure. John Ruskin regarded restoration, and by extension adaptation, as a deceptive portrayal of the thing destroyed; he argued that it expunged the spirit of the previous age and was merely a false description of the thing that was replaced. He called for care and maintenance, arguing that the 'buildings belong partly to the generation that constructed it and partly to those who have subsequently occupied them, but the present generation has no right to tear it down or damage it, just care for it' (11).

A ruin could be regarded as an acknowledgement of the force of history, of nature, climate and culture. It is a sign of an obsolete society, a monument to a distant time of different priorities and values. The preservation of a building in a ruinous state recognises this. The Seminary has become a memorial to a long lost culture of isolated education, but also, because it has been appropriated by young artists hoping to escape from the restrictive atmosphere of the well ordered city and enjoy the freedom that the shell of the Modernist masterpiece can offer, it has also become a symbol of the resilience and resourcefulness of the twenty-first century. Things are often admired not so much for their beauty, but for their association with a phase of our past; a retrieval from the original ideal condition. Unburdened by notions of architectural importance, the ruinous building can reveal its actual significance as a monumental example of a widespread condition: that of an abandoned space being given a new and romantic role.

References

1. Pevsner, N. (1980) "Ruskin and Violett-le-Duc" from Eugène Emmanuel Violett-le-Duc. P. Farrant, et al. London: PUBLISHER, p. 50.
2. Gallent, N. and Robinson, S. (2013) Neighbourhood Planning: Communities, Networks and Governance. Bristol, p. 10.
3. Jackson, J. B. (1980) The Necessity for Ruins and Other Topics. Amherst: The University of Massachusetts Press, p. 120.
4. Jenkins, K. (1991) Re-Thinking History. London and New York: Routledge, p. 60.
5. Barndt, K. (2010) "Memory Traces of an Abandoned Set of Futures" from Ruins of Modernity. J. Hell and A. Schonle (Eds). Durham and London, p. 270.
6. Jackson, J. B. (1980) The Necessity for Ruins and Other Topics. Amherst: The University of Massachusetts Press, p. 89.
7. Art & Design Museums Basel: www.youtube.com/watch?v=9-xo 89DxM, accessed 26 June 2017.
8. Benjamin, W. (1998) The Origin of German Tragic Drama. trans. J. Osborn. London.
9. Pallasmaa, J. (2005) The Eyes of the Skin: Architecture and the Senses. New York: John Wiley and Sons, p. 51.
10. Sebald, W. G. (2003) On the Natural History of Destruction. London, p. 39.
11. Brooker, G. and Stone, S. (2013) From Organisation to Decoration: An Interiors Reader. London and New York: Routledge, p. 262.

6

MEMORY AND ANTICIPATION

The Existing Building and the Expectations of the New Users

Introduction

Rudolf von Laban was a dance theorist and teacher whose studies in human motion provided the intellectual foundations for the development of modern dance. His analysis of forms in movement, known as choreutics, was a non-personal scientific system designed to apply to all human motion. Based on the individual's relation to surrounding space, choreutics specified primary directions of movement derived from complex geometric figures. Interestingly he also applied his theories of movement beyond the domain of the dance environment to include factory and office workers, as well as other athletes. He described this process:

> Existence is movement. Action is movement. Existence is defined by the rhythm of forces in natural balance. (…) It is our appreciation for dance that allows us to see clearly the rhythms of nature and to take natural rhythm to a plane of well-organised art and culture.
>
> *1*

Laban developed a theory to classify movement in space. He viewed spatial direction as the most significant element of bodily movement. The whole complexity of movement and dance could be reduced to essential directions that are derived from the basic orientation of the person in space. These related to the vertical and the horizontals of the three dimensions; that is height, width and depth. He regarded the most important components in movement as: bodily participation, spatial-direction participation, the shape of the moving body, and sequence. Every movement prompts the body to abandon its own equilibrium and to deviate from the natural and resting vertical position into one or several of the innumerable oblique directions. These directions can be correlated with common conception of the three dimensions: vertical, forward-backward, and side-to-side horizontals. Thus, Laban's view was that movement concerns the relationship between the body and the space that it occupied (2).

These theories have massively influenced the development of dance in the western world. Upon arrival in the studio, the dancer will 'centre themselves'. This is a double process that eventually becomes intuitive. The centring will begin with the self, and the mindful awareness of the core of the body; it will then focus upon the surrounding space. The dancer needs to be aware of their position within the room. In order to move freely within the confines of the space, they need to be acutely conscious of its parameters and responsive to these physical limits.

Dancers have extremely exacting space requirements. Just as they have rigorous expectations of themselves, so they demand it from the environment that they occupy. They need to know exactly how big the space is without ever having to think about it, it has to be so perfect that they don't even notice that it is. A dance studio space is designed to mirror a performance venue, which means a wide rectangular area. Irregular-shaped spaces make it difficult for dancers to easily determine the proportions of the space and particularly to recognise the front of the room. The space has to be sufficiently large for uninterrupted movement, especially across the diagonal, and it also has to be tall enough for even the greatest leap or lift. Other highly precise requirements within this extremely exacting space are: a sprung floor, as the wrong type can seriously damage joints and muscles; seamless mirrors on the walls; the space should be illuminated with an even top light; and the heating should be maintained at a comfortable 21°c, never going below 18°c (the liminal spaces where the dancer rests or warms up should be much warmer so as to avoid stiffness and injury). Ideally thigh-height radiators should be positioned along the blank wall to allow the dancers to lean upon them, thus keeping their legs warm while awaiting their return to the floor. Thus for the intuitive response of the dancer to be uninterrupted, the pure rectangular space, or ideal form of the rehearsal space, needs to be perfect.

Given the sheer precision of the meticulous expectations from the space, it is surprising how many dance based organisations are situated within remodelled buildings. The studio is a pure rectangular space that cannot be compromised. Other rooms, such as the support spaces, the circulation, even classrooms if it is a school, can be miss-shaped or deformed but the studio has to be faultless.

Malcolm Fraser Architects has developed a reputation for creating dance studios within existing spaces. The practice has completed a number of projects including the Dance City in Newcastle, Dance Base in Edinburgh and the headquarters for Scottish Ballet in Glasgow, all of which are enclosed and logical, yet contain high ceilings and vast glass skylights that connect to the world outside. The practice recognises the needs of the dancers. 'When you are dancing, whirling about, you really need to understand the simple geometry of the space you are in,' says Fraser, whose interest in dance also translates to Scottish country dance lessons (intermediate level). 'I know that dancers like our buildings because we are not trying to impose something on their art form – we are trying to help enable it' (3). Always within these projects, the first consideration was whether the given site could accommodate the dance studios. Given the necessity for such exact requirements, unless they could be inserted into the available space, then the project could never be built.

The architects needed to be completely certain that the new function would fit happily into an existing building if the adaptation was to be both convincing and appropriate. However masterful or clever a piece of design is, if the new spaces are not suitable for the new users of the building, then it doesn't work. The architects were acutely aware of the requirements of the users and these were predominantly the dance studios and the need for these Ideal Forms (4) to be inserted into the available space. Once the position of these elements had been established, then the other servant activities could be distributed.

This collage-type of approach allows for regular forms to be accommodated within a much larger irregular context. Schumacher describes this as urban deformations, but it can equally apply to the construction of the interior. (There is an obvious and great affiliation between urban and interior design theory; architecture is the mediator between the two.) 'Ideal forms can exist as fragments, "collaged" into an empirical environment' (5). The dance studios exist within the buildings as pure or ideal forms, with the deformed spaces of the ancillary activities distributed around them, thus all of the available space is filled. The studios are treated very much like exterior courtyards or squares, as figural voids within the landscape of the building.

Dance Base in Edinburgh was the first purpose built National Centre for Dance in Scotland; it consists of four dance studios on a dog-legged site in the centre of the city. The complex is a combination of reused existing buildings, new structures and the natural landscape. Edinburgh's Old Town topography is a jumble of multi-layered streets and historic buildings, with connecting closes and stairways all descending down from the rocky pinnacle of Edinburgh Castle. The steep south-facing slope of the Dance Base is hemmed in by adjoining tenements, so the approach that the architects took was to dig the support spaces into the hill and float the studios above this, thus the studios are scattered in section and in plan up the slope from the historic Grassmarket to the Castle. The principal consideration within the project was whether the studios could be accommodated. Given the importance of the purity of the dance studio space, if this was unachievable, then the project could not have been built. Each of the pure rectangular dance studios is modelled upon a different type of dance and has its own distinct character created through a combination of the quality of light, the materials and the structure. They are linked together by a series of ramps and staircases that seem to cavort through the space. Thus the Dance Base could be described as a collage of studios and routes (see Figures 6.1, 6.2 and 6.3).

Dance City in Newcastle is the leading development organisation for dance in the north east of England. It was the first of the series of Dance Bases that Malcolm

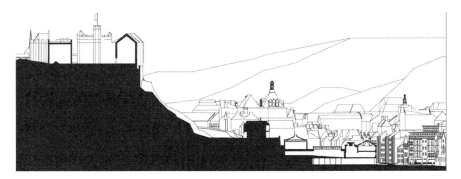

FIGURE 6.1 Dance Base, Edinburgh, Malcolm Fraser Architects, 2001. The section shows how the building nestles into the pattern of the Old Town beneath the towering masterful Castle above.

Credit: Malcolm Fraser

FIGURE 6.2 Dance Base, Edinburgh, Malcolm Fraser Architects, 2001. Architect's sketch shows the direct relationship between the orthogonal dance studios and the magnificent Castle.

Credit: Malcolm Fraser

Fraser completed, and it served to provide the design stimulus for all of the other buildings. Although it is a new construction, the tight site and the importance of the creation of pure space makes it relevant to the discussion. The building is organised as a series of ideal spaces situated around an internal public square. The highest block to the west contains the dance studios and associated activity. The second lower block to the north relates to dance performance (the theatre) and the third L-shaped block contains all administrative related activity. These wings come together to create an enclosed social and circulation space. This is the core from

FIGURE 6.3 Dance Base, Edinburgh, Malcolm Fraser Architects, 2001. Long horizontal natural light floods the studio; note the radiators positioned in every window reveal, exactly the correct height to keep a dancer's legs warm while resting.
Credit: Malcolm Fraser

which all activity is generated, however, the exact size and shape of this element was very much secondary to the formation of the key spaces: that of the clean dance studio and conventionally shaped theatre. This key communal area is formed from the left-over space, the remnants or remaining available room once the pure space of the studio and theatre had been installed (see Figures 6.4 and 6.5).

The exterior of the headquarters building for Scottish Ballet in Glasgow is a tough, robust and somewhat uncompromising metal-clad shed; however the interior is an intricate and fastidious accomplishment. The sheer scale of the dance studios dictates the plan, but even so, these huge orthogonal spaces are skilfully arranged around a top-lit communal area. It is from here that the intricate three-dimensional relationships that have been created within the building are visible. This central circulation space, formed from the spaces remaining after the pure studios have been considered, is a theme that unites all of the Malcolm Fraser dance projects. This timber-clad interior exudes the kind of warmth that the dancers need to keep their muscles supple. The studios themselves are regular, uncluttered and clean, and all have been designed as naturally ventilated spaces, which reduces running costs and carbon emissions. The space itself is graduated, so that the busyness of the ceiling space seems to recede into the greyness, leaving

FIGURE 6.4 Dance City, Newcastle, Malcolm Fraser Architects, 2005. The internal public square is the hub of the building, somewhere that all activity has to pass through and around which the studios revolve.

Credit: Malcolm Fraser

FIGURE 6.5 Dance City, Newcastle, Malcolm Fraser Architects, 2005. The studios are ideal and pure spaces that have a necessary exactness that the dancers need to be able to centre themselves within the space.

Credit: Malcolm Fraser

FIGURE 6.6 Scottish Ballet Headquarters, Glasgow, Malcolm Fraser Architects, 2009. The building has an uncompromisingly tough exterior.

Credit: Malcolm Fraser

FIGURE 6.7 Scottish Ballet Headquarters, Glasgow, Malcolm Fraser Architects, 2009. The central circulation space is clad with warm timber, and provides access to the surrounding dance studios.

Credit: Malcolm Fraser

FIGURE 6.8 Scottish Ballet Headquarters, Glasgow, Malcolm Fraser Architects, 2009. The pure top-lit studios are positioned at the top of the building. Natural light is filtered through great lanterns to provide the space with a slightly ethereal quality.

Credit: Malcolm Fraser

the pure white walls of the lower area to define the studio itself (see Figures 6.6, 6.7 and 6.8).

The final dance-space project under discussion is the Royal Conservatoire of Scotland, in Spiers Lock, Glasgow. It provides a teaching space for students at the school and contains dance studios, production facilities and social spaces. Not all refurbishment projects are in listed historic buildings, and the adaptation of this 1980s portal-framed brick-clad warehouse building forms part of a wider regeneration strategy for a much larger rundown area of the city. The brief was to extend the Conservatoire's reach into dance with four new studios, and provide teaching and technical facilities for the various trades that support drama. The architects employed the same approach as the earlier projects. They established the position of the regular space of the dance studios first, then accommodated all of the service area, including the circulation and social spaces within the remaining available space. This building is much more rectangular in form, and therefore the residue space much more coherent; but the simple approach and the distinct functional requirements that had to be fulfilled before the project could begin meant that again the position of the pure studio space was established first, then the support spaces accommodated within the residual areas. It was a subtle balancing act to generate light-filled dance studios with a sense of security and privacy, with the controlled ancillary space, all of which were needed to create a new landmark building for the arts (see Figures 6.9, 6.10 and 6.11).

FIGURE 6.9 Royal Conservatoire of Scotland, Glasgow, Malcolm Fraser Architects, 2011. The reclad 1980s brick building has been remodelled to contain a feeling of grace and movement.

Credit: Malcolm Fraser

Process and Examination

As part of the analytical procedure for every remodelling project, the programmatic requirements of the new function need to be examined to ensure compatibility between the old and new. It is not just a question of size but also of harmony. Those who will occupy the new spaces may not be completely aware of the best method of arrangement or current thinking as they are likely to be influenced by the current arrangements and associations of their existing organisation. Architects and designers need to be extremely confident that the requirements of the new users of the building will fit well into the adapted building. The client may not always fully understand these requisites themselves and sometimes request something that is very similar to their present situation, not fully appreciating the opportunities that are possible. There is a need for the designer to be completely aware of the requirements of the users of the remodelled building. This could be a chance for the architect to reorder the manner in which they operate as well as reorder the space.

The activities that are completed within the new building will need examination. For example, it may be important that certain areas are shielded from direct sunlight or indeed from any natural light at all and conversely some activities would positively benefit from contact with the afternoon sun. Some functions may require small individual rooms and others large open spaces and the intimate hierarchy of

FIGURE 6.10 Royal Conservatoire of Scotland, Glasgow, Malcolm Fraser Architects, 2011. The position of the studios was established first, thus the size, shape and position of the central circulation area was dependent upon what remained.

Credit: Malcolm Fraser

those who are to occupy the spaces needs to be appreciated. The analysis completed by the architect or designer will identify the basic requirements of the users and work with them to create a viable and appropriate solution.

The Irish Film Centre in Dublin was created through the remodelling of nine different adjoining structures. The programmatic requirements of an independent cinema are quite exacting. There is a great financial outlay in the day-to-day running and management of the complex, and one of the greatest cost implications is the projectionist. This cinema has two theatres both of which had to be served by the same projectionist, so the position of this seemingly inconsequential little room was crucial to the design of the whole project; if these exact physical relationships

FIGURE 6.11 Royal Conservatoire of Scotland, Glasgow, Malcolm Fraser Architects, 2011. Additional privacy within the top-lit rectangular studio space was established through the use of sound muffling curtains.

Credit: Malcolm Fraser

could not be established, then the cinema would not be financially viable. Therefore the first exercise that the architects, O'Donnell + Tuomey, completed was a spatial examination of the various components of the site, and upon confirmation that the two cinemas served by one projection room system was possible, they then proceeded with the intimate design of the project (see Figures 6.12 and 6.13).

Interior and occupation theory is continually progressing; so, for example, opinions about the organisation of the office have evolved since the mid-twentieth century. The ideas underpinning office design have developed since the vast expanses of the open-plan office landscape of the Bürolandschaft. This egalitarian method of office organisation was intended to provide a collaborative and humane work environment that encouraged all levels of staff to sit together in one open floor to create a non-hierarchical environment that increased communication and collaboration. The last decade of the twentieth century saw a massive shift away from this attitude towards the creation of New Office environments. The post-modern, post-industrial society has placed different demands upon the office. They are no longer highly regulated spaces dedicated to production, but inventive, inter-active environments that have to encourage creativity and interaction among those who work within them. Contemporary office design is based upon the creation of different spaces, each with a particular character so that distinct activities can be carried out in particular places. Instead of the space changing to accommodate

FIGURE 6.12 Irish Film Centre, Dublin, O'Donnell + Tuomey Architects, 1992. The complex is an accumulation of different structures clustered around a covered courtyard. Credit: Sally Stone

different types of work, it is the worker who moves, continually changing their position within the office in respect to the different types of work they are completing.

Frank Duffy was one of the first commentators to articulate this change. Beginning in the late 1970s he wrote a series of texts about society and spaces of non-manual

FIGURE 6.13 Irish Film Centre, Dublin, O'Donnell + Tuomey Architects, 1992. The entrances are hardly apparent from the main street, thus the complex is almost hidden within the dense urban block.

Credit: Sally Stone

production, including the seminal book *The New Office* (6). Here he set out his thoughts upon the evolution of the office environment; from one with a traditional hierarchy, individual offices and a very vertical line of communication to a sleek series of different spaces each with a vastly different character and a much more liberal, intuitive and spontaneous communication system. Duffy created a taxonomy of spaces, built not upon personality and position, but upon task, assignment and undertaking. He argued that the massive changes that technology has wrought means that the type of work completed has also radically changed, and therefore, so has the space in which it is completed. As the environment of the office became less solitary and more plural, so the balance between space given over to individual workstations, and that allocated to group activities, rapidly shifted. Work had become varied and therefore could be broken into four different organisational types: individual processes (Hive), group processing (Den), transactional knowledge (Club) and concentrated study (Cell). He proposed that offices could be organised according to the processes that occurred within them, rather than by the hierarchy of the personnel. Workers would no longer have a dedicated space, but would use the space most suitable for the task that they were completing. He used analogies to come up with appropriate names for the different types of space, and thus the Hive is characterised by individual and routine process work that has low levels of interaction and autonomy, a call centre would be typical of this type of space. The Den is a space for group work; it is suitable for short-term highly interactive, often noisy, work such as a team-brainstorming event. The Club is a space that encourages intimate interaction in a quiet and often private environment; an example of this type of work would be a confidential meeting. The fourth and final category is the Cell. This is a space for concentrated individual study that needs little or no interaction or interruption. In 1997, he described the scenario of occasional autonomous and sporadic work in a closed environment. Today the Cell is a space that need not even be situated within the office itself.

Methods of production have radically changed; the traditional organisational hierarchy of the working environment is no longer workable. The idea that the leader or boss would simply tell those further down the hierarchy what to do and how to do it has proved to no longer be viable in the post-industrial world. Office space has to encourage interaction and creativity if it is to embrace the new modes of production so prevalent in the new century. It has become obvious that the productive office environment is compromised by its physical organisation and it is definitely ready to evolve. Another development within office design is the recognition that conversing with the other workers is both healthy and productive. Chance meetings, water-cooler moments and impromptu conversations are thought to be beneficial, constructive and aid creativity. Official meetings are often time consuming and irrelevant to the majority of the attendees; current thinking is to reduce the size and shape of these events and replace them with much more impromptu and spontaneous get-togethers. Organised coincidence not only encourages productivity in that decisions can be made more quickly, and promotes an attitude in which collaboration is thought of as normal, but it is also beneficial to health and wellbeing in that it discourages isolation and supports human interaction.

Thus to understand the exact requirements of those who are to occupy the remodelled building, the designer must be aware of both the personality of those users combined with contemporary ideas about how space is occupied. It is their responsibility to inform the client of theoretical developments that will affect the manner in which space is used. The buildings that we occupy shape us all; we are constrained by the limitations of the spaces we inhabit, so a new building or interior is an opportunity to pose questions about organisation, relationships, expectations and requirements. Spatial patterns are primary means of communication and habits are formed by the manner in which the building is inhabited, that is, we organise our lives around the design of our environment. The architect and designer needs to be very confident that the requirements of those who occupy the space will fit happily into the remodelled building, and will conscientiously make a great deal of effort to understand what these are. Those who occupy the remodelled building genuinely want to feel that it is theirs, that their functional requirements have been met and yet the past has not been obliterated but incorporated and embraced as part of the pattern of the present.

References

1. Laban, Rudolf von. (1974) The Language of Movement: A Guidebook to Choreutics. Plays, inc.
2. de Gruyter, Vera Maletic Mouton (1987) Body, Space, Expression: The Development of Rudolf Laban's Movement and Dance Concepts. Reprint 2010 edition (1 February), p. 58.
3. www.telegraph.co.uk/culture/art/3662218/A-dance-to-the-music-of-light.html
4. Ideal Form refers to the rectangular purity of the shape of the space. It is a term that probably originated with Plato in his Theory of Forms.
5. Schumacher, Thomas L. (1971/1996) "Contextualism: Urban Ideals and Deformations. Cassabella no. 359–360" 79–86 from Theorizing a New Agenda for Architecture. Kate Nesbit (Ed.). New York: Princeton Architectural Press.
6. Duffy, Frank (1997) The New Office. Conran Octopus.

7

CONSERVATION

A Future Orientated Movement Focussing on the Past

The Search for Authenticity

Conservation plays an important role within the wider process of development and change in the existing built environment. Inevitably there is a conflict between the aims and ideals of the conservationist and those of the (interior) architect who is to transform the building to make it fit for new users. The goals of one group do not necessarily correspond with those of the other; indeed it could be argued that they do not even overlap.

The etymological origins of the word show the differences in attitude. Conserve is derived from the Latin verb conservare, composed of cum meaning with, and servare: to keep, maintain or take care of. Thus the sense seems to be to keep together or to maintain something in such a condition so that it cannot be altered. Transformation is also derived from Latin, the verb transformare, which is made from trans, meaning further, and formare: to give form to. So, the sense of transformation is the exact opposite of conservation, that is, to change, to modify or to convert.

The fundamental divergence in the two approaches is a continual source of disagreement within the profession. The conservationist may want to keep the building or monument in the exact condition that it was found in, while the (interior) architect will possibly expect to make massive changes to facilitate the new users of the new building. The situation is further complicated by the contemporary expectation that the narrative of the building should be exposed. All buildings have an interesting story to tell, to be exposed and retold within the adaptation. How can the architect and the conservationist come to an agreement about which period of history is to be shown, how much is to be conserved, exactly how much is to be let go and how this is to be achieved? Inevitably some sort of compromise must be reached.

Conservation is the general term that covers the process, but the subject can be more finely divided. The different aspects are based very much upon the balance between the active conservation of the structure and the productive adaptation.

Preservation is the category in which the conservationist has the most control; it is the highly intricate process of assessing the worth of the existing and safeguarding its continual existence. This approach exposes the patina of age and wear, and expresses the sense of time within a structure. Renovation generally refers to the process of updating a building to make it fit for use, but not generally making extreme changes; so, for example, the services may be improved, things such as the plumbing may be updated, the electricity distribution improved and Wi-Fi installed. This is not a new approach; indeed at the very end of the nineteenth century, Somers Clarke introduced electric light into Sir Christopher Wren's magnificent St Paul's Cathedral in London. Ten years later he also installed a hot-water heating system using a series of pipes that ran in large channels beneath the crypt floor and along the walls of the upper gallery; something that made the building vastly more habitable for the Edwardian congregation (1). Interestingly, these actually replaced the Gurney Stoves that had been placed in the crypt in 1868 by the then Cathedral Surveyor, Francis Penrose. This incredibly crude system encouraged the movement of moist warm air through convection. The stoves were installed in the crypt and several holes were cut directly into the vaults of the crypt above them, which allowed hot air to simply drift up into the cathedral. The holes were merely covered with cast iron grates (2) (see Figure 7.1).

The practice of restoration is possibly the most controversial of all conservation practices, as it could be thought to be the one that really contains the least authenticity. The building will be returned to a chosen historical condition, a moment in time will be selected from somewhere within the past life of the building, and the structure artificially returned to that state. This is not considered to be authentic because it is neither true to the original building, in that the pristine condition now depicted may never have actually existed, nor is it true to the contemporary period that the building now exits within. The patina of time is lost, and so it denies both the present and the past. Restoration is really a mixture of preservation and renovation, and although widely practised, it has been condemned since the middle of the nineteenth century as something that, because it did not maintain sharp separation between historical periods, violated the authenticity.

Adaptation is the process of unashamedly changing the building, of making it fit for new users with distinct expectations in a different time. The practice is also called remodelling and reuse. The (interior) architect will normally make a thorough reading of the building and thus have a complete understanding of the character, structure and context before embarking on a series of sometimes-irreversible changes.

Upheaval and Beginnings

Existing buildings provide a sense of connection with the previous ages. They reinforce the relationship that those who dwell in a place have with it and they

THE LONDON
𝔚arming and 𝔙entilating ℭompany
(LIMITED),
ABINGDON CHAMBERS, 12, ABINGDON STREET,
Westminster, S.W.
MANAGING DIRECTOR AND SECRETARY, MR. WOODCOCK.

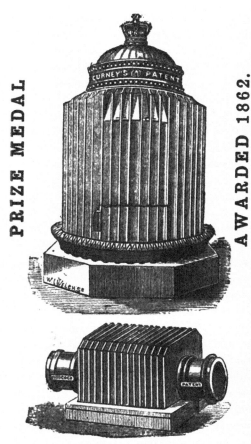

PRIZE MEDAL

AWARDED 1862.

Churches, Greenhouses, Offices, and Buildings of every description warmed by means of a modification of the plan successfully used by Sir Goldsworthy Gurney in both Houses of Parliament.

Steam, Hot Water, Gas, and in open or enclosed Fireplaces, Coal and Coke are equally available for the process.

The cost is less and the effect greater than that of any other known means.

For ordinary Sitting Rooms a patent fresh air grate is made use of.

The Horticulturist will find herein an instrument of new and important powers.

The apparatus may be seen at work in the *Houses of Parliament*, the offices of the department of *Science and Art*, in St. Paul's, *York Minster*, and 14 other *Cathedrals*, besides 1,000 *Churches* in England, and Government and other Public and Private Buildings, too numerous to name in an advertisement. Particulars and testimonials forwarded on application.

N.B.—In order to meet constant applications for the heating of smaller rooms a small Coke Stove has since last season been produced, suitable for Sitting Rooms, Bed Rooms, small Halls, Offices, and Conservatories. Prices, from 34s. and upwards.

[27-Lo.

FIGURE 7.1 The Gurney Stove: a quite simple form of heating provided some degree of environmental control in many public buildings including St Paul's Cathedral.

Credit: Grace's Guide Ltd

can become part of the collective memory of a society. Our perception of the past is very much based upon our reading of these buildings. The conservation of such buildings is a complex process that combines the need to preserve as much of the existing structure as possible with a new, and often conflicting, function. It is a somewhat controversial subject, not just in the manner in which it is carried out, but also the selection of the buildings to be conserved. Attitudes towards the subject are continuously changing and it promises to become more difficult as the need for sustainable redevelopment becomes greater and our attitude towards the past is reassessed.

The conservation of architecture is really a Modern concept; it is bound up with ideas of value and worth (3). Buildings and monuments are valued for their historical age and their aesthetic appeal. Both aspects are highly contentious. It is questionable whether a structure should be valued just because it is old, while aesthetic significance is directly connected with the culture that is making the assessment and is thus subject to the whims of that society. A very sad example of this conflict between historical and artistic value and the culture of the society that is making the assessment is the destruction of Penn State Railway Station.

When Pennsylvania Station opened in New York in 1910, it was widely praised for its majestic architecture. It was constructed by the New York architectural practice McKim, Mead and White, from pink granite in the Beaux-Arts style with a huge colonnade wrapping around the exterior. The main waiting room, which was inspired by the Roman Baths of Caracalla, was then the largest indoor space in the city at almost a block and a half long with vaulted glass windows soaring over a sun-drenched chamber. There are many freely available historical images of this incredibly theatrical space that depict the sheer drama and excitement that was then contained within rail travel. Beyond the waiting room, the trains emerged from below the ground to deposit passengers on an extraordinary top-lit steel framed concourse (see Figure 7.2).

By the late 1950s, with the advent of cheap air travel and high-quality highways, the attraction of the station was dwindling. Apparently the Pennsylvania Railroad could not even afford to keep the station clean. In 1962 plans were revealed to demolish the terminal and build the entertainment venue Madison Square Garden on top of it. The new train station would be entirely underground. Despite massive protests, most notably from the architecture critic and theoretician Jane Jacobs (1916–2006), the station was demolished. However, the sheer outrage was a major catalyst for the architectural preservation movement in the US. In 1965, the New York Landmarks Law was passed, which helped save the Grand Central Terminal and more than 30,000 other buildings from a similar fate. Ironically, since the demolition of Penn Station, train ridership has grown tenfold in the US. The new station, an oppressive tangle of subway lines and commuter railways, is now the busiest terminal in the country. Thus the station was not sufficiently valued by the society that demolished it, and yet today, given the massive shift in attitudes towards the existing environment, we consider this attitude as wanton destruction.

FIGURE 7.2 The magnificent foyer of the now lost Pennsylvania Station, New York.
Credit: Library of Congress

Before the Enlightenment, the rapid rise in industrialisation and the need for countries to have a definite identity, buildings were valued for their usefulness. If structures within the pre-industrial age needed to be expanded or changed to facilitate the needs of the users, they were simply added to in the style of the day. There are many castles and stately homes in Europe that show a definite chronology of construction, for example Prague Castle which dates from the ninth century and is regarded as the largest coherent castle in the world. It is an enormous composition of palaces and ecclesiastical buildings of various architectural styles, from the remains of Romanesque-style buildings of the tenth century through Gothic modifications of the fourteenth century. The Slovenian architect Josip Plečnik was responsible for adapting and updating the Castle in the time of the First Republic after the First World War. Thus it has been in a state of almost continual change for over a thousand years.

Old and disused buildings were also often used as quarries of easily accessible and already worked building material. There are many instances of the pillaging of parts of post-Reformation Abbeys and Priories in northern Europe. Complete elements of the buildings were simply transported across the country and installed into a new building. Spolia describes this practice of recycling existing architectural elements by incorporating them into new buildings. The word itself is derived from the Latin *spolium*, a phrase used to describe the act of taking trophies, usually armour and weaponry, from the enemy after a battle. The spoils of war would either be worn as trophies or used to decorate the victors' houses and temples. In architecture and design Spolia traditionally refers particularly to the reuse of the elements of the classical column – the shaft, base, capital and entablature – but can also mean complete architectural elements. The great Forum in Rome was, by the end of the first millennium AD, an incredibly impressive walled settlement. St Peter's already existed as a marvellous church and next to that was the Schola Anglorum, a hospice for travellers that was more than 100 metres long and could accommodate over 3,000 worshipers. Across the river was the Forum containing the gigantic arch of Septimus Severus, the temple of Castor and Pollux, and the fluted column of Phocas. This was a seventh century addition to the Forum and completely assembled from recycled stone. It was over 30 metres high and clad with gilded bronze: the product of looting and plundering radiating the strength and worth of the great empire (4) (see Figure 7.3).

The practice of using Spolia is a method of construction that relies on contingency, availability and ease of supply. It relies on the materials that are to hand and the ease of their reuse and it is a process that exploits a collage-like approach to reconfiguring buildings. A small example of this practice is the reuse of parts of Samlesbury Hall in Lancashire in the north west of England. The Great Hall of the half-timbered black and white mediaeval house was built around 1325 as a family home for the de Southworth Family, whose descendants quite peacefully occupied it until the late seventeenth century. The vastly extended collection of buildings was then sold to Thomas Bradyll, who never actually lived in the house, but stripped out many of the interior features to use in his main home, Conishead Priory, which is in Ulverston, about 60 miles to the north. These elements of Spolia were the elaborately carved wall panelling from the Long Gallery and the chapel screen. This building had a much more bloody history; it was founded as an Augustinian Priory in the twelfth century. After the dissolution of the Monasteries in the sixteenth century when the crown seized it, the building belonged to a succession of different barons and knights. It was Thomas Bradyll who renovated the building to transform it into a gentleman's residence using a collection of different elements removed from smaller houses in the area, and these included the oak panelling and the screen from Samlesbury (see Figure 7.4).

Ancient Monuments

Miles Glendinning argues that the aggressive and avaricious attitude of the French led by Napoleon was in someway responsible for the rise in the respect for ancient monuments and the consciousness of the need for the conservation of national treasures (5). The French Revolution of the late eighteenth century meant that the ideas of stability and ownership were destroyed. This, combined with a thirst for knowledge that Napoleon fuelled within the French population, led to much of the great artistic worth of Europe being hauled to Paris. Napoleon wanted to collect all of antiquity together to create a crucible of national heritage. What couldn't be moved, such as the Colosseum in Rome, which was then under French rule, was

FIGURE 7.3 The fluted column of Phocas, constructed completely from recycled materials.

Credit: MM (DecArch) via Wikimedia Commons

FIGURE 7.4 Many elements of Spolia were used in the reconstruction of Conishead Priory, Cumbria in the north west of England.

Credit: Michael Beckwith via Wikimedia Commons

repaired, mended and reconstructed. This did create a great deal of consternation, much of which fuelled a type of nationalism in which countries sought to find their own identity. Around this time a number of the great European countries were becoming more permanently fixed, more complete, for example Italy was formed from an amalgamation of many different states to become a unified country in the nineteenth century. These new nations needed a fixed and cohesive identity and many of them sought this in the adoration of historic monuments.

Interestingly it is about this time that the term 'vandalism' was conceived by Joseph Lakanal in a 1793 report on heritage to the UK National Convention. It was popularised by the antiquarian Abbé Grégoire, who is probably best remembered for his description of the revolutionary iconoclasts as barbarians whose destruction of France's material heritage was an attack on the nation. The Vandals was the name of the Germanic tribe that sacked Rome in 455 under Genseric; it comes from the Latin *Vandalus*, which is derived from the tribe's name for itself: *wandljaz* (wanderer).

Modern Conception of Conservation

It was from this upheaval that the modern conception of conservation emerged. The Age of Enlightenment combined with the beginnings of the industrial revolution meant that society was moving from a stable traditional religious based culture towards a modern, technologically based one. The pursuit of progress combined with the search for identity meant that cities, districts, buildings and monuments became intellectually contested areas of conflict. Some argued for the replacement of many structures with more up-to-date buildings that would serve the needs of those that occupied them more fully, while the opposite argument was for the preservation of these edifices so that they could epitomise the values of the nation (6).

The conservation lobby had its beginnings in the Anti-Scrape Movement and especially the book *Contrasts*, which was written in 1836 by A. W. N. Pugin (1812–52) when he was just 24 years old (7). This was a somewhat revolutionary book, dealing not with proportion and construction, as most previous books on architecture had (think Vitruvius or Palladio), but it was a manifesto; a social programme that redefined architecture as a moral force imbued with political and religious meaning. Pugin condemned the mixture of improvement and restoration that violated the authenticity of old buildings. He considered that authenticity was something that could only be achieved by maintaining a clear separation between old and new.

John Ruskin (1819–1900), who spoke of buildings possessing a life of their own, took up this architectural rhetoric of good versus evil. He argued that this agency went far beyond the purely stylistic value, something that had previously been used to judge the worth of an object. The monument, building or perhaps even a piece of furniture was considered to be significant because of its age. The historic patina of time, that is the exposed narrative or story of the piece, imbued within the object great authenticity.

Ruskin was one of the most outspoken and influential advocates for the formation of a conservation society. He argued that identity could be found in the pass-times and customs, in the vernacular and within the monuments that already exist. He felt that the authenticity lay within the age of an object and that the authenticity of a building or indeed a piece of furniture or a city rested within its historic style. He railed against the practice of repairs and even adjustments that were carried out in the accurate historic style of the original structure, because it became impossible to ascertain the difference between the old and the new. This he regarded as one of the great deceits, akin to a lie: 'It is in becoming memorial or monumental that a true perfection is attained by civil and domestic buildings … the greatest glory of a building is not in its stones nor in its gold. It is in its age' (8). Ruskin felt that imperfection was essential to life; it was an indication of progress and change. The Arts and Crafts movement, under the mantle of William Morris in particular, also recognised that the actual material oldness of the object was of the upmost importance. Morris combined Ruskin's anti-modern passion with the romantic concept of the value of honest labour to create an artistic movement inspired by egalitarianism and the vernacular.

Morris (1834–96) was instrumental in the formation of SPAB (Society for the Protection of Ancient Buildings, 1877) (9), which was established in response to the work of Victorian architects whose enthusiasm for what he regarded as harmful restoration caused irreparable damage. This organisation was of immense importance to the development of the conservation movement and could be regarded as the ancestor of all modern conservation campaigning societies. It was very much part of the late nineteenth century explosion of social reformist voluntary environmental groups (others in the UK include Royal Society for the Protection of Birds 1889, Footpaths Preservation Society 1899, and the National Trust 1895), all of which were not averse to confrontational public agitation on a national scale.

The Search for Authenticity

The SPAB Manifesto was written by William Morris, Philip Webb and other founder members in 1877, and although it was produced in response to the conservation problems of the nineteenth century, the organisation is still highly active and the Manifesto has been extended to provide protection to all times and styles and as such still remains the basis for the Society's work. It contains this plea:

> to put Protection in the place of Restoration, to stave off decay by daily care, to prop a perilous wall or mend a leaky roof by such means as are obviously meant for support or covering, and show no pretence of other art, and otherwise to resist all tampering with either the fabric or ornament of the building as it stands…
>
> *10*

It is interesting to observe how far this concept of what is important has progressed in the twenty-first century. A good illustrative example of this is the Cathedral of Santiago de Compostela, which is undergoing a massive amount of conservation work. The building is being completely cleaned and structural repairs are being conducted, this includes rectifying the mistakes that were made really quite recently, including the replacement of the far-too-heavy concrete roof. This will ensure that the building is fit for use for many generations to come.

It is the main gate, or Portal of Glory (Pórtico da Gloria), that is especially pertinent to this discussion. This Romanesque portico was once the main gate to the cathedral and dates back to the consecration of the building in 1211. Although it is now contained behind a protective eighteenth century Baroque façade, the once polychromatic archway is elevated at the top of a flight of stairs, and was designed so that the pilgrims could see it from afar as they entered the Cathedral Square. The tympanum was originally brightly painted, predominantly with the most precious and expensive colour, ultramarine blue; a colour already associated with holiness, humility, virtue and especially with the Virgin Mary. Over the next millennium the façade was repainted a number of times, and the decoration was a clear expression of what possessed value and worth in that day; and so as blue paint became more ubiquitous, gold was used (see Figure 7.5).

The objective of the present-day conservation work is to clean the sculptures, remove the grease and dirt that the city has placed upon it, and thus expose the patina of time. Traces of the earlier paintwork are still attached to the statues and these have been allowed to remain, but really the façade has become a study

FIGURE 7.5 Detail from the decorated tympanum above the magnificent Pórtico de Gloria of the Cathedral of Santiago de Compostela, Spain.

Credit: Sally Stone

of the pure three-dimensional beauty of the figures. On no account will the entrance be repainted. The exposure of the age is important, as is the revelation of the layers of history as shown in the fragments of paintwork that still cling to the crevices and folds combined with the weathered stonework that is being shown. As in previous times, the most precious material has been used to convey the worth of the revered sculpture, and in the twenty-first century, this is time. It has taken a huge amount of time and effort for the highly qualified, expensively trained conservators to carefully clean and preserve the sculptures. Time is our most precious commodity, it is the thing that we most commonly waste, and testament to the preciousness of time is the rise of the need in the western world for experiences rather than possessions. The present-day contemporary pursuit of 'art and form' through the application of subjective feeling fuels the tourism industry. As more of our basic needs are met, we increasingly expect sophisticated experiences that are emotionally satisfying and meaningful. These experiences will not be simple products. They will be a complex combination of products, services, spaces and information (11).

Human labour is the most expensive element of any work of conservation, therefore to show the consideration for any precious piece of art, the longer, deeper and more labour intensive the process, the greater is the inherent value of the object. This representation of the life of the façade shows how subjective the artistic evaluation of any ancient monument is. The precious blue paint and the valuable gold leaf are no longer regarded as the most treasured material. The fragments of these combined with the patina of time are the prized beyond anything else. A century ago this concept would have seemed barmy, but now it is the prevalent attitude.

Eugène Viollet-le-Duc (1814–79) took a completely different attitude towards conservation. He was a radical architect, wholly forward looking, who would courageously use new materials; he was also, at one time, the busiest restorer in France. For Viollet-le-Duc, the purpose of restoration was to define the artistic essence of a building, and recover an ideal unified authenticity for the benefit of the present. He was very much part of the desire in mid-nineteenth century France to use increasingly ambitious efforts to reconcile modernity and heritage. He developed a philosophy called 'Inventive Restoration' in which artistic freedom allowed the architect to speculate upon the possible aesthetic character of a building. Restoration included rebuilding in the style that the architect thought fitting, which was not necessarily true to the actual building, but was derived from the spirit of the structure. The monument existed not as material substance, but as an abstract ideal somewhat removed from historical reality. He felt that he was fully authorised to fill-in-the-blanks of damaged buildings. For him, the building could (and indeed should) be restored to a condition that was 'pristine', which may indeed be a condition that might never have actually existed: 'To restore a building is not to preserve it, to repair it, or rebuild it; it is to reinstate it in a condition of completeness that could never have existed at any given time' (12).

Viollet-le-Duc, who combined historical fact with creative modification, proposed a number of conjectural restorations in his Entretiens sur l'Architecture including the repair of an open-sided market with dramatic V-shaped pairs of cast iron columns. He was not afraid to use iron, which was then a radically new structural system, and he combined it with stone to create wide-spanning vaults and decorative ribs.

Le Château de Pierrefonds is an enormous mediaeval castle built at the end of the fourteenth century just to the north of Paris, France, by Louis, Duke of Orleans. It was pretty much destroyed by a petulant Louis XIII in retaliation against a rebellious governor. The ruins, hidden in the forests of the Valois, subsequently became a romantic haunt of artists. Napoleon III proposed the restoration; he was very much a keen moderniser determined to create a great legacy and was responsible for commissioning the great Haussman plan for the reconstruction of Paris (see Figure 7.6).

Viollet-le-Duc was appointed to provide a suitable setting within the mediaeval fortress, something that recreated the atmosphere that the romantic authors had created within the ruins, but with the facilities suitable for the users of the mid-nineteenth century. To begin with the restoration of the exterior of the building

FIGURE 7.6 The Chateâu de Pierrefonds was extensively restored by Eugène Viollet-le-Duc in the nineteenth century. The approach was one much more of interpretation rather than preservation.

Credit: Pierre Andre Leclercq via Wikimedia Commons

was fairly straightforward, the excavation work established the exact dimensions of the original building, the position of the structure and the extent of the damage. Viollet-le-Duc then, with deliberate asymmetry, creatively reconstructed the north and east wings and linked the two with an exterior staircase, decorated with mythical beasts and an equestrian statue of Louis d'Orleans. He then constructed a series of small defensive towers outside the perimeter wall, which would have served no useful purpose in medieval warfare. The interiors were much more extreme and fanciful, and here Viollet-le-Duc had creative licence to interpret and recreate the romance of the medieval period for a much later period. Cats and salamanders perch on the windows and sit on the walls, while the great courtyard staircase is decorated with eagles, storks and dragons. The architect reinvented medieval forms; he designed the furniture and the wall coverings, and he himself actually painted a frieze depicting the education of a young knight in one of the bedrooms. This restoration consciously selected a moment in time and to a certain extent was true to that moment. Thus the Château acquired the charming and picturesque quality of the idealised feudal period.

The intention of this approach to preservation was to return the entire monument to a form of hypothetical historical artistic integrity; that is, an ideal state, which was recovered from the found condition of the original building. Josef P. Kleihues used a similar approach within the 1989 conversion of the Carmelite Monatery and Church in Frankfurt into the city's Museum of Pre-History. The roof of the Church had long since been destroyed and the deconsecrated space was used to house the main gallery. Kleihues consciously echoed the shape of the original roof structure, but created it from laser-cut steel. This structure is oddly similar to the expectations of the original but also strangely different. The steel is highly contemporary and extremely delicate. New constructional techniques have been used to solve the practical problem of restoration without losing the unique atmosphere of the space. As a poetic rationalist, the strength of Kleihues' work lies in the endeavour to transform the reality of an original site into a new ideal reality in which historical elements, building structure and the building's context are adapted to his own architectural vocabulary, creating a relationship where building typology and urban form are synthesised. Thus Kleihues uses the same artistic imagination that Viollet-le-Duc advocated to creatively complete the building (see Figure 7.7).

Middle Ground

Aloïs Riegl (1858–1905) was one of the founders of art history as a discipline. He brought complex philosophical considerations to bear on art and its history, which took into consideration not just the object itself, but also the role of the spectator in the contemplation of the artefact or building. In 1903, he was responsible for one of the most significant of all texts on conservation: 'The Modern Cult of Monuments: Its Character and Its Origin' (Der Moderne Denkmalskultus) (13). It built upon Ruskin's idea of the monument as a living rather than dead thing, but furthered

FIGURE 7.7 The Museum of Prehistory, Frankfurt, Joseph Paul Kleihues, 1986. The new roof structure, constructed from laser-cut steel, is a contemporary interpretation of the timber beams of the original church.

Credit: Sally Stone

the discussion by arguing that authenticity is derived not from the origin of the building or artefact, but from the present-day reception of that object.

He reasoned that the monument was an idea of the modern age: a substitute for religious statuary, erected for the purpose of keeping particular human deeds or endeavours 'alive and present in the consciousness of future generations' (14). All monuments have historical value since they represent a particular stage in the development of a culture and that everything that has gone before forms an irreplaceable and inextricable link within the evolution of a culture.

Riegl described how the value of the monument could be subdivided into practical values versus oldness value; a division that reinforced the tension between artistic and historic motives for conservation. Historical value is imbued upon something because it is old. Things are often admired not so much for their beauty, but for their association with a phase of the past. It was once the case, for instance, that a furniture maker would construct a chair or cabinet in a particular style that reflected the environment of the place it was to be situated within. But Riegl considered this idea of copying a historical style as inauthentic, and that a piece of furniture, however well observed and beautifully constructed, would be given the derisory value of 'reproduction'. Inauthenticity was achieved not through the beauty of the craftsmanship, but because of the denial of the historical providence of the object.

Artistic value, however, is independent of the position of the object within the developmental chain of history. Therefore, artistic value is completely subjective, and is contingent upon the conceits and impulses of the particular society that is judging it. Riegl argued that given this particular situation, there is no such thing as eternal artistic value but only a transient modern value, thus the preservation of a monument should just take into account the historical worth.

Riegl described the simple tangible oldness of an object as Age-Value (Alterswert), and if artistic value is regarded as transient and therefore unimportant, then the consideration of all monuments should be based solely upon their age-value. This would mean that all objects are in essence equal. He agreed with Ruskin that monuments should not be shielded from the loosening effects of the forces of nature, something that is realised through a peaceful and regular continuity. But he differed from Ruskin in that he was not against restoration per se, but supported reconstruction and rebuilding of (broken pieces of) a monument if it supported the historical character of the object.

This attitude, that it is the present-day reception of the object that provides the authenticity, placed Riegl in the middle ground of the contested territory of the conservation debate fought over by Eugène Viollet-le-Duc, for whom intellectual history and complete restoration were important, and John Ruskin, who believed that the greatest glory of a building lay not in its stones, but in the patina of its age.

A contemporary example of this middle ground is the careful restoration of Rainham Hall, an early eighteenth century five-storey Merchants house sited on the north bank of the Thames in East London, and its conversion into a visitor attraction, café and education centre for The National Trust by Julian Harrop

Architects. The house was comprehensively restored, but essentially unaltered; however, the ancillary buildings were extensively remodelled to accommodate visitor facilities. The architects inserted a new lift and staircase into the two-storey stable block and integral brew-house. The form and appearance of the new elements was appropriated from the beer barrels, copper vats and gantries common to eighteenth and nineteenth century brewing houses, and it was the architects' stated ambition for these modern insertions to reinforce the understanding of the buildings' original use. A small extension to house the new entrance is obviously derived from the local Essex vernacular. Thus the conservation and remodelling works have the character of having always been there, but with the undoubtedly contemporary appearance of the twenty-first century.

This idea that it was possible for the ancient and the modern to viably exist side-by-side, for each to enhance and compliment the other, is another relatively modern idea. Whether within the urban environment, or the individual building, the quite subjective manner in which the city and the buildings developed meant that artistic considerations of balance and harmony were once not considered as important as they are now.

Written at about the same time as Riegl's great essay, Camillo Sitte (1843–1903) recognised the level of destruction that was occurring within many places and proposed the concept of Altstadt in his 1889 book *City Building According to Artistic Principles* (15). Here he established the basic principles of urban design, and strongly criticised the modern city planning that valued logic and mathematical solutions over artistic considerations. Within the book he developed the idea of integrating existing historic monuments into the living town. The old town and the artistic city could coexist.

This idea that old and new could exist harmoniously together was generally at odds with many of the prevalent ideas of the time, especially those of Haussmann and the massive regeneration of Paris, where huge swathes of the city were destroyed to make way for a grand vision. Sitte discussed the concept of the artistic analysis of urban space, genius loci, conservation and civic enhancement; that is, a cautious piecemeal and place sensitive approach. Thus new buildings and elements would be integrated into the existing environment, but would also serve to liberate that environment. These ideas of collaging the new elements into the historic environment are somewhat similar to those put forward by Colin Rowe and Fred Koetter almost 150 years later in their highly influential argument against the destructive power of Modernism: Collage City.

Patrick Geddes (1854–1932) placed value in the ensemble and encouraged regeneration through modern development within an historic core. He was a pioneer of the idea that social reform could be achieved through improvements in living conditions. He was a biologist, and had observed symbiotic relationships within nature, and he applied the same argument to the living conditions of the working class. He was deeply convinced that social structures and behaviour were related to spatial form and environment; so that by changing the surroundings and environment of a society, it was possible to change the structure and behaviour of that society. These ideas were developed at a time of increasing idealism, when other great social visionaries were developing their own concepts for a more fair and egalitarian future. The Mathildenhöhe in Darmstadt, Germany, designed by Joseph Maria Olbrich, and the Village of New Lanark in Scotland by Robert Owens, are just a couple of examples of new ideal villages constructed around this time. However, Geddes' interpretation of these ideas included the essence of community that had already been established within a specific location.

This belief was tested in a particularly run down and deprived area of the Old Town in Edinburgh, Scotland. The area had been effectively abandoned to slums in the early 1700s when the New Town was developed, so that almost two centuries later it was indeed a squalid place. Geddes was instrumental in the formation of the Edinburgh Social Union in 1885, which operated a socially conscious property management system; buying up housing, improving them and then leasing them to the poor at a fair rate. However, Geddes felt that he could do more, and in a bold effort to prove his theories correct he actually moved his family into the Old Town.

Geddes believed that those who occupied the area should have the ability to break the cycle of deprivation themselves. Improvements couldn't be imposed upon people, but if they were shown and encouraged, then change could be effected, others would join in and the momentum of change would happen. He actually carried out some of the initial physical work himself: painting walls, mending windows, clearing the rubbish from the streets.

One of his favourite ideas was the creation of gardens in disused and derelict areas. This was part of his commitment to a fairer greener world; he regarded gardens as important places that could help a family to thrive, somewhere that would bring the natural world into the heart of the built environment. These open spaces would provide a relief from the claustrophobic and overcrowded living conditions of the local residents and a social space to meet the other residents – somewhere that allowed people to mix that wasn't a public house or bar. He considered that the benefits of the city and their art should be for the many not the few.

This idea of careful reconstruction, renewal and repair, rather than demolition, was described by Geddes as Conservative Surgery (16). This was a process of amending and improving the urban quarter by minimising the destruction of the existing buildings, thus preserving the sense of community that already existed in the area. He considered that cities should be understood from three viewpoints: the historical, the geographical and the spiritual; these were aspects of the city that respond to place, work and folk and were closely interrelated. The existing alignment of the roads and lanes, the position of the key buildings and the established relationships between them was an expression of the local culture, and as such it was important to preserve them. Individual buildings, independent of age, style or period, had potential historic value that made them worthy of consideration. He thought that historic buildings must be used in order both to keep them alive and to guarantee the city's functioning as an organ for the transmitting of the cultural and social heritage. The value may not be obvious, but it may still be an important historic witness as part of a larger ensemble, or as a typical representation. The memory of the city was permanently stored within the buildings and monuments that made up the built environment.

Conservative Surgery relied upon judgements about the historic value of the buildings, and Geddes ensured that a stocktaking exercise of all of the possible aspects of a town was made before any work could begin. This survey included: visual images, written sources, statistical tables, diagrams, lists of historical buildings, three-dimensional models, maps and the like. Interestingly, each aspect was considered from a historical and a contemporary point of view. The historic survey was a narrative or story, rather than a scholarly tract, and as such, a process of selection by interpretation was required.

In this respect Geddes differed from Morris and many of the other early campaigners for the preservation of the existing environment, in that he did not object to improvements that brought the building up to modern levels of hygiene. He was not afraid to add to or even substantially change a building as long as it could be incorporated into the collection of historic architecture.

Geddes' work in Edinburgh can be seen as a direct precursor to the much more contemporary work of the group Assemble, which in 2015 was awarded the highly prestigious UK based Turner Prize, for its rehabilitation projects in the back streets of Toxteth in Liverpool, England. The collection of redbrick terraced (or row) houses was constructed for artisan workers at the beginning of the 1900s, but was suffering from neglect.

When the whole area was threatened with demolition and reconstruction the residents refused to move. Instead they commissioned the architects Assemble to develop a proposal to bring positive life to the area; one which would not lose the sense of community that had evolved within the place. The architects worked very much with the existing; each property was intimately assessed and then an individual solution developed. Some houses were beautifully restored, while others were very much left in the dilapidated condition that they had fallen into. One property now has a double-height living room, a reflection of the collapsed ceiling, while another, which was so badly damaged, has been converted into a lovely winter garden within the brick shell.

Geddes would have approved of this attitude, for he also felt that part of the process of saving a building was to reuse it. There was no point in preserving a building just for the sake of it, and it was here again that he differed from Morris, for whom the act of conservation itself was sufficient. Crosby Hall in the Bishopsgate area of London was the last remnant of a mansion house constructed in 1466 by Sir John Crosby. In 1908 Geddes organised the careful and painstaking removal of the building and its reconstruction in the former garden of Beaufort House, the place where Thomas Moore and Desiderius Erasmus deliberated upon the future of education and the pursuit of knowledge. The rebuilding of Crosby Hall allowed it to contribute towards the role of Chelsea as the place for intellectuals within London and thus the building reinforced the emerging character of the area.

The work of Geddes can be seen to encompass the altruistic attitude of the day, but it is still highly relevant to contemporary society in that he believed that romantic ruins should not be kept for the amusement of tourists or as an inspiration for artists, but should be used and reused. It is an important aspect of the twenty-first century that everything possible is recycled, including buildings. These sustainable ideas were not actually described as such by Geddes, but he can be seen as a pioneer of the environmental movement.

By the twentieth century, buildings began to occupy a more important role in society, both rationally and emotionally, but it was during this important period immediately preceding this that the contemporary attitudes towards conservation were formed.

Conclusions

Conservation embraces a vast range of subjects, environmental politics, urban economics and digital futures. The present-day contemporary pursuit of 'art and form' through the application of subjective feeling fuels the tourism industry. The existing situation is something that is constantly evolving, and as such can accommodate change, so it is possible to create a multi-level environment that embraces this evolution, rather than continually restarting without appraisal of the present situation. The manner in which the individual elements occupy the city respond to the individual situations of the city, buildings react to the location; Tabular Plena rather than Tabular Rasa.

Today authenticity of an object is derived not from the original or eternal values, but from the present-day reception of that object. While the artistic value is not attributed a transient or timeless status, it is a present-day concern. Over a century ago, Aloïs Riegl argued that of development: 'We call historical all things that once were and are no longer' (17). However, history is now regarded as a progressive activity. Indeed conservation is often described as a future oriented movement focussing on the past.

Thus it is the historical significance of an object that is valued. Its worth is not depend upon the quality of the object, the skill with which it was constructed or the materials that it is made from. Value is simply attributed through age. Reproduction is frowned upon and pastiche is ridiculed, because the sense of time and history are regarded as lost when these techniques are employed. Blemishes show age, something that Ruskin was much in favour of. The patina that comes with custom and use that appears after many generations have handled an object is considered to be of much greater value than something that reproduces the original piece or object, however well made.

Today's attitude towards conservation means that there would be a horrified reaction to a proposal to repaint the tympanum of the Portal of Glory in the Cathedral of Santiago de Compostela. The integrity of this once highly decorated sculptured infill over the doorway is preserved through the visual knowledge that it is very old, that it has survived as cultures and societies change and has remained constant through the ages. But of course it hasn't remained constant; the visual impression of the tympanum has changed as society's attitude towards what is precious has altered.

It was blue when that was the treasured colour, it was covered with gold when that was the most valuable material, and now that time is our most cherished commodity, it has been painstakingly cleaned to expose the sense of history inherent within it. Conservation is a constant search for authenticity, and as attitudes towards what is regarded as authentic evolve, so have methods and theories of conservation.

References

1. Schofield, J. (2016) St Paul's Cathedral: Archaeology and History. Oxford: Oxbow Books 177.
2. Schofield, J. (2016) St Paul's Cathedral: Archaeology and History. Oxford: Oxbow Books, p. 109
3. Jokilehto, J. (1999) A History of Architectural Conservation. London: Routledge, p. 29.
4. Crane, N. (2016) The Making of the British Landscape. London: Weidenfeld & Nicolson 277.
5. Miles Glendinning, M. (2013) The Conservation Movement: A History of Architectural Preservation. London: Routledge 67.
6. Miles Glendinning, M. (2013) The Conservation Movement: A History of Architectural Preservation. London: Routledge, p. 65.
7. Pugin, A. W. N. (1836) Contrasts. Originally self published, printed in London by James Moyes.
8. Pevsner, N. (1980) "Ruskin and Violett-le-Duc", from Eugène Emmanuel Violett-le-Duc. P. Farrant, et al. London, p. 50.
9. Morris, W. and Webb, P. (1877) The SPAB Manifesto. The Society for the Protection of Ancient Buildings: www.spab.org.uk/about-us/spab-manifesto, accessed 23 December 2017.
10. Morris, W. and Webb, P. (1877) The SPAB Manifesto. The Society for the Protection of Ancient Buildings: www.spab.org.uk/about-us/spab-manifesto, accessed 23 December 2017.
11. Svabo, C. and Shanks, M. (2015) "Experience as Excursion: A Note towards a Metaphysics of Design Thinking" from Experience Design: Concepts and Case Studies. P. Benz (Ed.). London, p. 26.
12. Pevsner, N. (1980) "Ruskin and Violett-le-Duc", from Eugène Emmanuel Violett-le-Duc. P. Farrant, et al. London, p. 50.
13. Riegl, A. (1903/1996) "The Modern Cult of the Monument: Its Character and Its Origin" from Historical and Philosophical Issues in the Conservation of Cultural Heritage. N. Price (Ed.). Canada.
14. Riegl, A. (1903/1996) "The Modern Cult of the Monument: Its Character and Its Origin" from Historical and Philosophical Issues in the Conservation of Cultural Heritage. N. Price (Ed.). Canada, p. 69.
15. Sitte, C. (1889) City Building According to Artistic Principles.
16. Welter, V. (2002) Biopolis: Patrick Geddes and the City of Life. Cambridge MA: MIT Press, p. 116.
17. Riegl, A. (1903/1996) "The Modern Cult of the Monument: Its Character and Its Origin" from Historical and Philosophical Issues in the Conservation of Cultural Heritage. N. Price (Ed.). Canada, p. 70.

8

THE SUSTAINABLE ADAPTATION OF THE EXISTING BUILDING

Introduction

One of the greatest concerns for the twenty-first century population is the search for a sustainable future; there is a growing global awareness of limited resources, expanding ecological footprint and climate change caused by excessive carbon emissions. Thus a reduction in the sheer amount of energy consumed is one of the most urgent challenges for all architects and designers today, and so a very sensible option is to extend the lifespan of the existing building stock. The built environment needs to be able to accommodate growth while also reducing consumption.

The sustainable adaptation of the existing situation is the reuse and modification of existing buildings, structures and places in an environmentally sympathetic manner. It is an alternative to the traditional system of demolition and reconstruction. The adaptation can be conducted without compromising the historic value of the existing structure; it can upgrade the building to cope with the demands of the new users, and it can encourage these occupiers to inhabit the building in a sustainable manner.

The environmental movement's international slogan, Reduce/Reuse/Recycle, is a manifesto for the way to live in the twenty-first century, and is especially pertinent to interior architecture and the adaptation of structures. The embodied energy in these elements can be saved through upgrade and reuse, and through adaptation the amount of natural resources required to construct a building is greatly reduced and the building can be adapted to be used in an environmentally kind manner.

The reuse of extant structures and situations to house new users is a very environmentally friendly approach to the creation of contemporary space, not only because the structure is already in place and quite often many of the services might already be on the site, but also because existing buildings can be seen as an important cultural, social and architectural resource for shaping the future. Architecture that is site specific is extremely sustainable. Good ecological design that results from context is adaptive, resilient and reflective – it is born of place and honours the land. Adaptive design is even more supportable. Sustainable construction aims to reduce the impact buildings have on the environment by making use of knowhow and technologies to create a sustainable environment that meets the needs of the present generation without jeopardising the ability of future generations to provide their needs; sustainable adaptation is a key element within this approach. A seminal example of building reuse, which was in direct opposition to Modernist advancement of the last century, was the Solar Pavilion. It was built in Wiltshire by the architectural partnership Alison and Peter Smithson as their own weekend retreat from 1959 to 1962. The new two-storey pavilion was superimposed upon parts of an old structure that was decaying in the courtyard of a group of farm buildings. The remains of the original cottage not only offered a framework to anchor the new wood and glass structure; they also provided a direct connection between the new building and the immediate context. Although it was not discussed at the time, this is a self-conscious attempt to escape from the technological consumption of Modernism and construct something in an ecologically sympathetic manner. The building took full advantage of the heating effect of the sun, the windows opened so that a breeze could cool the spaces when necessary, and the occupiers accepted that when the environment outside the little building was too cold for comfort, they had to put another layer of clothing on; thus retaining a direct connection with both the context and the climate.

Elements of Sustainable Adaptation

The sustainable adaptation of the existing building can be viewed as having two distinct components: the first is the manner in which the building is changed; this can be subdivided into three sections: environment, society and economy. The second consideration is that the adapted spaces are designed in such a manner that the new users of the building are actively encouraged to occupy it in a sustainable manner, and think about their environmental footprint as they go about their daily activities. Thus sustainable adaptation of an existing building contains four main components: environment, society, economy and inhabitation. The manner in which the adaptation of existing buildings addresses each of these factors reinforces the idea that adaptation is a sustainable strategy for the future development and redevelopment of the built environment.

Environment

All architecture is intrinsically linked to context, in that all buildings are constructed to occupy a particular place, situated within a distinct climate, orientated in a particular direction, and surrounded by a certain environment. Dean Hawkes asks whether this relationship with the prevailing conditions of the immediate environment is advantageous, something that can be used to the benefit of the building, or something to be fought? 'Do we design with or against climate? That is our choice' (1).

All buildings are distinct, and thus any project that attempts to modify the existing structure or situation has to take into consideration the particular characteristics of the original. Existing buildings can be remade, recreated, remediated and reclaimed with the discriminating use of the vernacular and traditions combined with cutting-edge technological innovation. The selection of suitable best practices for the holistic deep renovation of buildings, adapted to local traditions, using traditional bioclimatic devices, the most modern available materials and systems for implementing energy technologies can all be used in historic buildings. The recent developments and most up-to-date refurbishment techniques in built heritage rehabilitation, as well as the potential of traditional bioclimatic devices and techniques in energy-driven renovation of historic buildings, can be selected.

Many of the sustainable strategies that are commonly used in the construction of new buildings can be applied to reuse projects. Techniques such as the use of passive methods for heating, cooling and ventilation, orientation towards or away from the sun to encourage or discourage solar gain, thermal storage, the use of locally sourced or renewable materials, the use of innovative materials that reduce glare, high levels of insulation, the use and reuse of grey water, energy generation from wind, water or sunlight, boreholes, earth coils and other thermal systems are all transferable. It can also be argued that sustainable architecture is unambiguously linked to vernacular architecture, and that there are lessons that this architecture of the past can teach us in the future.

Reclamation and remediation projects involve a trajectory of strategies in repurposing, transforming and recalibrating; strategies such as subtraction, substitution, implantation and addition. Technological breakthroughs make it possible to reconfigure existing buildings with their own locally sourced energy, renewable energy, optimising building performance using highly engineered and integrated technologies. Buildings can be reconfigured to function as power plants – generate energy from the sun, wind, garbage, hydro, geothermal. They can employ techniques for environmental control – sensors, displacement ventilation, automatic shades, thermal control and ventilation control. Architects can specify add-ons to facilitate further ecological economy such as: photovoltaic panels, wind-blades, hydrogen batteries and heat pumps, thus diminishing energy consumption for internal conditioning. And architects can design buildings that generate more energy than they consume with the aim of optimising the building performance, improving the quality of the interior environment to increase comfort and productivity.

However all add-ons have a visual impact, and for the architecture to be truly radical, the project can embrace change without resorting to unattractive or inappropriate additions, that is, extensions, appendages, attachments, accretions or just unattractive and inappropriate protuberances that compromise the character and veracity of the existing building. To possess real integrity the architect and designer can choose to remodel the existing building in a manner that does not compromise either the original or the new; that is, the creation of something that fuses the character of both. This is an architecture that is totally relevant to the twenty-first century, that uses contemporary technology and is suitable for the needs of today. This means not resorting to pastiche, but remodelling and adapting buildings and interiors that are visually and operationally applicable to the present day.

Retrofitting is a term that is used to describe the process of refurbishing and remodelling buildings to achieve reductions in the operational energy consumption. It is an especially useful technique for saving large twentieth century structures, particularly apartment blocks, hospitals and other municipal buildings. These are structures that were constructed at a time of plentiful fuel and consequently paid little attention to such practices as insulation and double-glazing.

Given that reuse is a sustainable strategy, it is exceptionally difficult for a remodelled building to be awarded a very high classification from energy rating agencies. For example, the USA Agency LEED (Leadership in Energy and Environmental Design) is a green building certificate programme that recognises outstanding building strategies and practices, and BREEAM (Building Research Establishment Environmental Assessment Methodology) is a European based design and assessment method for assessing sustainable buildings; both of their assessments include aspects related to energy and water use, the quality of the internal environment, materials, waste and management processes. It is somewhat ironic that given how sustainable the practice of reuse is, that it is very difficult for conversion projects to be awarded a high status. This is because of the difficulties of compliance; the existing situation may contain insufficient natural light, little insulation and poor air-tightness. The U-Value of an existing building may be vastly different to that of a sustainably constructed new one. The walls may be inadequately insulated, and to add insulation to a historic building can be very difficult without drastically affecting the cultural character of the original structure. There are some fine examples of insulation added to the exterior of the building, thus not compromising exquisite interior finishes, and other examples that show how insulation can be applied to the inside, thus leaving the historic character of the exterior intact. But how is the situation resolved if both the interior and the exterior have historic worth? The rating agencies measure the amount of natural light that enters a building; the size and position of the opening within an existing building will normally already be in place, thus making it very difficult to alter the amount of light admitted into the interior of the structure without making unsuitable alterations.

Society

It is well recognised that cities consume less energy than the suburbs or the countryside; urban density is more efficient than sprawl and it is no longer sustainable to encourage unregulated expansion. It is necessary to develop a model that is no longer linked to perpetual horizontal development: a city needs to be able to grow in upon itself, it needs to become less consumptive and more efficient. As the function of an existing structure becomes obsolete, so different users with different needs can move in to take advantage of the already constructed. It may not provide a perfect fit, but it is possible for the building to be adjusted; that is, to be tailored to accommodate the needs of the new users. The existing building can be altered, remodelled, reclad and refurbished. Most buildings have resilience; that is, the ability to recover from disturbance, to accommodate change, to function in a state of health. Resilient, adaptive, sustainable design can stimulate a thriving environment and therefore includes economic and ecological health, and cultural vitality. The architect can develop an approach to the existing based upon a detailed examination and understanding of the existing, combined with a knowledge of the possibilities of transformation and an intricate comprehension of the needs of the users. Every solution is different, depending upon the nature and position of the existing building and the needs of the new users, so there is no one-size-fits-all solution.

Places that contain a rich and varied heritage are highly valued. At the beginning of the twenty-first century over 50% of the world's population live in cities; it is estimated that by 2050, the percentage may be as high as 66%. Interestingly it is not any city that most people want to inhabit; it is old cities. Urban environments that contain history, tradition and culture, that is, places that have naturally evolved over many years to contain an abundance of memory, are multidimensional and are diverse.

The idea that new economic and sustainable growth might fundamentally depend on the built environment possessing a good stock of old, distinctive buildings was put forward by the American urbanist Jane Jacobs over 40 years ago. Jacobs was writing at a time when wholesale redevelopment of great swathes of cities was being planned and carried out on both sides of the Atlantic. (A fine example of a building that Jacobs campaigned against its demolition, but which has been lost, is the Pennsylvania Street Station in New York.) She cited multiple reasons for the importance of existing buildings: they provide character and interest, they are adaptable, and available in the different scales, they can often be taken on easily and quickly, they are cheaper to occupy than new build and so are attractive to innovative, risky businesses that need to keep costs down (2).

US economist Richard Florida's 'creative economy' theory actively links the importance of heritage districts and buildings with economic growth. His book, *The Rise of the Creative Class*, extensively credits and updates Jacobs. He describes how active and creative people want to inhabit environments that contain character, which is of course something that is very difficult to create from scratch. Personality of place develops over many years. He describes historic buildings as a primary location for businesses working directly within the creative economy: 'Our older industrial age cities are potentially cauldrons of creativity … filled with just the sorts of warehouses, factories, and other buildings that can become the figurative garages where start-ups are incubated' (3).

The attitude that the reuse of existing structures and situations can be culturally beneficial, even if it is not necessarily the easiest or most straightforward strategy, was articulated by the late Florian Beigel. Developers and architects may want to make a contemporary statement, the users may not be an exact fit, adaptation may be difficult, and efficiency difficult to achieve, but given the important cultural value of the historic environment, razing and rebuilding may not be the most responsible solution:

> We think there can be significant cultural value and therefore use to structures of the past, even if they seem to be obstructions to change or efficiency. This is not a plea for conservationism but an acknowledgement that change is not a good thing in itself.
>
> 4

The layers of meaning within the city are a narrative that can be explored and analysed before further developments are embarked upon. In her seminal, *The City of Collective Memory*, Christine Boyer elaborates upon this idea that through the careful analysis of the existing situation, the architect or designer can facilitate changes that are appropriate and welcome:

> The name of a city's streets and squares, the gaps in its very plan and physical form, its local monuments and celebrations, remain as traces and ruins of their former selves. They are tokens or hieroglyphs from the past to be literally re-read, re-analysed, and re-worked over time.
>
> 5

Contextualism is an approach to the architecture and the design of the built environment that uses the process of analysing and understanding the nature and the qualities of place to develop new elements. The architect and designer can work with the identity of a place, to create architecture that is appropriate to its location and does not destroy the nature or character of an area. Kenneth Frampton, talks about the need for architecture and design to have the '…capacity to condense the artistic potential of the region while reinterpreting cultural influences coming from the outside', for the building to show a great understanding of both place and tectonics, and to '…evoke the oneiric essence of the site, together with the inescapable materiality of building' (6) (see Figure 8.1).

Contextualism emerged as a reaction to modernism and is now more than a generation old, but is a theory that is still highly relevant at the beginning of the new millenium. The twenty-first century post-modern society has the need to embrace ideas of memory and experience and this means that Contextualism is at the forefront of theories about contemporary architecture, urban design and interior design. For centuries architects and engineers have dwelled upon the problem of how to create controlled and conditioned environments for social relationships in buildings. Society lives under the same sun, shelters from the same rain and resists buffeting from the same wind as the ancestors, and yet within contemporary architecture ever more resources are devoted to the search for ever more complexity in solving these problems.

Smith, Lommerse and Metcalfe describe this link between context and sustainability as Social Sustainability. This is characterised by a strong connection to place,

FIGURE 8.1 Community interaction within any society is recognised as both highly sustainable and beneficial to the health of the residents. The Northern Quarter in Manchester has been transformed from a somewhat neglected and dilapidated area into a thriving and vibrant environment.

Credit: Sally Stone

to building capacity and contains resilience to external forces. They further explain that just as sustainable development could be described as being eco-centric, so social sustainability has an anthropocentric approach which focuses upon human relationships combined with the needs and quality of life:

> Social sustainability is the ability of a society or an individual's lifestyle to continue in a way that suits their needs and those of subsequent generations. The values and spiritual aspirations of the people should be complimented in their interior environment, and in the processes and activities involved should respect their history, current needs and future potentials beliefs and rituals.
>
> 7

Thus strategies such as reusing historic buildings, preventing urban sprawl, redeveloping town centres, reducing pollution, reducing carbon footprint, preserving open space and implementing sustainable design are all interconnected.

Economy

There are considerable cost savings when the existing building is in good condition and when many of the services are in place, however, completing the actual modification and preservation work can be expensive. Historic buildings were generally constructed at a time when skilled labour was cheap, and to viably match that high level of craftsmanship in the twenty-first century can involve considerable expense. Upgrading a building requires the specification and construction of individual specially made elements; it is very difficult to mass-produce the components of conservation. To upgrade any building to a very high level of environmental specification involves many different consultants and craftspeople with particular requirements, each of which is specific to that individual building. Thus it does normally take more time and at a greater expense to remodel than it does to build new. Generally it is accepted that renovation work uses twice as much labour but half as much material as new construction.

But this expense has to be weighed against the increased economic worth of the remodelled property. A higher property value is likely to bring a more advantaged population to the particular urban area, who can actively contribute to its economic development.

Inhabitation

Buildings can be remodelled so that they are occupied in a sustainable manner, thus architects and designers can help to implement behavioural change. For example, rain and grey water can be recycled and high levels of insulation will cut the necessity for massive amounts of artificial heating and cooling. The architect can design buildings that actively reduce demand, and increase efficiency, that encourage a less carbon-intense lifestyle and develop a respectful relationship with the natural environment.

In highly industrialised countries the building sector – through the construction and operation of buildings – accounts for about 50% of total CO2 emissions. In Germany for example, 20% stems from the production and transportation of materials, and 30% from heating cooling and ventilation (8). If carbon emissions are to be addressed, then the overall life-cycle of the building needs to be confronted, not just in the construction of the building, but also in its operation, heating, cooling and lighting. The argument for this reduction is well known: the imperative to reduce carbon emissions, combined with the imminent possibility of fuel poverty and the rising price of energy, means that we must consider a more responsible future. It is well recognised that a significant proportion of the reduction can be achieved through the modification of behaviour, at both the individual and the organisational level. 'Replacing incandescent lightbulbs with compact fluorescent lightbulbs is good, but turning off the lights when not needed is better' (9).

A change in human behaviour can bring about a reduction in energy demand and architects and designers can help to implement that change; it can be made straightforward for the user of any building to ask themselves: What temperature is realistically comfortable? How important is it to turn off the lights? Can waste be sorted into its individual components? And controversially, will the existing be adequate? Is a new replacement really necessary?

Attitudes that underpin these questions are bound up with collective responsibility and human rights, but the designer can help by making the questions easier to answer, with simple design decisions such as ensuring that the interactive elements of the design are easily accessible with simple modifications available – by ensuring that the recycling bins are easy to access, by making certain that the cooling and heating systems are easy to operate, by having windows that open to allow fresh air into the building and by specifying that the light switches are situated in a visible position.

Case Studies

Two case studies that were developed almost a quarter of a century apart show how ordinary buildings can be adapted to accommodate the needs of new users. They both take advantage of the immediate context in which they are situated and aim to control the environmental quality of the interior. Advances in the manner in which materials are collected and used are illustrated by the projects. Both are laudable, but it is obvious how much the understanding of the possibilities of materials has evolved in the time between them.

Office for Greenpeace UK, London, Feilden Clegg Bradley, 1990

Feilden Clegg Bradley Architects converted a 1930s factory and office building into the headquarters for Greenpeace UK in 1990. This was a pioneering project; it was one of the first to really take seriously the concept of sustainable adaptation. The client recognised the importance of not using more resources than necessary, so chose to occupy an existing building rather than construct a new one. The building they selected was a former laboratory in North London. Greenpeace wanted to minimise CO2 emissions as much as possible, to allow as much natural light and ventilation into the building, limit the amount of mechanical environmental control and to reduce the impact of the various materials used.

The existing building was selected not just for its integral strength and uncomplicated construction and therefore the ease with which it could be adapted, but also because of the substantial amount of exterior glazing. The structure is a simple striped brick exterior with interior cast iron columns. The previous occupants demanded a huge amount of natural light, and the remodelling made maximum use of the considerable window area for the access of both natural light and ventilation. The new function was quite unlike the original, and Greenpeace intended to occupy the building in a different manner; they required office space rather than laboratories. This meant that natural light needed to reach the centre of the building; it was not sufficient for it to illuminate the desks situated at the perimeter of the space.

The architects used the existing organisation of the building to inform the new elements of design. They conducted little more than conservation work to the exterior; it was within the interior that they made huge sculptural interventions to mark the circulation areas. Feilden Clegg hung dramatic steel and timber staircases at strategic moments in the building; these not only facilitated movement, but also signalled the dramatic intent of the new occupants. The architects solved the problem of how to throw natural light into the centre of the space with a series of ingeniously designed screens. Pivoting awnings were fixed to the window frames at the same point internally and externally. These acted in two ways: to control the levels of sunlight entering the building and to throw it deep into the middle of the space. First, as sunlight enters the building it is bounced at a high level off the pivoting reflectors, across the room to reflect again from natural cotton ceiling-mounted canopies and into the centre of the deep office. The pivoting screens also stop any direct penetration of sunlight or excessive solar gain from entering into the building by acting as louvres on the exterior of the building. Small casements at the top and bottom of the windows open; this encourages cross–ventilation and the movement of clean air into the depths of the building. The centrally placed open stair admits natural light into the centre of the building and aids ventilation by encouraging the stack effect. Greenpeace needed to make a statement about the environmental possibilities of reusing an existing building, Feilden Clegg Bradley fulfilled all their expectations.

Edinburgh Centre for Carbon Innovation, Edinburgh, Malcolm Fraser Architects, 2013

A fine example of sustainable adaptation is Edinburgh Centre for Carbon Innovation (ECCI). It is a collection of buildings that were modified to accommodate new occupiers with different demands to those who originally inhabited the spaces. The proposal for the ECCI was for a world-class interdisciplinary research and teaching facility focused upon the key climate related challenges facing society. The intention of the ECCI was to bring together high-quality research facilities that address the significance of climate change, that inform political decision-making and establish Edinburgh as a leading university in the field.

The ECCI could be described as pioneering in that the client insisted that the conversion should be awarded the BREEAM status of Outstanding. BREEAM (Building Research Establishment Environmental Assessment Methodology) is one of the world's foremost environmental assessment methods of assessing, rating and certifying the sustainability of buildings (10). The assessment includes aspects related to energy and water use, the quality of the internal environment, materials, waste and management processes. It is somewhat ironic that given how sustainable the practice of reuse is that it is very difficult for conversion projects to be awarded this status. This is because of the difficulties of compliance as the existing situation may contain insufficient natural light, little insulation and poor air-tightness. The ECCI was the first remodelled building to be awarded this status.

The ECCI involved the alteration and extension of the Category B listed Old High School building, Infirmary Street, Edinburgh, Scotland. The project included the consideration of the adjoining buildings and proposals to reinvigorate the land within the High School Yards, to the boundary of Infirmary Street at the front and the enclosed space of Surgeon's Square to the rear. High School Yards had always been a significant architectural site and has had many incarnations since its beginnings as Blackfriars Monastery (from 1230), including the Royal High School, where Sir Walter Scott was a pupil.

In 1578 the first school building was built on the site to replace the educational function of the monastery. A larger Royal High School was then rebuilt in the same location in 1777 (Sir Walter Scott's initials can be seen today among the eighteenth century graffiti on the wall by the entrance to the building). As great numbers of people moved out to the New Town in the early nineteenth century, the old school was closed and in 1832 the building re-opened as a Surgical Hospital, in which the University of Edinburgh held its Anatomy classes. At this time a rear building, square in plan, was added to contain the surgical lecture theatre. The Surgical Hospital then formed part of the Edinburgh Royal Infirmary (at the time located on the site of Dovecot Studios on Infirmary Street), which had become short of space. By the latter stages of the nineteenth century, the old hospitals were reaching the end of their useful life and throughout the twentieth century the University acquired the Old High School building to house a number of different disciplines, including Engineering and Science, Geography and the Dental School.

Malcolm Fraser Architects was confronted with a collection of significant yet problematic buildings. The approach that they took was to tie the disparate elements together with a new atrium, staircase and social spaces, which were stitched between and around the original historic buildings. This central circulation route served to tie the various new and old elements together and also provide a passive heating and cooling system. The architects then used a very limited palette of

FIGURE 8.2 The Edinburgh Centre for Carbon Innovation, Edinburgh, Malcolm Fraser Architects, 2013. This complex of buildings was the first adaptation project to be given BREEAM status of outstanding.

Credit: Malcolm Fraser

materials: sustainable cross-laminated timber, recycled copper and locally quarried Cullalo and Blaxter stone to adapt the collection of buildings for the twenty-first century users (see Figures 8.2 and 8.3).

The primary structure of all new work consisted of a locally sourced cross-laminated timber (CLT) frame and floor panels system. The CLT is said to lock in four–five times more carbon than it takes to produce and is considered an innovative solution to use within an existing building. The existing Cullaloe and Blaxter stone was conservatively repaired and any new stone needed for construction was sourced locally from Fife. (This natural stone, when supplied and worked locally, provides an exceptionally low energy and durable material, which can easily be repaired and recycled.) The bronze cladding (80% copper, 20% tin) is lightweight, which reduces demand on structure, and the copper itself was made from up to

FIGURE 8.3 The Edinburgh Centre for Carbon Innovation, Edinburgh, Malcolm Fraser Architects, 2013. The individual structures are clustered around a new internal courtyard that serves to facilitate the circulation, and encourage the movement of clean warm air through the building.

Credit: Malcolm Fraser

30% recycled material. The architects ensured that most of the ventilation is controlled passively through the use of stack ventilation in large spaces and trickle ventilation in smaller rooms, plus all of the new and existing windows have operable sashes. The ventilation control is determined according to the function of specific rooms and is ventilated passively most of the time but offices and teaching rooms do sometimes require temperature control through mechanical ventilation; heating the air is not the main purpose of the ventilation but rather circulating the outdoor air into the building as well as maintaining the indoor air temperature are the key environmental aspects of the design. The air is recycled through air suction vents in the roof that filter the air to the Air Handling Unit located in the attic. The air is filtered, and in the summer it is cooled through chilled beams and recirculated into the building at a constant temperature. The high ceilings of the indoor spaces provide natural air circulation within the building and allow a constant control of air temperature through air-tight double entry controlled areas and thick open vapor walls. Most of the heat is self-generated indoors by activities, equipment or mechanically through radiators that are powered by the district Central Heating and Power unit; this reduces the CO_2 emissions by 38%. The window openers are automatically activated to release excess heat throughout the summer thus maintaining indoor temperature at comfort levels. The main windows and sashes are manually operable which gives direct control of the ventilation to the users of the building but the automatic management of roof-light windows allows for non-occupancy ventilation control. The spaces all have large windows that open to almost all directions giving adequate illumination within the building. The efficient heating and ventilation systems allow large southern windows to be exploited within the design without risk of overheating in summer or heat loss in winter. The internal and external lighting is low energy (including LED where appropriate) throughout, with zoned control and sensors to reduce usage. Fluorescent lights were preferred in the study areas, which allowed long periods of activity and were supplied by PV energy. By carefully considering the surfaces of the building mass, which are subject to the highest levels of renewable solar gain, the PV panels have been strategically situated on the south-facing pitches of the original existing roof-lights. They cover 30m2 in total and are the primary energy supply for the building; excess power is sold back to the grid. Thus the remodelled building is extremely environmentally sound, the heating and cooling systems are highly effective, the embodied energy in the new elements is relatively small and the occupants of the building are encouraged to be very aware of their carbon footprint as they use the buildings.

Conclusions

The historic environment is somewhere that a large proportion of society wants to inhabit, as can be observed from the massive areas of gentrification visible in many older cities. The historic city is interesting, full of character and provides a direct link to their own personal and collective memory, it lacks the anonymity that new developments contain. These all contribute to the pattern of the twenty-first century and the sustainable adaptation of the existing can play a very important role in this progress. These environments can be adapted in an environmentally sound and sustainably friendly manner that encourages energy efficient inhabitation.

It may not be the easiest approach, but it is a very sustainable process to reuse existing buildings, most simply because of the massive amount of energy required to build new, mainly in the materials but also to a certain extent in the man-power that does not have to be expended. It is of an even greater benefit if the conversion is made using sustainable techniques. The designer can select materials that do not contain huge amounts of embodied energy, that have been sourced locally and that do not harbour toxic or hazardous chemicals. Additionally, remodelling can be made more environmentally sound by considering how the building is used. It can be designed so that the minimum amount of energy is expended in the day-to-day use and so that the environment that created is beneficial to everyone who occupies it. Specific decisions are important to ecological urbanism and design: the individual and society can become less consumptive, they can practice conservation and restraint, reduce demand and increase efficiency, energy use can be curtailed, efficiency maximised and carbon footprint reduced.

References

1. Hawkes, Dean (2015) "The English Climate and the Enduring Principles of Environmental Design" from Sustainable Building Conservation: Theory and Practice of Responsive Design in the Heritage Environment. Oriel Prizeman (Ed.). RIBA Publishing, p. 35.
2. Jacobs, J. (1992/1961) The Death and Life of Great American Cities. New York: Vintage, p. 33.
3. Florida, R. (2005) The Rise of the Creative Class; And How it's Transforming Work, Leisure, Community, and Everyday Life. London: Routledge, p. 1.
4. Florian Beigel, F. (2013) An Art of Living. Domus 973 / October, p. 69.
5. Boyer, C. (1994) The City of Collective Memory: Its Historical Imagery and Architectural Entertainments. Cambridge MA: MIT Press, p. 21.
6. Frampton, Kenneth (1983/1996) "Prospects for a Critical Regionalism" from Theorizing a New Agenda for Architecture an Anthology of Architectural Theory 1965–1995. Kate Nesbitt (Ed.). New York: Princeton Architectural Press, p. 471.
7. Smith, D., Lommerse, M. and Metcalfe, P. (2011) Perspectives on Social Sustainability and Interior Architecture: Life from the Inside. Curtin University Interior Architecture Publication Series, Pencil and Paper Press, vol 1, p. 1.
8. Richarz, C. Schulz, C. and Friedemann, Z. (2007) Detail Practice: Energy Efficient Upgrades. Basel – Boston – Berlin: Berkhäuser, p. 3.
9. Mostafavi, M. and Doherty, G. (2010) Ecological Urbanism. Harvard: Lars Müller Publishing, p. 516.
10. Building Research Establishment Environmental Assessment Methodology (BREEAM): The Worlds Leading Design and Assessment Method for Sustainable Buildings: www.breeam.org, accessed July 2015.

9

SPATIAL AGENCY OR TAKING ACTION

Introduction

Private social agencies that are engaged with the provocative design of social spaces are filling the voids in the city – subsidised housing, students, young people, temporary occupation, pop-ups. These are people and activities for whom the historic urban environment is valuable; it is interesting, full of character and provides a direct link to their own personal and to the collective memory. They feel that they can make a difference, not through the traditional craft of architecture but through non-antagonistic, small, local interventions, whether they be social, physical and/or temporal. As custodians of the built environment they use non-traditional models of practice to generate a feeling of civic responsibility within the local population of urban users and dwellers. This is a provocative and absolutely hands-on method of adaptation and interpretation. Raoul Bunschoten in his chapter 'Points, Spirals and Prototypes' likens it to the intuitive art of cookery: 'To stir a city you have to first get its ingredients sorted out, then feed them into the cooking pot one by one, each one prepared in the manner that gets the most out of them' (1).

The De Anderen Studios is a somewhat crazy and dynamic collection of free-flowing creative spaces situated within an old railway arch in Glasgow. The architects Baxendale have created a sculptural suspended mezzanine from reclaimed timber, second-hand pallets and old packing cases. It contains a flying platform, a suspended balcony, a cantilevered desk and a really quite dangerous spiral staircase. At ground floor level the space is subdivided with a series of bespoke movable screens, which define specific workspaces for individual designers and artists, or are simply shifted to the edge of the space to create a large interactive studio. The archway was quite basically lined with sheets of pale grey painted corrugated steel to provide adequate environmental control and thus a completely clean space that was then occupied in this creative manner (2) (see Figure 9.1).

FIGURE 9.1 The De Anderen Studios, Glasgow, Baxendale Architects, 2013. The installation was constructed collectively ensuring that all of those involved with the project were invested in it.

Credit: Thomas Manley

The project was a collaboration between the facilitating architect and artists who occupy the space. It was much more than just a design task for Baxendale, but also an on-site hands-on construction project. This allowed the design to evolve as the project developed, as more material arrived and as the collaboration developed.

Baxendale regularly work with people and places, they facilitate this public agency in the re-imagining of place through collaboration with the users of the space combined with active making. The practice believes that conceiving ideas, prototyping interventions and creating local capacity to enact sustainable change can be an organic and responsive process that brings communities together to work towards common goals. Their projects occur at a variety of scales and duration, from immediate and improvised interventions within public space, gallery installations and public art to the establishment of permanent pieces of physical architecture.

Baxendale works with communities and individuals, with the ambition to improve their experience of life through intervention in their social, economic, physical and cultural environments; this includes the coordination, guidance and support of volunteer and non-professional people in the construction of community spaces. Collaborative working was at the base of another intimate installation of theirs, the Nadfly Shop, which was situated beneath the main staircase in the Trongate 103 Arts Centre, again in Glasgow. This little pavilion created from reused wooden pallets was lined with colourful reclaimed carpets and used self-assembled construction techniques to create a temporary shop, which sold products designed by artists from unwanted or recycled items for the festive period. Trongate 103 is an arts centre situated within a converted Edwardian warehouse in the centre of the city. It is on a constrained site, hemmed in by busy roads and the main shopping area. The highly professional design project, by the architects Elder and Cannon, is finished to an exceptional level to simply create open spaces for the artists to occupy. The juxtaposition of the colourful carpet and raw timber against the pure white walls of the gallery is extreme and definitely highly amusing (see Figures 9.2 and 9.3).

FIGURE 9.2 Nadfly, Glasgow, Baxendale Architects, 2010. This pop-up installation is an exploration of reclaimed materials and self-assembled construction.

Credit: Thomas Manley

FIGURE 9.3 Nadfly, Glasgow, Baxendale Architects, 2010. The structure is formed from old wooden palettes, lined with colourful reclaimed carpets to create a dynamic improvised shop unit.

Credit: Thomas Manley

Encounter and Exchange

This uncovering of alternative practices can define a different way of working. Small temporary interventions within a place can change its meaning by highlighting, juxtaposing and transforming features, thus the interventions become a spatial collage. Temporal changes can make visible the potential of a building by changing the users' perception of a place, and so the practice can encourage the place to be viewed differently, to be studied from an altered angle, to be reconsidered. The idea of the pop-up shop or unit is something that has definitely moved away from the subversive into the mainstream. This is always an inevitable process; cutting edge artists develop an idea that to begin with is seen as alternative, rebellious and challenging, the idea is then appropriated by the majority and becomes if not exactly normal, certainly accepted. Graffiti art or flash mobbing are fine illustrations of this process, but here are many other examples. Hermès, the luxury high-end accessories retailer, recently created a series of pop-up installations within their own shop units, something that they called: Hermèsmatic. These pop-ups were quirky, temporary and deliberately fun installations that allowed the company to show a more eccentric personality than their usual products and identity communicated. The style of the installation was a bright orange 1950s launderette. The interior space was painted brilliant orange with white detailing, and filled with stacked Pop Art inspired cardboard boxes. Hermès have used the ephemerality of the pop-up idea to create a playful and transferable concept, far from the normally sedate and respectable image of the luxury brand, something radical and fun designed to attract a new younger clientele (see Figure 9.4).

The future of the 'high street' is highly questionable; this has to a certain extent been caused by changes in shopping habits brought about by the use of digital

FIGURE 9.4 The Hermèsmatic installation for Hermès takes the pop-up concept far from the improvised make-do environment into the high-end luxury area of the retail market. This installation was created in Manchester by Up North Architects.

Credit: Sally Stone

services. Shopping is now something that can be done out of hours, at home, while doing something else. So town centres have to rethink how they are to attract customers into them, how to encourage them to spend money and therefore support the local economy; after all, the shopping areas will not be sustained by just interactions that are completely personal; that is, 'Coffee Shops and Hairdressers'. Encounter and Exchange will be the future of these places and it is interesting that within the digital age, the real, homemade and handcrafted have become valued. The idea that the economy will be rescued by huge numbers of individuals making things and selling them may seem barmy, but it is possibly something that will supplement the products purchased online from the retail giants as they pull out of the city centre.

The pop-up economy has become more ubiquitous; it generates interest and has great pulling-power. This movement has become legitimised. Agencies now organise the pop-up market, thus making it much easier for start-ups and temporary businesses to thrive. A shop doesn't have to take a long lease on a unit, they can stay for a week, a year or as long as they feel they need to survive. Digital interaction means that it is possible to move without losing the client base. The pop-up agents will even supply the furniture, so this quick-footed, somewhat subversive, movement has started to move into the centre ground abandoned by the establishment.

Urban Activists

Interventions can subvert how people think and feel about a place and are often used to start finding out what, if any, changes local people want. Participants and instigators play a more active role in this category. Instigators of these methods tend to be artists, community groups and other informal collectives. Interventions can be a positive way of stimulating ideas for an area, and can make people aware that changes are happening. These principles, which are embedded in the climate, the context and the people, are based upon the idea that we celebrate what is good and distinct about what we already have: vernacular food, clothes and buildings that have evolved directly from the individual place or region, with a commitment to community and the environment.

Places are defined by the people who live within them. As individuals and communities, deep significance is attached to familiar places, and thus complex relationships can develop between the residents and the place that they inhabit. This quality that is present in the nature of the buildings and the streets is often generated by the ordinary actions of local people, many of whom believe that their identity is essentially tied to the place that they inhabit. Most people live relatively close to where they work, and therefore their activities form the environment and create the character of the place. This local distinctiveness is characterised by the activities that occur within the specific environment. Thus, significant markers are formed, in both the present and in the past, which will allow a society to relate to a particular environment. Events that hold value in a community are often manifested in physical form, and therefore allow a population to trace back meanings and connections with their past. This organisation of the past seems to stimulate social cohesion and the feeling of being part of a community, and so, physical links with the past are often important elements within the cohesion of a community.

Thus all environments are different, and all have evolved their own and individual characteristics. Places, whether interiors, buildings, situations or larger urban developments, are particular to their own situation and have been formed by a huge collection of different factors. Meinig and Jackson celebrate these circumstances: '… one of the greatest riches of the earth is its immense variety of places … individuality of places is a fundamental characteristic of subtle and immense importance' (3). The relationship between the building and its wider location has often been seen as somewhat ambiguous and yet it is possible to describe some spaces as encapsulating, in miniature, the characteristic qualities or features of a much wider situation. The interior has an obvious and direct relationship with the building that it occupies, the people who use it, and also it can have a connection with the area in which it is located.

The position of the designer or architect, in the last generation, has radically changed. The role is far greater than Le Corbusier's aphorism: 'the masterly, correct, and magnificent play of masses brought together in light' (4). Dan Hill, in the foreward to Rory Hyde's book, *Future Practice*, describes the designer as: 'Community Enabler, Contractual Innovator, Educator of Excess, Double Agent, Strategic Designer' (5). A new type of generalised design practitioner is developing, one who is involved with horizontal connections across disciplines. And on the very edge of this, beyond the Strategic Generalist and those engaged with Multidisciplinary Orchestration, is the designer, architect or activist engaged with Disruptive Change Agency. People for whom the built environment is important feel that they can make a difference, not through the traditional craft of architecture but through non-antagonistic, small, local interventions, whether they be social, physical and/or temporal. As custodians of the built environment they use non-traditional models of practice to generate a feeling of civic responsibility within the local population of urban users and dwellers. Guerrilla Knitters and Embroiderers are a fantastic example of this type of activist; local people who bring attention to specific elements and fixtures in the city by decorating them. The 'Slow' movement is also a fine example of this type of gentle activism. From Slow-food, to Slow-homes, the idea is that things are prepared in accordance with local customs and practices, using high-quality locally sourced ingredients. These principles, which are embedded in the climate, the context and the people, are based upon the idea that we celebrate what is good and distinct about what we already have: vernacular food, clothes and buildings that have evolved directly from the individual place or region. Slow-food, which was founded in 1989 in Italy, is a global, grassroots movement that now has thousands of members around the world. It links the pleasure of food with a commitment to community and the environment.

The urban activist is not actually a twenty-first century phenomenon. Patrick Geddes used a process of darns and repairs to create collective public gardens from disused and abandoned patches of land in Victorian Edinburgh. Geddes championed a mode of planning that sought to consider primary human needs in every intervention, engaging in constructive and conservative surgery rather than the massive swathes of reconstruction that were popular in the nineteenth and early twentieth centuries. Geddes encouraged close observation as the way to discover and work with the relationships among place, work and folk. In this sense he can be viewed as prefiguring the work of seminal urban thinkers such as Jane Jacobs (6) and other highly contextual region specific planning movements, by encouraging the planner to consider the situation, the inherent virtue and the potential in a given site, rather than an abstract ideal that could be imposed by authority or force from the outside. He firmly believed in these ideas, and chose to live in a remodelled home, rather than build something new. He also instigated the renovation of a number of important buildings in Edinburgh, arguing that the adaptation process was much more productive that simply razing the structures and erecting something new. This was a hands-on process: he was acutely involved with the renovations, actively participating, actually wielding the hammer, climbing the ladders and mending the windows. He also instigated collective gardens; little places that belonged to the residents and offered a moment of relaxation and peace away from the crowded home or loud and possibly dangerous workplace. These gardens allowed the residents to actively contribute towards the upkeep of the area; they also encouraged them to reappraise the area, to look at it from a different point of view, and maybe appreciate to a greater extent the inherent quality of the place (7).

This participative approach challenges the more traditional configuration of power relationships. An architectural design project is usually organised through a top-down distribution of power. However, participatory projects can subvert this through the instigation of action at a microscopic level, at the level of the collective and individual desire. Neighbourhood associations, self-managed organisations, experimental institutions and alternative space groups can all play an active role in the decision-making process within their own environment. Projects that respond to the needs of the neighbourhood enable the inhabitants to participate directly, to organise themselves in the manner that they want, with the knowledge that sometimes community desires differ from those of the public or private body. Community desires are not governed by profit, but are constrained by the need for all of the participants to be heard, that is for everyone concerned to participate in the process. This creates a 'bricolage structure' (8) in which both the users and the professionals become equal members in the structure of the project. This process may not necessarily produce the results that are expected; it is spontaneous, reactive and open to unexpected conclusions.

Participation is an active process that is both progressive and evolving. It requires the participants to continually adjust their opinion and thus their situation. The energy generated through people acting within their own environment can lead to a network of mutual support, an interest in the immediate surroundings and direct involvement with any changes that are taking place. This is certainly the ambition that Geddes had for the deprived area of Edinburgh that he chose to live in. Autonomy could not be realised by imposition, but by the creation of a living society, one which is continually shifting to accept the unpredictable nature of the environment. The position of the architect or designer within this process is as one of the participants. The blurred border between the architect and the user invites all of the participants to find ways to adapt and reinvent everyday life concerns.

Participation

Assemble is a London based collective whose work addresses this disconnection between the users of a project and the authorities, often including the architect or designers, that implement it. They were awarded the prestigious UK based Stirling Prize 2015 (9) for their work with a community in Liverpool. The residents of the terraced houses were facing eviction and relocation as their homes had become so neglected that the condition was close to dangerous. Assemble worked directly with the community to save the collection of buildings. Each house was intimately examined and an individual approach for each was developed. So, for example, one home that was just too badly neglected, the condition was just so bad that it couldn't be saved, was changed into a courtyard garden, while a different house, the condition of which was much better, was completely restored (10).

Another project that actively engaged the local population is the Waterside Neighbourhood project on brownfield land close to the city centre of Leicester. Brownfield space is an area of land or collection of premises that has been previously used, but has subsequently become vacant, derelict or contaminated. This term is derived from its opposite: undeveloped or 'greenfield' land. Many post-industrial cities have large areas of such land. It is not always contaminated, but it is often difficult to reuse. The cost of clearing the site for reoccupation can be prohibitively high, while the impetus for adaptation and reuse is often not available. Government sponsored projects, like the Dock area in Gdansk or Copenhagen, can deliver wholesale gentrification; however, smaller areas within less high profile cities are often burdened with much more difficult propositions (see Figure 9.5).

Brownfield sites typically require preparatory regenerative work before any new development can go ahead, and the situation can also be further complicated as they can sometimes be partly occupied. Thus Brownfield Regeneration is often seen as both expensive and complicated. Quite often the easiest approach is to simply wipe away everything and start again. However, these urban sites are full of existing buildings, places, systems and people that have accumulated over time. Such dense urban sites encourage architects and designers to work across the fields of architecture, historic preservation and urban planning, to develop cooperative projects that benefit the existing community without creating a massive disturbance.

Waterside is one such area, in an advantageously close location to the city centre of Leicester, a post-industrial city in the middle of England. It is situated at a strategically important position where the Grand Canal meets the River Soar, and has been continually occupied for over two millennia; the principle street patterns were actually established at the time of the Roman occupation. It was once home to wholesale trading and warehousing, however the area has declined rapidly since

FIGURE 9.5 The systematic and highly effective government sponsored gentrification of run-down and neglected areas of cities, such as the docks area of Gdansk, has created vibrant and desirable places that people want to inhabit.
Credit: Diego Delso via Wikimedia Commons

the loss of Leicester's industrial base in the 1970s. The site has a varied collection of sturdy buildings and a group of committed local residents and businesses. This area could be regarded as one of the city's significant hidden assets.

The city council originally proposed to raze the whole area and begin again, but the local population were against this, and they collectively formed the Waterside Adaptable Neighbourhood. This organisation saw the opportunity for the incremental adaptation of the area in response to changing economic and cultural scenarios. This forward looking and provocative group approached the architects Ash Sakula to develop a vision for the area; one that was empowering, inclusive and intelligent, that could be developed as the neighbourhood needed, and at a pace that that they could keep control over.

Cany Ash from Ash Sakula Architects has a reputation for working with what they refer to as Adaptable Neighbourhoods. These are projects that differ from the normal process of development, to create dynamic publicly owned collaborative areas that are enriched with ideas of history, community and place. Their approach is to instigate incremental regeneration by working directly with the people who live and work in a neighbourhood. This is a gentler approach to renewal, something that is opposed to the tabula rasa idea of starting again. They encourage the neighbourhood to adapt organically to new opportunities, to celebrate low property values as an opportunity for young people to invent new businesses and encourage older people to continue with businesses that have declining order books but still serve a purpose. As architects they can help see the way that under-appreciated buildings and whole areas can eventually find new audiences (11) (see Figure 9.6).

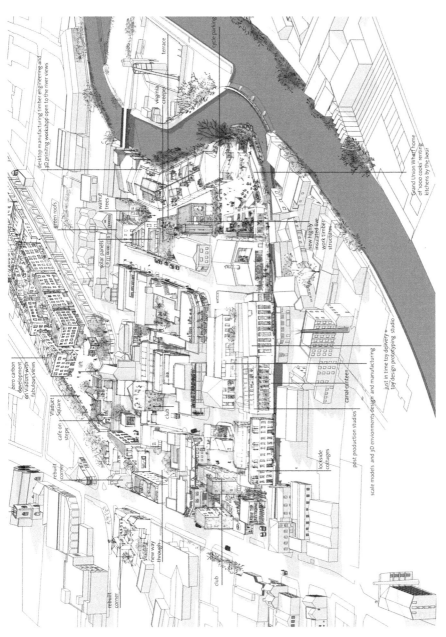

FIGURE 9.6 Proposal for the community regeneration of the Waterside Neighbourhood in Leicester by Ash Sakula Architects.

Credit: Ash Sakula Architects

Initially the architects worked with the highly committed local population of Leicester Waterside to create an inventory of the area; to carefully study the physical nature and character of the place and produce a catalogue of what was already there. This included a substantial survey of the history, the buildings (including the more mundane as well as the valuable and the listed) and also the infrastructure, as well as ephemeral aspects such as the flora and fauna that occupied the banks of the river and the canal, and of course, the stories of the people who live and work there. They also created a forum that put everyone in touch with each other, and through this, create an opportunity for collective goodwill, energy and impetus for change. This powerful sense of the place then formed the basis of a proposal for regeneration.

The starting point of the proposal was to create a collection of small interventions to encourage more visitors into the area; this included things like new signage to catch the attention of commuters on the ringroad immediately adjacent to Waterside. This shouted about the things that were happening, the shops and the events. This would be reinforced with a series of festivals, again to encourage visitors in Waterside and increase the expectations of the place; these were festivals of music, food and upcycling. Another suggestion to bring large numbers of new people to the site was an outdoor cinema and a pop-up garden and nursery. Gardening enthusiasts could also help soften the border with the main road by planting lots of shrubs and other florae that effectively started to green-up the place. Buildings would be adapted to contain big openings so that the street comes alive with activity. The viaduct would be opened up with grand steps, just like the Highline in New York, and it could become a favoured route into the city centre for many commuters. A new public square by the canal could be created to accommodate the new activity and could be flanked by a permanent home for the market and gallery. The vision was for families to move in, and thus encourage more activity, new work opportunities to mingle with existing enterprises, all of which would attract the attention of the media, and thus the cycle of self improvement for the area would continue.

There is a final postscript to this story. In the early spring of 2018, the City Council completed the compulsory purchase of the existing properties in the area with the intention of completely flattening everything and replacing it with housing, which is admittedly much needed. The project is designed in a sympathetic and distinctive manner with some regard for the existing street pattern, but the sense of place that has evolved over hundreds of years will be lost (12). It is a wasteful squandering of resources to throw away the substantial physical and personal neighbourhood. The place could be enriched through gentle, slow, incremental but creative development which allows the place to prosper without losing the sense of the character of the area.

Alternative Futures

The architect has certain skills, they understand the built environment and can envisage alternative futures for it. Architecture is formed in the imagination and architects have effective techniques for envisioning alternative futures. They can use this ability to lever support for the conservation of important elements of heritage. They can act as curators of the built environment, something that draws upon the creativity of the other participants to envisage a new future. This form of participation emphasises the connectedness and individuality of the users while questioning the authority of the political power of those in authority.

Two projects that effectively illustrate the ability that architects have to understand and generate alternative proposals for specific buildings are both in Preston, a small city in the north west of England. Both use the creative power of the architect to summon support against the prevailing opinion of the governing body. The first project saved an important building from well meaning but irrevocable damage. The second project mustered up support for the preservation of an existing building and the contribution that the small team made to the protection of the structure meant that it was given listed building recognition.

Preston is a small provincial city well positioned on a ridge above the estuary and the flood-planes of the River Ribble. The town made an important contribution to the affluence of the industrial revolution, and although it is now somewhat less significant, the civic elements of the Minster, the open Flag Market Square, the Victorian cast iron covered markets, the Town Hall, the Brutalist bus station and the Harris Art Gallery are testament to the once great wealth and ambition of the city.

Nikolaus Pevsner describes the Harris Art Gallery as '…one of the most remarkable Victorian public buildings of Northern England'. It was constructed in 1877 by the largely unknown architect James Hibbert, and stands on an elevated point in the centre of the city facing the large market square, close to the Minster and the main shopping area. Pevsner continues, 'This is a monumental and entirely classical building. It comes off completely and is an ornament to the town as well as a powerful demonstration of the arts it wishes to serve' (13).

The giant portico entrance consists of a decorated pediment upon six fluted ionic columns. These sit upon a huge blank podium. The design of the portico is based upon the Rostra Augusti from the Ancient Forum in Rome, and the podium directly references the speaker's platform. The building was designed at a time when museums and art galleries were the preserve of the educated, of those who could afford the time and had the confidence to visit them. But in the twenty-first century, an entrance as forbidding or intimidating as this one is not so desirable.

The Harris commissioned a proposal from an internationally known architectural practice to open up the gallery, to make it less intimidating and much more approachable. This was with the laudable intention of updating the institution and making it fit and accessible for a twenty-first century population. However, the proposal was to simply and quite crudely cut a huge hole in the magnificent podium. This undermined the principle of the building, its relationship with the wider urban context and would irretrievably alter it.

Continuity in Architecture, a postgraduate atelier for design and research at the Manchester School of Architecture, felt that this was a mistake, and so demonstrated that it is possible to change the perceived situation without irreversibly altering the building by designing alternative proposals (14). Architects have the ability to imagine alternative futures for buildings, they can visualise ideas and therefore show things that maybe others consider difficult or impossible. The student architects made architectural proposals that looked specifically at the entrance to the Harris Museum, and so provided different visions for the museum, which contained a more inviting entrance sequence to the present situation, but without affecting the fabric of the building. They created a collection of propositions that would facilitate the needs of the users, but not cause gratuitous and irrevocable damage to the land-mark building. This was an opportunity to use the cultural power of architecture strategically; it was an appropriate time to make explicit how things could be better. The gallery, who had begun to realise that they may have made an awful mistake, exhibited the drawings, showed them to the funding authorities, and they were also featured in the local press. There were other agencies who were also involved in the campaign to stop the destructive proposal, including the Victorian Society. This opposition led to the gallery withdrawing the destructive proposal and seriously rethinking their approach to the updating of the building (see Figure 9.7).

The second example is the Preston Bus Station, a 'marvellously Brutal' building (15) constructed in 1969 by BDP Architects. It is an incredibly long and elegant

FIGURE 9.7 Projects by students from the Continuity in Architecture atelier at the Manchester School of Architecture, which were developed in direct opposition to the proposed scheme to irreparably damage the Harris Gallery and Museum in Preston, Lancashire, England.

Credit: Sally Stone

building, and is reputedly the largest bus station in Europe. The building contains a series of car parks, situated on extended floor plates with upturned curving parapets, which appear to float over the double-height space of the public concourse.

The urban configuration of the building is essentially flawed. It is positioned beyond the eastern edge of the city centre and effectively stops regeneration of that area and makes movement difficult. The situation was compounded by the intro-duction of the ring road in the 1980s, thus there is a largely redundant area on the edge of the city centre which could be seen as preventing the development of the city. Interestingly the building had been somewhat neglected over the half century since it was constructed, so it had not had to endure any refurbishment over the course of its life. So the original timber benches and divisions, the white tiles and the rubber flooring were all still in place and still in good condition, so the pure Modernist character of the building had not been adulterated.

The building was scheduled to be demolished as part of a massive regeneration project, but with the rise of the internet and the downturn in physical shopping (the future of the city centre really is coffee shops and hairdressers) this was abandoned. However, in a desperate attempt to instigate regeneration, in 2012, the council announced that the building was to be demolished and replaced with a surface carpark. This roused a number of national and local interest groups, and thus began a campaign to save the building. This included the Gate 81 project, which was a series of events and happenings in and around the building, including an open day with stalls, installations, biscuits and lectures, and a marvellous procession. Interested people carried a huge model of the building through the streets of Preston, not in an aggressive attempt to force through change, but in an attempt to celebrate the building while it was still standing (see Figure 9.8). Local projects focussed upon raising the profile of the building among the residents of the city. It is interesting to note that according to a poll in the local newspaper, during this period, the bus station went from being the most hated building in the city to the most loved. Meanwhile nationally, organisations such as the Twentieth Century Society lobbied government.

The combined force of these projects compelled the council to rethink their policy; they were, after all, elected politicians, and thus in a great moment of celebra-tion, reversed their attitude and began to commemorate the building and the sense of character that it bestowed upon the city, sufficient for them to spend upwards of £20 million on the refurbishment. Any development has to take into account this huge great Modernist masterpiece plugging up the edge of the city centre, but it is an example of people power, of a group of incredibly committed and interested people who can achieve what was at one time seen as impossible.

Conclusion

Architectural action is both intimate and specific. Architects and designers have the ability to imagine alternative futures; they possess the capability to make visible the spatial and material potential of a place. Therefore, architecture can be used as

FIGURE 9.8 Continuity in Architecture students at the Manchester School of Architecture paraded through the streets with a huge model of the Preston Bus Station in a creative and joyful attempt to stop the demolition of the important landmark building.

Credit: Sally Stone

a provocative cultural practice, not through aggressive, antagonistic and confrontational methods, but through the strategic use of the cultural power that architects and designers possess. This may include direct and provocative action, and also physical collaboration and communication. Urban activism, Art activism and Design activism are all practices of revelation. Desire, which Deleuze places before power, is the precondition of action, and although the audience may appreciate that the position that they find themselves in is not ideal, they may not have the foresight to remedy this. Architects and designers, who do have the ability to envisage a different future for a given situation, can therefore influence the manner in which the built environment is developed to the benefit of all those concerned.

References

1. Bunschoten, Raoul (2005) "Points, Spirals and Prototypes" from Architecture and Participation. Peter Blundell Jones, Doina Pettescu and Jeremy Till (Eds). Taylor & Francis, p. 246.
2. Baxendale Studio Ltd: http://baxendale-dco.com.
3. Meinig, D. and Jackson, J. (1979) The Interpretation of Ordinary Buildings: Geographical Essays. Oxford: Oxford University Press, pp. 33–50.
4. Hyde, Rory (2013) Future Practice: Conversations from the Edge of Architecture. Oxon: Taylor & Francis, p. 13.

5. Hyde, Rory (2013) Future Practice: Conversations from the Edge of Architecture. Oxon: Taylor & Francis, p. 13.

6. Jacobs, Jane (1961) The Death and Life of Great American Cities. New York: Random House.

7. Welter, V. and Lawson, J. (2000) The City after Patrick Geddes. Oxford: Peter Lang.

8. Petrescu, Doina (2005) "Losing Control, Keeping Desire" from Architecture & Participation. Peter Blundell-Jones, Donna Petrescu and Jeremy Till (Eds). London and New York: Taylor & Francis, p. 49.

9. Stirling Prize: www.architecture.com/awards-and-competitions-landing-page/awards/riba-stirling-prize.

10. Assemble: https://assemblestudio.co.uk.

11. Ash Sakula Architects: www.ashsak.com.

12. Ash Sakula Architects: www.ashsak.com.

13. Hartwell, Claire and Pevsner, Nikolaus (2009) Lancashire: North: The Buildings of England. Yale University Press, p. 519.

14. Continuity in Architecture: http://continuity.msa.ac.uk.

15. Hartwell, Claire and Pevsner, Nikolaus (2009) Lancashire: North: The Buildings of England. Yale University Press, p. 510.

10

SMARTNESS AND THE IMPACT OF THE DIGITAL

Introduction

The twenty-first century has brought substantial advances in digital technology, which when combined with fundamental changes in the expectations of the manner in which life is conducted have brought about a necessary transformation in the way in which the built environment is occupied. Digital and smart technologies mean that we are increasingly able to interact with our built environment. Smart cities provide an environment for the residents' needs by equipping them with the ability to better inhabit it; whether this is with access to information or by providing a platform for interaction. A smart city is capable of responding to the changing needs of the inhabitants in response to the rapid speed at which urban culture is evolving. The British Standards Institution defines the Smart City as: '… the effective integration of physical, digital and human systems in the built environment to deliver a sustainable, prosperous and inclusive future for its citizens' (1).

Smart technologies are set to revolutionise the manner in which we all interact with the built environment. From self-driving cars that instinctively locate parking spaces, to sensors that detect human presence in a building and automatically turn off the lights when everyone has gone home. Things are going to radically change. Hopefully this will be for the better, indeed it is often discussed that what smart technologies fundamentally and actually do are all the things that you would really like your mother to help you out with. Even given this, the pace at which this is developing means that even before you read this, the examples shown will be out-dated.

This technology will probably become invisible; it will become so much part of the fabric of the spaces that we inhabit that its presence will not even be noticed. Cameras are somewhat unreliable; they need a line of sight to be effective, so digital interaction may be supported through voice or touch. For example, voice controlled interactive audio systems, or conductive paint, which can be applied to the interior walls of a room and reacts to human finger tips with carefully spaced tiny electrodes, in the same manner as a smartphone. These are the type of things that will allow the occupants of a building to control equipment within the space almost without perceiving that they are doing so.

An environment that is sufficiently sensitive to respond to human presence is said to exhibit ambient intelligence. This is a building or interior that can respond to the needs of humans, and it is foreseen that it could especially aid those who need support. That is, those that may need reminders about their own home, for instance dementia sufferers or others who may have physical, sensory or cognitive impairments. But this support will probably be much more universal and ambient intelligence will become an integral part of all built environments. Grossman suggests that 'The next stop on the road to the fourth revolution is ambient computing or ambient intelligence, where we continuously interface to the always-on, interconnected world of things' (2).

This threshold, interface or point of interaction with the smart technologies relies upon the complete acquiescence of all of those involved, it assumes that everyone is in agreement and that public surveillance is normal and privacy is something that is not necessarily available. The Internet of Things and importance of digital connections to aid the smooth running of many aspects of today's world demonstrates the manner in which technology and innovation is radically transforming the manner in which the population interacts with the world. From the manner in which healthcare is delivered to patients, smart motorways that will be automatically connected to in-car SatNavs and provide advice of alternative routes if there is a build-up of traffic, to more simple devices that automatically connect with stores to replace depleted necessities. Potentially most of life will be digitally connected so that the boring stuff doesn't have to be thought about.

Sometimes this acquiescence needs to be pointed out to people, to be accentuated so that it is not invisible or taken for granted. 0point3recurring, an artists-collective that works with light and sound, built an installation that collected fragments of images of the users of the Preston Bus Station. This was as part of the Gate 81 project series of events that were organised to bring greater attention to the building. The images of the people in the building were distorted, and then projected onto the tiled interior wall of building, thus making the users acutely aware of their own movements and the association that they had established with the building. This broke the threshold or interface that existed between digital technologies and the people who use them; it made the unconscious relationship uneasy by accentuating the unwitting agreement the visitors have with digital technology (3).

Fragmentary Living

The contemporary manner in which the built environment is occupied can be described as fragmented, in that it is used as the receptacle or environment for a collection of individual adventures. The idea of the collected experience, the notion that everyone will be doing the same thing at the same time, is now seriously out-dated and has become a somewhat rare experience. Digital media and communications mean that everyone can create their own way of occupying the world. This unsystematic and disjointed approach has encouraged a new way of living in the urban and rural situations. Sabine Pollak suggests that: 'Maybe we cannot really speak of a "new culture of living", but the individual functions of living and working, recreation and public life are starting to mix in both time and space' (4).

The spatial patterns within the built environment were once the primary means of communication. This space was used to organise people and objects, and much of conceptual thought was traditionally generated through this organisation of public and private space. It is now obvious that this old world order is breaking down, and a fragmented and disjunctive logic of the modern city is rapidly being created. The idea of the city as a collection of fragments is not a new phenomenon; Walter Benjamin regarded the past as accessible only through ruins and fragments (5), while for Anthony Vidler, the fragment has a double standard, it is a reminder of a fractured past while also being an incomplete piece of a potentially complete whole (6). Indeed, this fragmentation of the traditional social structures and the old familiar social order can be likened to a cubist painting, in which the whole thing can no longer be ascertained, instead it is viewed as a collection of disjunctive actions.

However, fragmentation in the twenty-first century post-modern society suggests the disintegration of a previously existing unity to be replaced by a decentralised, chaotic model. William Mitchell in his seminal and prescient discourse of 1995, 'City of Bits: Space Place and the Infobahn', views the city as 'largely asynchronous in its operation, and inhabited by disembodied and fragmented subjects who exist as collections of aliases and agents' (7).

The obsessive impact that digital communication has had upon contemporary lifestyle means that there is no longer just a recognition of the fragment as the driver of lifestyle, but a celebration of it. The built and the natural environment are seen as a collection of not necessarily connected experiences. This approach to the use of the city by the contemporary population could be described as fragmentary because everyone chooses their own route or journey through time and space. We all create our own narratives; that is, the individual has control over the manner in which they live, and the way in which they interact with the city and its buildings, and those that occupy them. Rem Koolhaas presciently described architecture as a 'chaotic adventure' (8) and that is exactly how the modern dwellers live within the contemporary city.

Margaret Crawford describes this as everyday space, as something that the individual creates between the identifiable realms of the home, the workplace and the institution (9). It is the lived experience of the connective tissue that binds daily lives together. The way in which the individual occupies the built environment contributes to their character. Steven Jacobs quotes Judit Bodnár when he explains that as the manner in which it is occupied is increasingly accessed and facilitated by digital technology, so 'Personality is created in a web of group affiliations that have become truly global and increasingly virtual' (10). This has produced a previously unforeseen sense of freedom combined with extensive fragmentation.

Thus the existing building is seen as a small fragment in the chaotic disorder of the city. Digital technology has provided the already-there with greater worth and esteem. The existing is seen as an incoherent and unsystematic link with a disconnected past, it offers a nostalgic link to a time before digital technology which rendered everything clear, clean and ubiquitous. And yet, the digital has also liberated the existing situation, it has meant that the buildings and places are easily located, that they are connected to the people who want to use them. No longer do they have to stumble upon a new experience or adventure, they can be connected directly to it and use it as they want to. Computer technology offers immediate digital gratification, but what is interesting about this is the combination of this and the return to the sense of the real. Vinyl records are coveted, real coffee is vital, natural materials are important and the hand made, the exquisite, the home cooked have all become desirable. The need to occupy real places that contain heritage and character has advanced in line with digital technology.

Digital Parochialism

Hannah Arendt argued for the existence of a 'world in common' as a pivotal condition for politics. She reasoned that it is the experience of the common that defines the public sphere as the place where things and people can be seen and acquire the status of 'public' (11). The public sphere is defined by its commonality, and is created by a plurality of perspectives that are and remain separated. This world-in-common can easily be extended to the digital domain and would apply to public space not in the physical sense, but that shared space which is manifested digitally.

What is particularly interesting about the advent of digital technology is the extent to which it builds communities, not in the traditional sense of those living next to each other or in the same neighbourhood, but in the way that it allows like-minded people to immediately connect with each other. It encourages interaction beyond the physical limits of the immediate situation. Being together, yet apart.

The DIY Space for London is a community of like-minded people with a collected interest in a physical space. It is actually a cooperatively run social centre in South London that is managed in a non-hierarchical manner by its members, all of whom are volunteers (except for the book-keeper and the sound-technician). The community work together, sharing their time, skills and ideas (12).

The collective occupies the ground floor of a mid-twentieth century light industrial shed. An evangelical church uses the floor above. The building contains an events room to host gigs, screen independent small films, and support discussions as well as holding art and yoga classes. It has a practice space for musicians, a chill-out space for resting and a large communal room with a bar in it, as well as the support spaces expected in an organisation such as this, store rooms, a very cluttered office and gender-neutral toilets.

The building itself is situated within a quiet area of the city, there is little foot-fall in the street outside and the club gets very little passing trade. The front door is little more than a fire-exit with a hand painted sign above it, and yet within just two years of opening the club has over seven thousand members, four thousand of whom are active meaning that they attend some sort of activity every month (see Figures 10.1 and 10.2).

FIGURE 10.1 The entrance to the DIY Space for London is most inconspicuous. As befits an organisation that uses digital communication, it has very little exterior presence.

Credit: Sally Stone

FIGURE 10.2 Community interaction is encouraged within the interior of the DIY Space for London.

Credit: Sally Stone

The membership has grown mostly through word-of-mouth, or to be more precise through social media, rather than direct advertising; indeed the community does very little active promotion other than occasionally dropping off flyers at strategically selected stores, bars and clubs. DIY Space for London is a perfect example of the phenomena of digital parochialism; that is, the collecting together of people who have similar tastes or attitudes and who are attached together not so much by location, but through social media (13).

Attitudes towards connections have radically changed; digital technology can help build communities, it can help people stay in contact even when they are physically separated. It is no longer necessary to actually be physically together to consult over particular matters. Digital connections are spontaneous and informal; shared meaning is created through use, and community initiatives, habit-led interventions and placemaking can occur through virtual technology. The use of digital technology to facilitate these connections allows people to react to circumstances much more quickly and thus this somewhat counter-culture creates an atmosphere of continual evolution

DIY Space is a very apt name for the collective; the building certainly contains the quality of having been converted by highly enthusiastic but unprofessional people. Again, the collective spirit encouraged collaboration and community engagement. The initial volunteers spent several weeks over the summer before the building opened erecting the walls, constructing the doors, the bar and the stage, and installing the plumbing and the electrics. The members shared their skills and contributed what they could; so, for example, one member who was a structural engineer was able to draw the plans to apply for planning permission, while another who did have some building experience was able to show others the basics of joinery.

Thus the Collective found the space, installed the new interior to facilitate the new use and then created an online identity for the building. The formation of the Collective and the organisation of the club is primarily digital; this enables the collection of volunteers to communicate easily but also allows them the freedom to join the conversation at times of their own choosing. They communicate through the digital platform LOOMIO. This allows for several streams of conversation to be conducted at the same time

Without the digital interface, the building would not be able to function. The disparate lives of the organisers, the different jobs that they have, the dispersed places that they live and their unrelated day-to-day commitments mean that actually meeting face-to-face on a regular basis is difficult. The cooperative has fully embraced digital technology to enable them to create a community that has a distinct location.

The community has a lease for the building of just five years, which does place the organisation in a slightly precarious position. This short and temporary occupation of a place reflects the conditions that many emergent artistic cooperatives are forced to endure. Artists will move into an area because it is possible to rent a large space quite cheaply. Their presence immediately makes the area more popular. Artists have the vision to imagine the potential in a neighbourhood, they make it acceptable and so the place begins to be recognised as somewhere desirable containing worth and character. There are proposals to extend the Underground system to serve this area of London; this will allow easy access of just half an hour from the centre of the city, which is something that will definitely provide the impetus for gentrification. The difference in this case is that when DIY Space moves, the organisation will not be lost, they will be easily traced and their community will not be substantially harmed by any relocation. It could even be envisaged that they could exist without a home at all, but as a series of events and happenings at strategic sites in the city.

The city really will then become the interface. This concept of occupying the city in such a creative manner is of course not new. Frank Duffy discusses the peripatetic life that Samuel Pepys lived as a precursor to twenty-first century life and communication:

> Pepys as a young servant of the Crown was always on the move – leaving his house near the Tower to go to his office next door (he was nearly but not quite a home worker); visiting his uncle in the country; down the river by wherry to supervise victualling at the Naval Yards at Deptford; by carriage down the Strand to wait on his superiors and to be accessible to the Duke of York in the court of the Palace of Westminster; then to the tavern to make music on his way home; moving about the narrow London streets, singing here, drinking there, talking everywhere.
>
> *14*

A much more contemporary example of the city as home is Toyo Ito's Pao for the Tokyo Nomad Girl (1985) (15). It is a project of mobility and permeability within what was then the most technically advanced and one of the most densely occupied places on earth. The house of the urban nomad is scattered around the city, her dwellings are collaged from parts of it to create a user specific experience of place. The tiny family home of the Nomad Girl was somewhere just to sleep at night, all other activities are spread through the city, so cafés are her dining room, the gym for bathing, and bars are her living room.

Alone Together

The home is now a place where the boundaries between private and public, work and leisure have been eroded. Where work used to take place in a separate workplace, more knowledge workers now take work home to be continued both in evenings, and during any of the seven days of the week; working from home is now considered as normal.

Digital and smart technologies mean that we are increasingly able to interact with our built environment. Smart cities provide an environment for the residents' needs by equipping them with the ability to better inhabit it; whether this is with access to information or by providing a platform for interaction. A smart city is capable of responding to the changing needs of the inhabitants in response to the rapid speed at which urban culture is evolving.

The twenty-first century home has taken advantage of this revolution, allowing for shared space, shared conversations and shared ideas. Immediate communication is possible with almost anywhere in the world, including with other residents of the same dwelling. The need to communicate and the desire for connectivity is one of the most important distinguishing features of contemporary life. This level of digital communication allows for multiple types of interaction and, to a certain extent, multiple personalities engaging with that interaction.

What is most remarkable are the opportunities that digital technology offers, the level of connection that it provides with people and communities beyond the immediate physical context. A small example of the manner in which digital technology can create a sense of connection that the lack of physical proximity does not allow is the appropriation of video conferencing. For one reason and another, my teenage son now lives some 50 miles from his best friend. They text often and certainly communicate on Facebook (I take this on trust; to look at a teenager's Facebook conversation would be beyond the pale), however, on many evenings they use video-conferencing technology (Skype or Facetime) to communicate with each other; this isn't because they have anything important to discuss, it is much more about company. They complete their individual homework together, drink cocoa before bed and even jam along with their guitars to the same piece of music. It is almost like having the friend in the room. It is a very simple but effective acceptance of what this type of technology can bring.

Recently I was talking to my son, when this disconnected voice wished me a good evening. I bent over towards the computer to greet the best friend, whose image occupied the whole screen. Behind him was a mirror and reflected in the mirror was obviously his back and the computer, and on his screen was an image of me; and for a fleeting moment I could see myself reflected in the mirror of a bedroom some 50 miles away from where I was standing. I was shocked to see my real-time presence in a place so far away; intellectually I knew that it was merely a reflected image, and yet this whole process proved that physical distance was no longer an obstacle in the way of real-time visual and aural relationships. It was at this point that I realised how video-conferencing technology can bring everyone together in an intimate and personal way. The children had embraced the technology for their own purposes; they had no reservations or qualms about using it, and neither did they respect its limitations.

I was discussing this (face-to-face) with the best friend's father, who admitted that when he calls his own son downstairs for dinner, he often feels very guilty about not only leaving my son on his own, but also closing the door on him. So real was the feeling of togetherness that he had trouble disentangling the digital image from the reality of the situation.

This small example illustrates the fact that digital technology allows us to feel together, even when we are alone. It allows us to build social networks with people that we've never physically met, it allows us to conduct meetings, have impromptu chats, confidential discussions as well as individual and concentrated study from the security of our own living space.

Digital connectivity also facilitates the ability for people to be together but in essence they act as if alone. The family or group of friends can occupy the same space, they can enjoy the physical proximity of each other, but without actually interacting or engaging in conversation. This has the possibility of bringing people closer together; children do not need to retreat to their own rooms for privacy, office workers can carry out different tasks in close proximity and strangers can provide companionship.

Frank Duffy in effect predicted this in his seminal publication of 1997, *The New Office* (16). He developed a theory that suggested that within the contemporary workplace, there were just four types of activity: individual activity, group processing, transactional knowledge and concentrated study. Each of these, he argued, could be accommodated within distinct areas of an office, thus it would be the worker that moved to distinct places to conduct the different types of work that they needed to do. The Hive, Den, Club and Cell would provide the correct setting for the type of work to be completed. Digital technology has taken this idea much further, and the connectiveness that it provides means that some of these processes need not actually occupy the office at all.

The home has to be adaptable for a number of different activities and situations. It has evolved far from the notion of mere shelter to encompass all the different aspects of family life. The majority of homes are fairly small; the average family lives in a far more intimate way than would ever be acceptable in an office situation. It is normal for the different members of the family unit to be carrying out different tasks immediately next to each other. Digital and wireless technology has augmented this situation. For many years the family members were dispersed around the house, but wireless technology has once again allowed and encouraged a sort or comradeship. Other breakthroughs in technology mean that machines are smaller, not so much not-big, but they are flat and this means that they need less room. Whether it is listening to music, watching iPlayer, eating dinner, sewing, completing homework, this hub or kitchen table around which the family members circulate allows for the types of interaction that existed before technology really took over the world. The advent of the wireless office combined with the reduction in the size of technological equipment has enabled the user to reclaim the surface of the table; no longer is it cluttered with cabled, plugs and massive machines, it can now be arranged with objects that matter: books, pictures and artefacts that interest and stimulate thought, interaction and productivity. Ironically, this is a concept that has moved from the domestic interior into the office environment. When the Bouroullec Brothers were approached by Vitra to develop a range of office furniture for the twenty-first century, they declared that their aim was to de-specify furniture and create multi-task products. They felt that the manner in which furniture was designed was too prescriptive, it only allowed people to work in one particular way; it didn't encourage creativity, lateral thinking or serendipity. They developed a product that they described as the Common Table, one that allows people to communicate and to complete communal work. They started with the very old concept of the big family table, at which everyone sat and everything happened.

It is possible to contest that technology has allowed us to move much further than that. It is now possible to complete all activities that would normally be completed in the office at home. All of the different environments described by Duffy are freely available within the normal home.

Digital Design and Interrogation

The digital can also aid the actual adaptation and design of buildings and interiors. Digital methods contain the potential to have transformative effects upon the current architectural design expectations. Joined up programmes, interactive databases and shared platforms mean that innovative and collaborative is perceived as the normal approach to design.

The 'digital' is now ubiquitous within contemporary architectural practice. Its presence is felt in many ways: the first is a design tool, that is, to aid the design, delivery and production of architecture, often generating innovative and extreme shapes and forms. This has inevitably led to an advance in manufacturing and fabrication techniques including ornament and decoration, which have had to keep pace with these advances and the need to realise them.

The second use of computer and digital techniques is as an interrogative tool. The application of computer modelling can detect and exhibit the performance of a building: it can speculate upon structural and engineering capabilities, environmental performance can be predicted, the manner in which the building can change or evolve as the occupants needs alter can be predicted. The multidisciplinary interaction of different professions allows the capabilities of the existing environment to be measured, and as changes are made to it, they can be tracked. Various different design solutions can be tested before they are actually constructed.

Performance testing is especially pertinent to building reuse projects. Various options, for example increased energy efficiency, can be tested before they are implemented. The effect that the adaptation will have upon the performance of the building can be predicted, allowing the architect or designer to work from an informed position.

Another practical example of how the digital can aid the architect or designer in the adaptation of the existing structure is the 3D laser scanner. These are used more and more as surveying instruments for various applications. These are highly precise machines, capable of working in most real-world environments under a variety of conditions to create precise data of the environment in order to be able to have an as-existing documentation of the building or situation. The 3D laser scanner can create a 'point cloud' of data collected from the surface of an object, which is used to generate a highly accurate digital representation of the exact size and shape of the existing building, interior or landscape. The scanner can measure fine details and capture free-form shapes. This makes them ideally suited to the measurement and inspection of contoured surfaces and complex geometries that require massive amounts of data for their accurate description and where it is impractical to do this using traditional measurement techniques.

Conclusions

The physically real quality of the existing building is increasingly desirable in a world that is constantly changing; one in which digital representations can appear to be more authentic than the actual and genuine thing. However, information, big data, robotics, artificial intelligence and renewables can all aid this search for the authentic experience, it can connect like-minded people together, create communities and support a forward thinking attitude. Digital media seems to reinforce the process of parochialism; it can filter different lifestyles and help people stay in contact even when they are physically separated.

References

1. Designing Buildings Wiki: www.designingbuildings.co.uk/wiki/Designing_smart_cities
2. Grossman, G. (2016, 7 May). "The Next Stop on the Road to Revolution is Ambient Intelligence". https://techcrunch.com/2016/05/07/the-next-stop-on-the-road-to-revolution-is-ambient-intelligence/.
3. 0point3recurring: www.facebook.com/0point3recurring/.
4. Pollak, Sabine (2003) "Culture of Living. In Roberto Rizzi. Civilization of Living: The Evolution of European Domestic Interiors". Edizioni Lybra Immagine, p. 24.
5. Benjamin, Walter (1992/1955) "The Work of Art in the Age of Mechanical Reproduction" from Illuminations. Fontana Press, p. 40.
6. Vidler, Anthony (2008) Histories of the Immediate Present: Inventing Architectural Modernism. Cambridge MA: MIT Press, p. 109.
7. Mitchell, William (1995) City of Bits: Space Place and the Infobahn. Nai101 Publishers Rotterdam, p. 15.
8. Koolhaas, Rem and Mau, Bruce (1997) S,M,L,XL. Monacelli Press, p. xix.
9. Crawford, Margaret (1992) "The World in a Shopping Mall" from Variations on a Theme Park: The New American City and the End of Public Space. Michael Sorkin (Ed.). New York: Hill and Wang, p. 30.
10. Jacobs, Steven (2002) "Shreds of Boring Postcards: Towards a Posturban Aesthetics of the Generic and the Everyday" from Post Ex Sub Dis: Urban Fragmentations and Constructions. Rotterdam: 010 Publications, pp. 19–20.
11. Arendt, H. (1958) The Human Condition. Chicago: University of Chicago Press, p. §2.
12. DIY Space for London: https://diyspaceforlondon.org.
13. Conversation with founder of DIY Space for London, Chris Little, 5 November 2017.
14. Duffy, Frank (2008) Work and the City. London: Black Dog Publishing Limited, p. 50.
15. Tokyo Nomad Girl (1985) Japan Architect 8607.
16. Duffy, Frank (1997) The New Office. Conran Octopus.

11

ON TAKING AWAY

Introduction

In what is possibly an apocryphal tale that has now achieved legendary status, the artist Gordon Matta-Clark was once invited to create an installation for the 'Ideas as Models' exhibition at the Institute for American and Urban Studies, the glamorous architectural 'think-tank' in Lower Manhattan. He was one of an illustrious crowd, which included three members of the so called 'New York 5': the architects Michael Graves, Charles Gwathmey and Richard Meier. The institute, which was founded by Peter Eisenman, another member of the 'New York 5', was recognised as one of the most progressive forums for the exploration and analysis of architecture.

Matta-Clark's proposal was to place a photograph of a vandalised building from the South Bronx in almost every available window opening. In the others, which already contained cracked glass, he gained permission from the gallery director to actually break the glass and therefore emulate the images in the photographs. This piece, entitled 'Window Blow-Out', was a statement about the housing conditions of the city's poor.

However, some time during the night before the show, Matta-Clark turned up at the gallery, he was 'incredibly wrecked' and carried an air pistol. He then proceeded to shoot all of the windows on the floor of the institute, while raging hysterically about the self-important and pretentious concept of the abstract notion of modern architecture that was being presented by the other exhibitors in the exhibition, while the residents of the South Bronx lived in barely habitable apartments. It was a statement that directly reflected the character of the surrounding area; the context had informed the fury and the installation.

What has elevated this act of violence to legendary status is the reaction of the gallery elite. They did not embrace this radical and progressive action, instead the mess was cleared up and the glass replaced. An act of extreme violence was immediately countered with one of polite refusal. But strangely this didn't obliterate Matta-Clark's statement, it completed it; if this sort of action was intolerable in the well mannered and respectable surroundings of the gallery, then what made it acceptable in the South Bronx. This act of destruction commented upon what was there, the violence revealed the character of the area. Rather than abstracting and dignifying his reaction to the wrecked apartment buildings, Matta-Clark created a direct and aggressive statement, which was so destructive and offensive to the cultivated manners of the Institute that they had to remove it (see Figure 11.1).

This process of recognition led the artist to make a dramatic intervention within the interior space. The subtraction of elements from the interior somehow liberated the space; it was a statement that connected it with its immediate environment. Matta-Clark transgressed the boundaries of what was acceptable in 1976. His unconventional statement was the result of an analysis and understanding of what was there and using that information to inform his actions. He read the situation and revealed the underlying condition.

To transgress is to go beyond what is acceptable. In his project for the Institute for American and Urban Studies, Matta-Clark crossed the boundary between what was acceptable even by the fairly radical standards of the progressive New York 5. He acted in violation of the unwritten principles or conventions of the group and therefore, to a certain extent, society. Deliberately provocative behaviour such as this is now frequently observed even in the proposals for student shows and site specific reactions to particular situations are relatively commonplace. Art is no longer seen as only having a place within a gallery, but in 1976, Matta-Clark's interpretation of a particular and given situation was profound and provocative.

In the second decade of the twenty-first century, it is becoming increasingly difficult for the artist or designer to act in such a controversial and defiant manner, but it is possible for the architect or interior designer to use such an attitude as a tool in the design process. Matta-Clark exposed the qualities of the surrounding area. In a violent and challenging manner, he deliberately smashed the glass in the windows; this not only echoed the qualities of the neighbourhood, but also removed something from the building. His study of the context led him to interpret the immediate context in a brutal and savage manner. He took things away; he smashed bits of the building. This act of abolishing or eliminating these elements transmitted a message, he had made a statement; he had exposed the inequalities that existed within the surrounding area.

This is the same process that the architect or interior designer can engage with when remodelling an existing building. This will often result in equally destructive consequences, although of course, not usually so political. The process of taking things away, of subtraction, or removing elements of the building to reveal the underlying character or qualities is a common architectural and interior design strategy.

FIGURE 11.1 Gordon Matta-Clark, a radical and farsighted architect/artist recognised the important connection between community, food, art, architecture and life.

Credit: Richard Lantry via Wikimedia Commons

Analysis and Understanding

When working with an existing space or building, the architect or designer will use the analysis and understanding of the qualities of that context to provide the impetus for change. This process of investigation and examination promotes a certain kind of sensibility, an acceptance of what is already on or around the site, and the willingness to accentuate these found elements or narratives. This method of comprehension encourages a responsiveness and a sensibility that is described by Rodolfo Machado, in his essay 'Old Buildings as Palimpsest', as '…in remodelling, the past takes on a value far different from that in the usual design process, where form is generated "from scratch"' (1).

Stripping back, subtraction or even demolition can be considered as a process that actually precursors the real act of intervention; as some step, intellectual or intuitive, that the designer must pass through to reach the main or central point of the design process. The designer often sees this as an important but secondary stage, it has little more than a minor role in the creative method.

Fred Scott describes it as '…a means by which the designer can begin a negotiation between the ideal and the actual, and also begin the process of intervention by which disparate parts must be made to cohabit' (2).

To take this attitude further, this process can be viewed as the most significant and essential element of the design process. Taking away doesn't contain the glamour or the productive nature of intervention. It does not construct something new. It is not part of that most basic of human instincts, that is to create. It does not satisfy the sense of self-worth of the architect or designer. It is less than doing nothing; to take away is a process of reduction, or removal, it reduces what is available and what is there. It is a very strange process indeed and one which is much overlooked.

This process of removing elements of an existing building can convey many different types of message and contain a variety of meanings. The architect or designer can use it to respond to many different contextual factors. Matta-Clark's installation was a reaction to the social conditions surrounding the gallery. Other architects have responded to particular situations in a similarly deleterious manner.

The Bull Staircase by Josip Plecnik is situated in the far corner of the courtyard of Prague Castle, beyond the great expanse of the royal courtyard and behind the grand edifice of the Cathedral of St.Vitus, and yet this small, compact and beautifully detailed intervention is one of the most significant elements in the vast collection of buildings and spaces. Plecnik was commissioned to liberate the Castle after the First World War to make the new democracy visible. The approach he took was not to add a symbolic element to the Castle, but to do exactly the opposite; he cut a hole in the massive castle walls. This opening created a physical link between the royal palaces at the top of the hill and the city below it. The population of the town could enter and leave whenever they chose; the Castle was no longer an impenetrable fortress, but a playground for the townsfolk. The language of the staircase is intricate and delicate, the opening at the courtyard side is guarded by Minoan Bulls

FIGURE 11.2 The Bull Staircase, designed in 1931 by Josip Plecnik, established a physical connection between the Castle at the top of the hill, and the city of Prague below.
Credit: Sally Stone

sitting upon an elegant post and beam structure that has been draped with a canopy of copper. The staircase has three flights, and as it breaks the surface of the wall, it is supported by a single column; something that gives it an almost post-modern quality. The act of subtraction has liberated the Castle and aided the transformation from a royal palace to a seat of democratic government (see Figure 11.2).

Subtraction

Taking things away from a building can be more surprising; it can create a sense of excitement, wonder and revive a structure that is tired and rundown. The Caixa Forum in Madrid, which was once a brick power station, was converted into a museum by Herzog and de Meuron in 2008. This project contains two examples of quite brutal subtraction; the first was the extraordinary act of removing the whole of the ground floor of the building, thus bestowing upon it the impression that it is floating or gently hovering above the ground. The second destructive act was to demolish any extraneous structures immediately in front of the museum to create a new public square. The removal of the base of the building allows this new plaza to flow into the museum, thus creating spaces that are neither inside nor outside, they are under the building, but are not enclosed by it. This is a building that appears to defy gravity, it is full of wonder, ambiguity and whimsy. The architects have, through the visual removal of intrinsic elements necessary for the structural stability of the building and the razing of the surrounding buildings, commented upon the congested nature of the environment, the limited heaviness of the industrial society that created the buildings and the importance of the cultural industry to the twenty-first western societies. The project acts in direct violation of the urban environment, it transgresses the physical capabilities of the structures (see Figure 11.3).

FIGURE 11.3 The Caixa Forum in Madrid by Herzog and de Meuron, 2008, contains two elements of subtraction: the structure immediately adjacent to the gallery was razed to create an open public square, and the second equally strong move was the elimination of the ground floor level of the building.

Credit: Sally Stone

A project that exploits and accentuates the qualities of an existing building to the advantage of a new use is the old slaughterhouse in Landau. It was once a celebrated structure, but its limited size and position close to the city centre caused it to fall into disuse. Lamott Architeken BDA converted it into a library in 1998. They surrounded the abattoir with a new steel, glass and timber louvered skin, thus relegating the original stonewalls to internal partitions. These were then quite brutally carved into, almost butchered. The cuts and incisions facilitated moment through the library while making an illusory reference to the previous function (see Figures 11.4, 11.5 and 11.6).

These cuts and fissures echoed the function of the original building. An abattoir is something that the majority of the population does not want to engage with. It is a place that is acknowledged as necessary, but now-a-days is usually hidden some distance from urban areas. Meat is something that is almost divorced from its original source; it is carefully sanitised and innocuously packaged for the supermarket shelves. The act of reusing this building is definitely a radical act, although for reasons of sustainability and heritage, it is a very reasonable and sensible course of action. However, it is very provocative of the architects to make reference to the original purpose through the use of the two challenging methods. The first is of course the act of stripping out and

FIGURE 11.4 The Town Library in Laundau, Germany, by Lamott Architects 1998, was adapted from the old slaughterhouse.

Credit: Sally Stone

FIGURE 11.5 Lamott Architects make careful cuts and slices through the disused building to create the new Town Library in Laundau, Germany.

Credit: Sally Stone

carving up the original building, a direct reference to its former function. The second is the act of enclosing this carcass within a new screen wall. The uncompromising horizontal louvers of this protective enclosure are almost reflective of the pens and stalls that contained and controlled the animals prior to slaughter. Indeed, the stonework walls of the original building do seem to peer forlornly over the top of the modern wrapping. What makes this project so interesting is not only the manner in which the original building was gutted and butchered, and the fact that is has been enclosed within a cage, but also it is the infiltration of the memory of the original function into the narrative of the new building. A remembrance of the slaughterhouse is literally carved into the structure of

FIGURE 11.6 Lamott Architects caged the old building behind the new structures of the Town Library in Laundau, Germany, 1998.

Credit: Sally Stone

the library. Perhaps the new function is entirely appropriate; a building that in an industrial society produced food for the body, in a post-industrial era distributes cultural fodder.

Another project that uses the quite uncompromising act of subtraction is the extraordinary Centre for the Documentation of the Third Reich in Nuremberg. When constructed it was one of the most significant structures in Nazi Germany, but after the end of the Second World War, it lay dormant for years. No one quite knew what to do with it, but equally, its massive social significance meant that it couldn't be demolished. By virtue of its position within the German psyche as a city of great tradition, Nuremberg was in 1933 officially designated the 'City of Congresses', a privilege that entitled it to host the greatest gatherings of the Nazi Party. The great Nazi architect Albert Speer was responsible for the planning and development of a stadium for 400,000, parade grounds, Zeppelin fields, halls, barracks and other structures to house these spectacular shows. The site was linked to the centre of the town by a two-kilometre-long avenue. The centrepiece of the master plan was the Kongresshalle, designed by Ludwig Ruff, with his son Franz. It was a massive horseshoe-shaped auditorium intended to house 50,000 party officials. It was more than 275m wide by 265m deep, the colossal size and shape became a monumental backdrop for the huge rallies held there. The hall suffered from structural problems due to the marshy ground that it was built upon, the heaviness of the granite cladding and the sheer weight and size of the roof. It was never completed. The building was declared a national monument in 1973, and after reunification, the government held a competition to remodel the Kongresshalle to house the documentation centre; Gunther Domenig won it. However, the building is so huge that this project only occupies a small proportion of it, just the rectangular court-yarded hall to the north of the main semicircular buildings. The centre was designed to contain exhibitions, lecture rooms, film studios and workshops, the purpose of which were to provide a documentation of the events that took place within the city specifically focusing upon the Party Rally Grounds.

Domenig made a direct statement of intent which symbolised the new use. He inserted a dynamic diagonal cut directly against the grain of the original classically orthogonal building. This twenty-first century shard slices through the building. It begins as an entrance in the most northerly corner of the structure, brutally and uncompromisingly cuts through the rooms and the courtyard and emerges into the massive open space in the centre of the horseshoe building. This blade-like element lacerates the space to create a circulation route through the building (see Figure 11.7).

The remodelling is not a subtle statement, as this was not the time or the place for sensitive reappraisals and careful installations. The form of the new directly counterpoints the old. This is a bold proclamation on the history of the building and its relationship with the new function. The heavy masonry of the fabric of the Kongresshalle is literally just cut away to accommodate the

FIGURE 11.7 The new insertions deliberately smash through the classical structure of the original building in the Centre for the Documentation of the Third Reich in Nuremburg, Germany, by Gunter Domenig.

Credit: Sally Stone

insertion. The end of the shard opens out to form an entrance for the museum. Inside it links a series of rooms, which were originally intended as the meeting chambers and offices of the party and now form the exhibition spaces and the documentation archive. The 130m by 1.8m wide corridor is inclined, and rises through the space until it shoots out of the back of the building into the main central arena of the hall. Here the objective of the original architects becomes shockingly apparent as the enormity of the hall impresses itself upon the viewer. Domenig's intentions were to counteract, heighten and expose the existing building:

> I used oblique lines against the existing symmetry and its ideological significance. To contrast the heaviness of the concrete, brick and granite I turned to lighter materials: glass, steel and aluminium. The historic walls are left in their original state without ever being touched by the new work.
>
> 3

The scale and the orthogonal geometry of the existing building are extremely significant and Domenig undermines these with a direct, almost savage, slice through the very body of the structure. The edges of the cuts are unfinished; they are raw and jagged, uneven, rough and uncomfortable. The building is treated in a manner that is normally unacceptable. The unfinished, uncompromising nature of the new architecture is shocking. The building has been violated; there is no respect in this intervention. In any other building the level of finish and precision would be objectionable. The sheer rough crudeness of the untreated materials goes beyond the boundaries of what is normally accepted within the building industry. Equally, the function of the original building contravenes what is socially acceptable by an early twenty-first century society. The architect uses an extremely aggressive act to counteract that. The new function combined with the very symbolic event in this notorious building creates a building full of contrite contradiction.

The Castelvecchio Museum in Verona is a much gentler piece of architecture, but the architect was dogmatically uncompromising in the realisation of his vision for the project. Elements that had a direct connection with the site were retained, while the redesign of the building also involved the careful process of subtracting other parts of the building. The remodelling goes far beyond what was originally expected from the project, the narrative of the building has been unpicked and exposed. Huge areas of the buildings were torn away to reveal underlying layers of meaning and a small careful collection of interventions were used to accentuate the character of the castle.

The Venetian architect and designer, Carlo Scarpa, is recognised as the master of building reuse, he is noted for his profound understanding of the relevance of landscape and materiality within design, as well as his grasp of his native Venetian culture. He worked within the Modernist tradition, and it was with great skill that he was able to employ the progressive concepts of architectural promenade and transparency within the adaptation of classical buildings. The Castelvecchio Museum is generally considered to be his greatest work, and by many, as possibly the best example of building reuse ever constructed.

The approach that Scarpa took at the Castelvecchio was to create historical clarity within the building; he carefully identified the various historical strata within the complex of structures so that the layers of history were recognisable through the orderly uncovering of the various fragments. The buildings were originally constructed in the fourteenth century as a fortified castle for the della Scala dynasty, however there were already buildings on the site and the castle actually incorporated several existing structures which dated from Roman and mediaeval times, including the eighth century church of San Martino in Aquaro and part of the twelfth century city wall. The position was strategically important; it assured the family's control of Verona while also providing them with an escape route to the north via a fortified bridge. The original building was enclosed on three sides by a strong sheer wall with battlements and corner towers, with the open side open to and protected by the river. The buildings were transformed into a military garrison during Napoleon's occupation of the city. Two large barracks were constructed in the period 1802–6 along the north and east sides of the main courtyard, this effectively cut the courtyard off from the river. This is the basic form of the building today.

Arnaldo Forlati transformed the castle into a museum in 1923 by inserting a false gothic façade in front of the face of the barracks building. This created a pseudo-mediaeval palazzo with an Italian-style garden. Gothic doorways and window surrounds that were removed from local buildings were inserted into the courtyard façades. Also, five centuries of exclusive use of the bridge by the residents of the castle was ended by the opening of the road to the public. The result of this was to provide the residents of the city with a river crossing, but it also cut the castle in two along the axis of the ancient city walls.

Scarpa felt that this remodelling possessed an unnatural symmetry, which had the effect of presenting a false image of the building. He approached the project by carefully stripping away much of the detritus of time in order to be able to clearly present the layers of history. He carved away at the intrinsic balance of the structure to create something more asymmetrical, more irregular, uneven and unbalanced. This was the imposition of a Modernist agenda upon the more regular and balanced qualities of the classical building. He used three different but related methods to demonstrate the deposits of time.

Scarpa decided that the false symmetry of the Napoleonic barracks or north wing had to be broken, that the rhythm of the windows was at odds with the order of the façade. To achieve this he made it appear as if the façade was an attached stage screen. Although the elevation was left much intact, Scarpa purposely upset the artificial balance. The Napoleonic staircase and two rooms at the west end of the collection of buildings were demolished. The entrance was moved from the centre to the north east corner and a number of elements projected through existing openings to create a dialogue with the courtyard. The windows were recessed and so appeared as if part of another wall behind, the grid or rhythm of which was not synchronised with that of the façade. This strategy made it appear as if the façade was detached, as if it were an individual element that had been removed and was floating slightly in front of the original building. He wanted the façade to appear as a theatrical set, as a tacked on piece of scenery (see Figures 11.8 and 11.9).

Second, archaeological excavations had revealed the twelfth century passage linking the Porta del Morbio tower with the bridge over the Adige. This was exposed when the two Napoleonic rooms and the staircase were knocked down. This point was the last bay of the building and the point of intersection; it was the most complex part of the collection of structures. This created a pivotal space between the city wall, upon which the tower sat, and the north wing. The gap allowed the previously interlocked parts to be read as individual elements. The city wall connected to the bridge, the tower assumed its fortified position at the junction of the two, the façade of the nineteenth century wing was separated from these to appear as if it had been slid back to reveal the space, and in the midst of these dramatic frames and theatrical backdrops the famous statue of the original members of the family seated upon a horse; Cangrande 1 Della Scala was placed high up as a single highlighted enigmatic object. The roof of the north wing was extended in an irregular fashion to provide the statue with a degree of shelter.

The third method of explicitly depicting the evolution of the building was the very subtle use of negative space to separate the existing building from any new elements that were added to the building. This use of a shadow gap to define the historical layers of the building reinforced the earlier approach of separation. The depiction and emphasis upon the negative, the missing or the absent is a feature that drives the project. The character and nature and qualities of the original building are still apparent, these have not been completely removed. The histories of the building are made clear; they have been clarified by the strong, clear and incisive edited cuts to the building. This was a considered, yet violent act of ripping away at the building, of defiantly stripping away the accumulated detritus of years of misinterpretation.

This building does not look as if it has undergone a destructive or violent act; it has a warm and gentle honesty that hides the contravention of normal conservation practices. The archaeologist would maybe argue that the building has to be preserved in its found state, or that a particular moment in time is decided upon, and the building is preserved to recognise this. Scarpa did not take this approach, neither did he, in an attempt to provide historical clarity, deliberately try to contrast his alterations with the original structure. Instead he deliberately

FIGURE 11.8 The Castelvecchio Museum in Verona, Italy, by Carlo Scarpa (1959–73) is a masterpiece of careful and surgical removal.

Credit: John Lee

set out to tell the story of the building, to explain through the exposure of the layers of time, the narrative contained within the walls and spaces of the building. This did involve the subtraction of important historical and arch-aeological information. It deliberately upsets the enforced symmetry in such a

FIGURE 11.9 The new interventions within the Castelvecchio Museum (1959–73). in Verona, Italy, by Carlo Scarpa, deliberately contrast with the original building.
Credit: John Lee

manner that it almost mocks the previous scheme by Arnaldo Forlati. Small acts of destruction that purposefully separate the different era and elements of the building go beyond the polite reconstruction of the famous castle. The architect carried out a massive act of destruction of the precious heritage, but through this process of what he described as 'scraping away', created a building of great significance and worth.

Conclusion

Subtraction is an intrinsic element within the art of architecture and remodelling. It is a strategy that can be both productive and/or shocking. It is a process that scrapes away at the building, which can actually physically reveal the layers of meaning within the place and liberate the new architecture. It can be a violent and destructive act, it could sometimes almost be described as vandalism.

In 1985, the Spanish architectural historian Ignasi de Sola-Morales outlined a theoretical framework for understanding adapting buildings and remodelling them. In the ground breaking article 'From Contrast to Analogy – Developments in the Concept of Architectural Intervention', he described the development of remodelling as a concept that is closely related to understanding history. Sola-Morales also understood the foolishness of establishing a too rigid formula for remodelling buildings:

> It is an enormous mistake to think that one can lay down a permanent doctrine or still less a scientific definition of architectural intervention. On the contrary, it is only by understanding in each case the conceptions of the basis of which action has been taken that it is possible to make out the different characteristics which this relationship has assumed over the course of time.
>
> *4*

The violent act of subtraction is often overlooked in the process of adaptation. Architects and designers engage in the process of production, that is, the act of adding to what is already there. Destruction is a much more modest approach. The ego of the architect is not satisfied, they are not producing anything, rather they are engaged in a practice of expurgation or restriction. This method of revealing is an important tool in the armoury of the interior architect. It can be described in many ways: control, suppression, cutting, bowdlerisation, editing, but it is a practice that can have dramatic and expressive results.

This discussion has shown that the act of taking away is not something that is completely lost to the generation of the twenty-first century, an audience who are very difficult to shock. The use of subtraction as a primary method of remodelling buildings can produce results that are full of surprise, wonder and delight as well as deep understanding and symbolic judgement. It is an act that is usually a necessary stage in the process of architectural design, but for some projects it can be the most important, the most significant, central and vital method of communicating the character of the building.

'Every intervention results in some destruction. Destroy then at least with understanding' (5).

References

1.   Machado, Rodolfo (1976) "Old Buildings as Palimpsest" from Progressive Architecture. 57 (11) pp. 46–49. Stamford: Reinhold Publishing, p. 48.

2. Scott, Fred (2008) On Altering Architecture. Routledge, p. 113.

3. Cappezutto, Rita (April 2002) Confronting the Architecture of Evil. *Domus*, p. 90.

4. de Sola-Morales Rubio, I. (1985) From Contrast to Analogy. Lotus International No. 46, p. 37.

5. Snozzi, L. (2007) Cited in Architecture in Existing Fabric. Johannes Cramer and Stefan Breitling. Birkäuser, p. 29.

12

ON MAKING ADDITIONS

Assemblage, Memory and the Recovery of Wholeness

Introduction

The introduction of new independent elements into, between or beside an existing structure can often be seen as confrontational, and yet it is possible to establish surprising or sympathetic dialogues between the additions and the existing structure or volume. The prevailing argument is that this approach is most successful when the clearest possible distinction between the crisp new contemporary work and the crumbling antiquity of the existing is established and therefore the style, the language, the materials and the character of each are different. However, this is beginning to be seen as an out-dated approach, and there are many contemporary examples of additional elements that in a sense recreate or complete the original building to generate a new comprehensive structure. Gordon Cullen describes this process:

> There is an art of relationship just as there is an art of architecture. Its purpose is to take all the elements that go to create the environment: buildings, trees, nature, water, traffic, advertisements … and weave them together in such a way that drama is released.
>
> *1*

Although any addition to an existing structure is to a greater or lesser extent independent, particular qualities will always be derived from the original building. This is inevitable because there is always a direct architectural relationship with the absolute physical properties of the existing space and those of the new elements. Factors such as the scale and the dimensions, the proportions, the rhythm and the structural composition of the existing building influence the design of any new additions.

In a sense, building adaptation is always a duel process of subtraction and addition. The subtraction can sometimes be quite brutal, in that large areas of the existing structure are removed, or minimal in that the things to be taken away are little more than surface treatments or new openings made. Equally, all reuse projects contain an element of addition, of being supplemented or expanded. This can be the simple installation of new elements to facilitate the needs of the new users, such as new doors or windows, or can be massive extensions placed within or next to the building. Inherent within the additions is the agenda of the architect or designer. This is where they can exhibit their character, that is, their flair, creativity, sensitivity or intellectual judgement.

A number of systems of classification that catalogue the extent or method of the relationship between old and new have been developed. Philippe Robert was one of the first theoreticians to write exclusively about the practice of reuse as a design subject in its own right, rather than it being a mere adjunct of architecture. He uses the analogy of 'Architecture as Palimpsest' as the introductory title in his 1989 book *Adaptations: New Uses for Old Buildings* (2). He lists a series of projects, not by function or use, but by the level of interaction between the old and the new. So, the first few categories are: building within, building over, building around and building alongside. The constraints of the existing building are regarded as a stimulus to the imagination that 'enable architectural solutions to be developed that would never have been invented from scratch', but he also argues that for a conversion to be successful, there should be some symbolic memory of the original within the resultant structure (3).

Brooker and Stone, in their 2004 book, *Rereadings* (4) also create a taxonomy to classify the manner in which the existing building is added to. Again, they list projects not by function, but by architectural approach. They argue that the categories of adaptation can be ordered through the sheer amount of integration between the old and the new. This they catalogue into three sections: Intervention, Insertion and Installation. Of course, as with many taxonomy processes, there are exceptions to these categories, but it is surprising how few these are.

Intervention is the practice of the old and new becoming completely integrated with each other. The sheer amount of changes to the original building combined with the numerous new additions means that each can no longer be considered as independent. The old and the new rely completely upon each other for structural and spatial integrity. The most commonly cited example of this type of approach is the Castelvecchio Museum in Verona, Italy, remodelled in the middle of the twentieth century by Carlo Scarpa. Large parts of the existing building were 'scraped away' to reveal a narrative that told the story of the history of the building before new elements that facilitated the needs of the new users were applied as a contemporary layer of archaeology (see Figures 12.1 and 12.2).

If a new element is designed to fit exactly within the confines of an existing building, then the category is Insertion. This is usually a distinct and practical element, such as a circulation core or theatre. It is almost as if the new component is just conceptually lowered into place. A fine illustration of this is the contrasting

FIGURE 12.1 The Castelvecchio Museum in Verona, Italy, by Carlo Scarpa (1959–73). Meticulously positioned objects are placed at critical moments in the journey through the building.

Credit: John Lee

steel and glass stairs and elevator that the architects Foster + Partners sensitively slipped into an old and disused light-well at the Royal Academy of Arts in London (see Figures 12.3 and 12.4).

Installation is the process of the new additions simply inhabiting space within the confines of the old. The two will have a spatial relationship; after all, they occupy the same area, but it would be possible to remove the additions without affecting the integrity of the original building. This strategy is often used in historic buildings when great care has been taken over the conservation and it is important that the fabric is not altered. The Stirling Prize winning MAGNA exhibition centre in Rotherham, UK, illustrates this category well. Wilkinson Eyre Architects placed a number of expressive pavilions among the dirt and detritus of the disused steelworks to create a dynamic and animated visitor experience.

Adaptation is Cyclical

A brief historical survey of the manner in which additions have been made to existing buildings will compliment these classifications. Again, this is based upon architectural approach and the nature of the connection between the new and the

FIGURE 12.2 The Castelvecchio Museum in Verona, Italy, by Carlo Scarpa (1959–73). A dynamic tension is created between the building and the objects of art.

Credit: Paolo Monti via Wikimedia Commons

old rather than function or use. Form and function do have a strong link, but within building reuse projects there is always a much greater relationship between the form of the existing building and the resultant form of the adaptation.

There is a definite evolution of ideas and attitudes towards the adaptation and extension of original structures. The manner in which additions have been made to existing buildings shows a distinct correlation between the nature of the remodelling and that of the culture that did the work. Buildings can in microcosm represent the attitudes and culture of the society that occupy them. Inevitably this process of

FIGURE 12.3 The Sackler Galleries at the Royal Academy in London by Foster + Partners, 1991. The rhythm of the new elements deliberately contrasts with that of the existing building creating a visual distance between the two.

Credit: Sally Stone

addition and reuse is cyclical; ideas evolve and are reconsidered, so that attitudes that a generation earlier seemed barmy can become commonplace. Inevitably, making additions to buildings is also directly connected to ideas about conservation and restoration.

Before the industrial era, buildings that were considered to be of value and needed extending were either simply added to in the style of the day, or restored in a manner that paid no respect to the age or weathering. Reuse often took place without regard for the history or culture of the society that constructed the original building. Factors such as the picturesque or completeness would definitely be considered, but modern concepts of contrast and juxtaposition were unknown to those completing the work.

As the industrialisation of the western society and ideas of identity progressed, this position gradually evolved into the second method of conservation, which was much more vexing to nineteenth century aesthetes. Up until about the middle of the century, the prevailing attitude was for the weathered or worn areas of the building to be simply rebuilt in the original style. But the fundamental problem with this was the identification of what that style was and when it actually existed. The French architect, Eugène Viollet-le-Duc, who felt that he was fully authorised

FIGURE 12.4 The Sackler Galleries at the Royal Academy in London by Foster + Partners, 1991. The new elements almost fill the neglected space of the old light-well, which was rigorously restored by Julian Harrop Architects.

Credit: Sally Stone

to fill-in-the-blanks of damaged buildings, took this attitude to the extreme. For him, the building could (and indeed should) be restored to a condition that was 'pristine' which may indeed be a condition that might never have actually existed (5). But what does pristine mean? Viollet-le-Duc, who often combined historical fact with creative modification, felt that he could seriously reimagine the building. Within the fortified city of Carcassonne, for example, he designed new towers, extended the walls and developed a collection of picturesque pointed roofs.

The British historian and activist John Ruskin (supported later by William Morris, the founder of the Society for the Protection of Ancient Buildings) (6) recognised that few really old buildings have survived without alteration. He proposed that while their purpose was still fully vital, conservation must take such changes into account and usually retain them. Restoration, he argued, destroyed the spirit of the previous age and was merely a false description of the thing that was replaced. He called for care and maintenance, arguing that the 'buildings belong partly to the generation that constructed it and partly to those who have subsequently occupied them, but the present generation has no right to tear it down or damage it, just care for it' (7).

It is this basic argument, between creative restoration and complete preservation, that dominated the discussion about how the existing environment should evolve. Of course, there were many other practitioners and theoreticians involved with the debate about how an existing building should be adapted and enlarged, these included AWN Pugin, Aloïs Riegl and Georg Dehio. Such was the furore of the argument that it that led to the writing of the Charter of Athens in 1931. This was a forerunner of a series of international charters that would dominate the conservation movement; most notably the Venice Charter for the Conservation and Restoration of Monuments and Sites is a set of guidelines, drawn up in 1964 by a group of conservation professionals in Venice. These attempted to develop a systematic methodology through consensus and consolidation. It was agreed that old and new should be clearly different, and above all, what was wholeheartedly condemned was the use of pastiche. (Interestingly this word is the same in French and English.)

Thus it was generally agreed that if a building must change to be able to accommodate the needs of the new users, and that a fairly straight restoration will not suffice, then the general attitude that developed during the twentieth century was one of contrast and juxtaposition. The argument was that this was most successfully achieved when the clearest possible distinction between the shiny new contemporary additions and the decaying relics of the original building was established and therefore the nature and intent of each was visibly different.

Narrative Separation

From this attitude of extreme contrasts and definite difference, and in direct opposition to the prevailing view, emerged the architect Carlo Scarpa. He was the radical proponent of an approach that actively revealed the stratified account or chronicle of life of the building, and inspired several generations of architects and designers to pay great respect to the condition of the existing. A direct lineage between Ruskin and Scarpa can be drawn. Ruskin believed that authenticity was imbued through age and that the expressed patina of time revealed the true worth of a structure, while Scarpa considered that every building contained a narrative; that is, an inherent story, something to be uncovered and exposed. This chronicle of existence allowed the essence of the building to be displayed, thus showing the layers of history and use. He regarded conservation not as a scarifying practice, but as a creative life-giving exposé of the narrative of existence. His intention was to develop an understanding of the life of the building and recognise and reveal the strata of time, the patina of age and display the multi-layered history of its creation (see Figure 12.2).

Carlo Scarpa is perhaps the most celebrated architect of adaptation. The palimpsestuous approach to the remodelling of existing buildings that he developed through the systematic and intuitive process of carefully scraping away of the existing fabric and the meticulous placement of additions, he established a system that narrated the life of the building. This approach that showed the different layers or strata of history was exaggerated by the additions made by the architect, which were essentially a continuum of that history (8). It is an approach that was almost universally adopted from the time of Scarpa's design of the Castelvecchio Museum in Verona; a project which began in 1959 and was completed in 1973.

Wholeness

We have now entered what could be described as the next era of transforming or extending a building. Over the last generation, the attitude towards the existing situation and therefore the approach that the designer or architect will take to the remodelling of a structure has changed. It has evolved far from the Scarpa inspired approach of narrative separation into a new search for completeness or wholeness. This new method fuses the old and the new into a single and complete entity, one in which the individual historical layers are not necessarily visible, indeed the differentiation between the old and the new is not of particular importance. Neither is historical accuracy, as the past is just one element within the composite whole. The object is to create a complete and new entirety.

Walter Benjamin describes the idea of completeness as an attempt or an endeavour to remove something from its original system of classification and place it into a new expressively devised structure of organisation. What is decisive within the art of collecting is that the object is detached from all of its original functions in order to enter into the closest conceivable relationship with things of the same kind. This affiliation is the diametric opposite of any utility, and falls into the peculiar category of completeness (9). This accentuates the memory of the piece, while reducing it to an element of reference or catalogue entry. It is the opposite of utility, the reverse of usefulness. Thus completeness. (See Figures 12.5, 12.6 and 12.7).

The contemporary attitude towards remodelling does favour Wholeness. This act of completion can be observed in the work of, for example, Chipperfield's Neus Museum in Berlin, Kleihues' Museum of Pre-History in Frankfurt, Grassi's Roman Theatre near Valencia or within many of Herzog and de Meuron's recent remodelling projects. Within all of these projects, the original building has been adapted with reference to the history but accuracy is not regarded as particularly important. The building carries a sense of time and of transformation, but it is difficult to identify the strata of history within the whole building. Peter Zumthor completed the Kolumba Museum in Cologne in 2007. It has been made whole through the carefully constructions that have been built directly onto the ruins of the original building. The remains are not slightly detached objects of exhibition but are elements of the new building. The size and scale of the reconstruction is reminiscent of the original, but the materials, scale and function are all the products of the imagination of the architect. Thus, composition that is pristine, balanced and complete has been created.

It could be argued that this approach, that is to complete the building in a manner that creates a coherent whole but does not necessarily respect the language of the original, is the type of approach witnessed in much of contemporary

FIGURE 12.5 Neues Museum, Berlin, David Chipperfield, 2009. The original building was just sufficiently restored to become useable, thus it retains that patina of age and neglect acquired over many years.

Credit: Sally Stone

remodelling work. The building is given new life, the building is reconstructed, and is therefore enriched with perceptible meaning. This approach is also highly reminiscent of the attitude of the somewhat controversial nineteenth century French architect and theorist, Eugène Viollet-le-Duc, who often combined historical fact with creative modification, and felt that he could seriously reimagine the building. The new and the old were fused into a single entity to create a composite object. The past is just one element of the new whole and no effort was made to differentiate old and new.

City Archives of Bordeaux

A project that contains this contemporary idea of wholeness is the City Archives of Bordeaux, which is situated within a reused rail warehouse on the right bank of the River Garonne. Cargo trains actually ran lengthways through the open building, which once contained an elevated platform to facilitate this in the middle. It is situated in an area of the city that was previously cut off from the rest of the town, but is currently part of a large-scale urban redevelopment project and it forms the first link with the future eco-district of Bastide-Niel.

FIGURE 12.6 Neues Museum, Berlin, David Chipperfield, 2009. The new elements are visually separated from the original building, yet they support, compliment and complete it.

Credit: Sally Stone

The Belgian architect practice, Robbrecht en Daem, has unsentimentally interpreted the industrial history of the site within the remodelled building. They shifted the entrance, constructed an additional wing and created a new public space immediately in front of the building, thus welcoming new visitors and signalling the change of use. The old tracks of the Compagnie d'Orléans and the Napoleonic paving stones on the site have been preserved. The magnitude of the building is retained; and this enormity is matched by the robustness of the new building and a most formidable intervention within the open warehouse itself.

Five storeys of cantilevered boxes, which contain the air-conditioned spaces for the archive, have been placed into the vast uncluttered space. These enormous free-standing elements are simply stacked upon the old platform and smash their way through the roof. The principle is that of a big pile of boxes contained within a huge box. This great structure is positioned off-centre in the building, so the longitudinal view through the building is maintained, and the ground-level spaces around it can be used for other activities. The profile of the old roof was restored on the gables and the south façade, while simply lifted on the northern pitch to accommodate the massive archive. A new translucent wall was added above the original façade along the complete length of the building to accommodate the change

FIGURE 12.7 Neues Museum, Berlin, David Chipperfield, 2009. The hall that contains the great staircase has been reconstructed in a sympathetic manner that simply completes the building.

Credit: Sally Stone

in height. The reading room is located on the ground floor in the north side of the building and the concrete boxes cantilever over it. This creates an acceptable atmosphere for study and contemplation; while the smaller free spaces on the south side of the building are used for circulation. The supply of fresh air and the high inertia of the concrete structure guarantee a stable climate for the archives within the boxes themselves (see Figures 12.8 and 12.9).

FIGURE 12.8 The City Archive, Bordeaux, France, Robbrecht en Daem Architects, 2016. The additions that have been made to the building compliment the majestic size and scale of the original structure.

Credit: Sally Stone

FIGURE 12.9 The City Archive, Bordeaux, France, Robbrecht en Daem Architects, 2016. Trains used to run lengthways through the building, entering through the enormous archways at either side of the gable façade.

Credit: Sally Stone

The changes obviously signal a change of use; the building has been updated and given a new purpose, and the architects have strived to create an awareness of completeness within the buildings. The old and the new cooperate with each other to create a solid sense of wholeness.

The Roman Theatre in Sagunto

The Roman Theatre in Sagunto, Spain, dates from the first century and was originally built to take advantage of a natural depression in the land; this is something that provides excellent acoustics for open-air theatrical performances. It was constructed in the shape of a semicircle and once had capacity for 8,000 spectators. A lot of the blocks of stone from the theatre stage and from the stands have, over the years, been removed and used to build the local castle and various other houses. After many centuries of abandonment, in 1994, the theatre underwent a transformation and reconstruction by the architect Giorgio Grassi (see Figure 12.10).

The approach that Grassi took was to leave the original structure in place, plus those relatively modern additions that had accumulated over the last century, especially those that did not create too great a juxtaposition with the Roman remains.

FIGURE 12.10 The Roman Theatre in Sagunto, Spain, Giorgio Grassi, 1986. The building has been completed in a retrained manner, something that contrasts with the more decorated approach of the ancient structure.

Credit: Sally Stone

He then added to, or rather completed, the building in a manner necessary for the theatre to once again function. Grassi carefully investigated the practices of the ancient Roman engineers and used these as the basis of the new structures. He acknowledged the centrality of the fixed architectural stage set, with its principal and two lateral openings. However, large parts of the fixed sets were missing, so Grassi created a simplified version of the lower set, which was placed exactly as it would have been in ancient days. This mixture of new and old adequately narrates the story of the theatre while also providing a dramatic environment for the action.

The upper levels of the stage set and the backdrop were a much greater problem; these were completely missing. Grassi chose to illustrate the missing elements with an abstracted version of the theatre. He completed the building, not by simply recreating what had previously been there, and not through contrast or collision, but by constructing a contemporary simulacra or copy. This was something that intimated the size, scale and materials of the original but was obviously of the present day. The result is an extremely elegant and restrained project in which the old and new combine and support each other to create a new whole. The form of the original building generated the new elements; history is present in the reconstruction, but the architect did not feel it necessary to narrate the story of the building, to tell of its destruction and reconstruction, he felt it more important to create a sense of wholeness which in itself was a statement of completeness of the theatre and its connection with the past.

Conclusions

Within the modern age, attitudes to interior architecture and building reuse have evolved. We have moved from a pre-industrial approach of making necessary additions in the style of the day, through creative rebuilding, indiscriminate preservation, contrast and analogy to once again embracing an attitude of filling-in-the-blanks of the history. The post-modern approach is to create a new wholeness; that is, for the new additions to harmoniously complete the building (10). This sense of wholeness is not restricted to the visual, it often includes issues of sustainability, environmental concern, materials and smartness to create a radically new building that responds to the past and to the future.

References

1. Cullen, Gordon (1961) Townscape. Architectural Press, p. 10.
2. Robert, Philippe (1989) Adaptations: New Uses for Old Buildings. New York: Princeton Architectural Press.
3. Robert, Philippe (1989) Adaptations: New Uses for Old Buildings. New York: Princeton Architectural Press, p. 4.
4. Brooker G. and Stone, S. (2004) Rereadings. London: RIBA Publications.
5. Viollet-le-Duc, E. (1858) Eugène-Emmanuel Violett-le-Duc On Restoration (from Dictionnaire Raisonne, Vol 8, 1858). trans. Charles Wethered 1875.
6. Society for the Protection of Ancient Buildings: www.spab.org.uk.

7. Ruskin, John (1849) The Lamp of Memory. The Seven Lamps of Architecture. London: Smith, Elder, and Co., pp. 162–182.

8. Ghirardo, Diane (2013) Italy: Modern Architectures in History. London: Reaktion Books, p. 192.

9. Hanssen, Beatrice (Ed.). (2006) Walter Benjamin and the Arcades Project. London: Bloomsbury, p. 219.

10. Rowan, Moore (1998) The Architecture of Damage Ruins of Modernity: Erich Mendelsohn's Hat Factory in Luckenwalde Chair Mohsen Mostafavi. London: AA Publications, p. 50.

13

ITINERANT ELEMENTS

Portable Rooms

King John of England – he who signed the Magna Carta, was mocked by A. A. Milne and made legendary as the archenemy of Robin Hood – lived an extraordinary peripatetic life. Between 1204 and 1205 he stayed in over 100 different places, and not one of those for more than ten consecutive days (1). He was an uncompromising monarch who ruled over an extraordinarily discontented kingdom and therefore had to continually show himself as both alive and well, and thus still in charge. All Mediaeval Kings needed to be seen, and be seen to rule by as many of their subjects as possible. So, they were continually on the move, travelling from one castle to the next fortified home. And they brought with them great trains of courtiers, guards and hangers-on, as well as the machinery and officials of government. King John carried his whole household with him in what was described as the baggage train (2); the volume of stuff that was moved from point to point was quite considerable. Everything needed for the court and administration had to be portable; not only the royal beds, furniture and kitchen, but also the deeds and papers of government; for wherever the king was stationed was regarded as the temporary capital. These writs and royal orders were sewn together into huge rolls – difficult to read, but easy to carry (see Figure 13.1).

Upon arrival, it was the responsibility of the Royal Upholsterer to arrange the furniture, erect the tents, position the drapes, display the collection. One of the most intriguing pieces of baggage was itemised as pieces of glass; these were window pieces that John carried around with him on his travels, which were fitted into the apertures of the houses wherever he happened to lodge (3). This extensive collection of belongings meant that the baggage train could at times stretch for as long as two and a half miles.

Despite of, or maybe because of, his somewhat ferocious life, King John was a pious man, and the royal baggage would also have included a portable chapel for

FIGURE 13.1 Illuminated manuscript that shows King John out hunting on horseback. The royal party often rode ahead of the baggage train, which made a slow and cumbersome journey and was easily outpaced by the much more fleet aristocracy.

Credit: King John of England, 1167–1216. Illuminated manuscript, *De Rege Johanne*, 1300–1400. MS Cott. Claud DII, folio 116, British Library

worship. This nomadic room was carefully constructed by the Royal Upholsterer at every new dwelling and served to satisfy the King's need to celebrate Mass every single day. The chapel consisted of a portable altar, most probably with cupboards inserted into it. These would undoubtedly have held holy relics and probably a folding painted triptych. The walls of this portable room would not have been the actual walls of the castle or fortified home that the King happened to be staying in, but would have been a shelter constructed within the interior of the building; that is, a room within a room. These transportable walls will have been made from fabric; they would have been highly decorated tapestries. The tapestries served to contain the space, to form a thermal barrier and thus create some environmental control, and also to provide decorative images of religious scenes to help concentrate the mind of the King during the Mass.

The itinerant way of life encouraged the production of lighter articles that could be carried around. One of the reasons for the wide use and the value of textiles was the ease with which they could be packed into a travelling chest and transported from house to house. Indeed, tapestries and other wall hangings had a much greater worth than many other types of belongings.

This portable fabric construction provides a direct link to Gottfried Semper, his theory of the Four Elements of Architecture and the evolution of the primitive hut. Semper's Four Elements are: 1, a hearth, 2, an earthwork, 3, a framework, 4, an enclosing membrane. (Interestingly, Semper linked the hearth to the altar; that is, the spiritual nexus of architectural form.) (4)

The tapestry walls of the simple encircling chapel could be likened to this enclosing membrane. Semper argued that the carpet wall plays the most important role in the general history of art (5); he regarded the hanging carpets as the true walls, that is, the visible boundaries of space. The often solid walls behind them were necessary for reasons of security, for supporting load and for permanence of this support, but had nothing to do with the creation of space. 'Even where building solid walls became necessary, the later were only the inner, invisible structure hidden behind the true and legitimate representatives of the wall, the colourful woven carpets' (6).

Semper goes on to argue that the wall retained this meaning even when more robust and decorative methods of construction were employed. Stucco, bitumen plaster, ceramic tiles, panels of sandstone, alabaster and timber linings attempted to imitate the colourful embroideries of the carpet walls. And so the King's portable Chapel, a fabric room with a transportable altar, could be likened to the primitive hut. The hanging tapestry panels would be placed in front of the solid walls of the interior of the castle of the manor house creating the appearance of a different space. The tapestries transformed the cold alien room into a comfortable and familiar space that was decidedly refined and suitable for a highly cultivated prince or man of nobility.

While the upper-classes maintained a peripatetic way of life, it was more convenient to cover the walls with portable hangings, but when a more sedentary existence became more common, the greater efficiency and durability of wainscot in covering the walls and excluding the weather became apparent. The invention and common usage of the sawmill meant that wood was used for purposes that more commonly had been fulfilled by hanging fabrics. Wainscoting is a method of lining a wall with timber panels to create a complete and decorated interior. The timber panels were often richly decorated, sometimes with painted pictures or working upon the wood itself produced the patterns and ornamentation.

Cordula Seger discussed the material difference between the thickness of the masonry wall and the expanse of the surface of that wall; that is, between the constructed autonomy and a corresponding dependency on other constructional elements. Thus '…significance lies in the fact that cladding of any kind generates meaning' (7). Semper argued that there was a very different meaning between a wall that was simply built for reasons of construction and one which carries the symbolic meaning of containing and describing the space: '…even where solid walls are necessary, they are nothing more than the internal and invisible framework to the true and legitimate representation of the spatial idea, of the more or less artificially worked and woven assembly of textile walls' (8). Semper loved this role-playing. He declared: 'I believe that dressing-up and masquerade are as old as human civilisation itself' (9). Thus a difference exists between a building and architecture. The building is a purely assembled construction, while architecture, as John Ruskin established, contains significance and meaning.

These lined, highly decorated rooms were often small and private and were used by the nobility to contain the first collections of objects. These were not necessarily of great financial worth, but were of value for their rarity, historical or personal significance. These intimate rooms were originally referred to in English as cabinets. This is where such obvious expressions as the cabinet of curiosity and the more obscure relationship with the parliamentary cabinet stem from. The timber linings were still portable, and would customarily be moved from one home to another, not as an everyday activity, but as an inheritance. It is recorded that within his will, John Colet (10) ordered that his wainscot should 'remain forever in his lodgings', while Gilbert Spense directed that none of his wainscot or furniture should be removed from his house (11). Thus timber wainscot replaced tapestries as the true inner walls of the room, the outer walls acted to support the timber panelling and to keep the worst of the weather out of the space, but the true extent of the room was defined by the screens or panels.

Itinerant Rooms

It is not uncommon, even in a more contemporary period, for whole rooms to be removed and placed in a new location. The highly valuable disconnected lining could be transported from one location to another. Distinct parts of a building can be used and reused. An ornate doorway or fireplace is a valuable commodity, while whole screens, elaborate windows and the timber panelling can and have been transported to a new place. They can be exploited and manipulated; an elaborate artefact may enhance a somewhat dowdy building, and confer a status that may not have previously existed. But whole rooms have a much less anonymous quality, a more direct relationship between the different users and by virtue of their completeness, a much greater impact when relocated.

One such room is the Antichambre des Chiens, or the Room of the Dogs at the Chateau de Versailles in France, which was established by Louis XIV at the end of the seventeenth century. His son, Louis XV, was a much less flamboyant character, and made a number of alterations to the magnificent palace, which included the creation of a number of smaller and more intimate rooms. One such space was the Room of the Dogs. This room had an immediate proximity to the King's bedchamber and served two purposes: the first was as a waiting room for the courtiers who would accompany the King on the hunt; the second was as a room for the King's favourite dogs to sleep in. The highly ornate timber panels originally adorned Louis XIV's billiard room, but Louis XV turned that into his bedroom and the panels transferred to dog's room. A series of eight gilded wooden niches arranged on its perimeter. This gilded panelled room afforded the occupants, that is, the dogs, and the valets who cared for them and thus shared the room, great status. The room had been 'dressed up', with the application of the panelling, it had in effect been decorated; it had been given a disguise, a costume, a mask.

A much more contemporary example of a whole room that has been dismantled and reused is the Shakespeare Memorial Library. This interior space is positioned at the pinnacle of the new City Library, which was constructed in 2013 in Birmingham, England. The building itself is a highly contemporary decorated collection of concrete and glass horizontal slabs, which occupies a prominent position on the edge of the city centre of this post-industrial city. The highly expressive Dutch architects, Mecanoo, imagined it as a People's Palace, a centre for learning, information and culture that unites people of all ages and backgrounds. At the summit of this wondrous stack of carefully balanced decorated boxes is the prominent golden rooftop rotunda that houses the Shakespeare Memorial Room. This small but significant interior space has been painstakingly transferred from the City's School of Music to act as the most remarkable feature within the deliberately flamboyant post-modern landmark building. But this is not the first move that this tiny and intricate chamber has made, neither is it the second, but it is actually its third different transposition for the room.

This ornate and intimate room was constructed in 1882 and was originally situated in the Central Library. John Henry Chamberlain, a founder member of the city's Shakespeare Club, was responsible for it and for re-building the old Central Library after the original building was gutted by fire in 1879. The room is a timber lined highly decorated orthogonal library space with a painted barrel-vaulted ceiling. The design was highly praised at the time and is in what was then considered a highly appropriate Elizabethan style with carvings, marquetry and metalwork representing birds, flowers and foliage. Long before this building was demolished in 1971 to make way for the inverted concrete ziggurat-shaped Brutalist library by John Madin, the collection had outgrown the little space, and so it had become a slightly neglected reading room. Although it was the only part of the original building to be saved, the Shakespeare Library was thought of as unsuitable for the modernist masterpiece, and so it was stored at the city's Sheepcote Street depot, in what were reported to be extremely poor environmental conditions. In 1986, the room was reconstructed and placed within the Birmingham Conservatoire (see Figure 13.2).

Birmingham has no direct associations with Shakespeare and yet this little decorated room has become a somewhat self-conscious destination at the top of the city's most radical and progressive building. The timber-lined space is rectangular and yet it is situated within a golden cylinder, so the interior and the exterior are different. The decorated library shelves are what Semper refers to as the 'true walls' (12), that is, the visible boundaries of the space. The solid walls behind them are necessarily strong and environmentally secure, but do not create the nature, character or shape of the interior; they are an invisible structure concealed behind the true inner wall. The enclosure is a flamboyant signal or gesture towards the exquisite and detached interior within.

FIGURE 13.2 The Shakespeare Memorial Library is a complete room that has moved several times, it is now positioned at the pinnacle of the stack of contemporary orthogonal blocks of Birmingham City Library (Mecanoo Architects, 2013).
Credit: Sally Stone

The 11th floor of Richard Rogers' internationally acclaimed High-Tec Lloyd's building is famously home to the Adam Room, an eighteenth century dining room. It is an adaptation of the original dining room of Bowood House in Wiltshire, designed in 1763 for the first Earl of Shelbourne. Much of Bowood was demolished in the late 1950s; this coincided with the building of the new Lloyd's premises in Lime Street. So the architect, Terence Heysham, conceived the idea of recreating the complete interior in its entirety in the new building. It was purchased at auction, and was installed by George Jackson and Sons, who coincidently were the same company who fitted the room almost two centuries earlier. In 1986, along with the rest of the company, the room moved to the new Lloyd's building. There is, of course, a deliberate and striking contrast between the classical interior design of Adam and the post-industrial architecture of Lord Rogers (see Figure 13.3).

There are of course numerous examples of rooms that have been reconstructed as exhibition pieces within museums and galleries, sometimes as permanent exhibits, other times as temporary installations. A fine example of the preservation of a complete interior for the benefit of the public is Miss Cranston's Tearooms on Ingram Street in Glasgow, which were designed by Charles Rennie Mackintosh between 1900 and 1912. These were one of a number of tearooms that Mackintosh designed for Miss Cranston (including the more famous Willow Tearooms), but they are the only complete original set of Mackintosh tearoom interiors to survive. The interior

FIGURE 13.3 The Adam Room, an eighteenth century dining room, has been inserted into the 11th floor of Richard Rogers' High-Tec Lloyd's Building.

Credit: Lloyd's of London via Wikimedia Commons

FIGURE 13.4 Miss Cranston's Tearoom, an intricately beautiful interior designed by Charles Rennie Mackintosh has been carefully reconstructed in the Tate Gallery, Dundee.

Credit: Sally Stone

last functioned as a tearoom in the early 1950s, and by then it had been neglected, over-painted and was generally in a very dilapidated condition. The room has been carefully conserved and restored and is displayed in the Scottish Design Galleries at the new Tate Gallery in Dundee (see Figure 13.4).

A quite bizarre and extreme example of the conservation, relocation and exhibition of a complete interior room is the Studio of the artist Francis Bacon. In 1998 the entire contents were moved from London to Dublin. The room, including the walls and the floor, was completely covered with the creative detritus of his work. A team of archaeologists carefully catalogued the position of over 7,000 different items in the studio, which included books, photographs, canvases, drawings, paints and correspondence. This was then reconstructed in the same chaotic, disorganised and haphazard arrangement in the Hugh Lane Dublin City Gallery (see Figure 13.5).

A possibly even more extreme example of the preservation, repositioning and subsequent exhibition of a complete room is the installation Seizure, created in 2008 by Roger Hiorns. The artist, in a great act of audacity, flooded a small London apartment with 75,000 litres of copper sulphate solution. The flat was then sealed up for a month. When opened and drained, the interior contained a strange, beautiful and a not-a-little-bit menacing crystalline growth on the walls, floor and ceiling. The abandoned dwelling had been transformed into a wondrous grotto; it quickly became a place of pilgrimage. The social housing block was due to be demolished in 2011, and so Seizure was permanently encased in a steel cage and removed from its original site to a specially designed enclosure within the Yorkshire Sculpture Park. Adam K Architects created a new home for the installation; one which reflects the industrial-agricultural nature of the surrounding landscape and acts as a suitable foil for the brilliant room. The incredibly fragile installation is now transportable, so it can be lent to other institutions. The space has become truly itinerant, its original home has been destroyed and thus the true connection with place has been broken, so it is free to roam around from place to place, from gallery to gallery (see Figures 13.6, 13.7 and 13.8).

Nomadic Spaces

Interior spaces have a definite and individual character. Their nature is dependent upon many things, but does include the relationship with the building that they are enclosed within and the immediate context within and around that enclosure. There are consequences when this clear and distinct room is removed from this context; it will lose its connection with the land that it once occupied, and take on a different personality, not just of the new users, but also the itinerant or nomadic quality of something in transition, of something unsettled and uncertain, of having had to adapt and change. It is questionable whether this self-conscious uncertainty leads to a lack of definite personality or just a change in that character. The interior space will acquire a dual personality, it will be relevant to the culture that first constructed the interior, and will also have resonance with the society that reused it.

The installation Seizure was constructed within a ground floor of a council apartment, when it was removed to an idyllic part of the English countryside, therefore the connection with those who occupied the social housing and the utopian vision that constructed the building was broken. The installation has become

FIGURE 13.5 Francis Bacon's studio was catalogued then delicately transported to the Dublin City Art Gallery.

Credit: antomoro via Wikimedia Commons

something incredibly beautiful, and admittedly very interesting because of its original home, but it is questionable whether the sense of origin still exists and thus the importance of creating something exceptional within a very ordinary and dilapidated space is somewhat lost. However, the room has meaning within the Yorkshire Sculpture Park as an object of great beauty and scientific wonder. The

FIGURE 13.6 Seizure, an exquisitely beautiful installation inside a small ground floor apartment was created in 2008 by Roger Hiorns. It was transported to the Yorkshire Sculpture Park in 2014. Adam Khan Architects created an agricultural austere container for it.

Credit: Sally Stone

Shakespeare Library is testament to both the intellectual ambition of those that constructed it and also it has importance to the citizens of Birmingham as a symbol of the aspirational past of the city and the pluralistic and progressive attitude that is now prevalent in the city; the library is very much a symbol of the post-modern society. As Heidegger discussed, the building is a thing rather than a sign, and by extension, a room is a definite and real thing: 'It is language that tells us about the nature of a thing, provided that we respect language's own nature' (13). The rooms have become both self-conscious and multi-referential. The itinerant room contains distinct character and personality, but this is an individual feature, which transportation has altered and enlarged.

To return very briefly to King John and his baggage train: the procession was long; it had to carry not just the goods of the King and his servants, but also the courtiers and the other members of the court. When on the move, royal baggage trains are thought to have travelled an average of 20 miles a day, moving at walking pace. Distance was limited not just by the state of the roads and the weather but also by the weight of the wagons and carts. And of course, the baggage train got longer as the relentless journey wore on. Taxes were collected en route, and the soldiers felt it was their right to collect as much other stuff of value as they wanted.

FIGURE 13.7 Seizure, 2008, by Roger Hiorns, is contained within a strong and substantial container, something that is sufficiently robust to accommodate the big move across the country.

Credit: Sally Stone

This collection of loot would definitely grow as the procession moved from place to place, and all of this continually growing collection of plunder had to carried on the continual journey.

The baggage that all of the King's stuff was carried in had to be both strong and lightweight. Cabinet making was not particularly sophisticated at the time; indeed, the saw was still an underdeveloped tool. Wooden chests were heavy and cumbersome, and thus used only for the most precious of objects. The majority of the baggage, that is, the travelling or trussing chests, were made from leather bound with strong iron straps for rigidity and security. They were necessarily smaller and

FIGURE 13.8 The language of the new containing structure (Adam Khan Architects) is derived from the local farm buildings.

Credit: Sally Stone

less decorated than the great standing chests, which stayed permanently within a fortified home.

The Spolia on display would have been the weapons and other artefacts of war. Spolia is also an expression used to describe a collage-like approach to reconfiguring buildings. It relies on the materials that are available, the ease of their reuse, on contingency, availability and ease of supply. This act of transportation can be likened to the approach taken by the bricoleur. Jaques Derrida quoted Levi-Strauss when he describes such a character as:

> …someone who uses 'the means at hand,' that is, the instruments he finds at his disposition around him, those which are already there, which had not been especially conceived with an eye to the operation for which they are to be used and to which one tries by trial and error to adapt them, not hesitating to change them whenever it appears necessary…

Spolia is a strategy of reusing specific elements of a building or culture in a new or radical manner. It is a collage-like approach, using appropriated bits and pieces, which have been gathered together. This accumulation or assemblage of slivers and shards creates a compendium or miscellany of different styles, fashions and meanings (14).

Beat Brenk, in his essay, 'Spolia from Constantine to Charlemagne: Aesthetics Versus Ideology' (15), outlines the origins of the practice before discussing the opposing reasons for its application. Spolia, he explains, is an ancient practice of incorporating found, stolen or otherwise appropriated building materials into a new building or monument. The word itself is derived from the Latin 'spolium', which actually means 'removed hide of an animal', and the term has evolved through a soldier's booty or spoils of war, to the reused parts of architectural constructions. Thus it could be described as a building that has been stripped of its hide. According to Brenk, after they had made a conquest, the Romans used the spoils taken from the conquered cities to construct architecture that communicated their identity as the victors. The conquerors would display the spoils of war to show the extent of the victory and revel in the magnitude of the conquest. Thus the Spolia was a symbolic gesture intended to both humiliate the loser and bolster the esteem of the victor.

However, the taking of Spolia served two purposes: the first was ideological, the second aesthetic, so the other reason for the taking of architectural Spolia was actually both practical and visual. The building materials were useful; it certainly saved considerable time if columns did not have to be carefully carved, archways carefully calculated and keystones decorated. The cut stone was a useful and economical addition to any building and could add significant aesthetic value.

Conversely, Brenk argues that it was not always as simple as this. Both Constantine and Charlemagne also transported the precious Spolia over hundreds if not thousands of miles. This was neither cheap nor particularly convenient. Building materials were dragged from Rome to the conquered towns to become monuments of political propaganda. A solid reminder of the historic tradition and the all-encompassing might of Rome, which was placed in a strategic position within a conquered town, served as a reminder of the occupying force. A monument is a physical manifestation of the ruling or governing body. Emphasis was placed upon the continuity of history of the victors, and thus the population of the beaten community would be constantly reminded of their pledges towards that occupying force. So the monument had the double function of being an aide de memoir, and also a guide to behaviour and attitude. Brenk cites the example of Charlemagne's 'abduction of building material' from Theodoric's Palace at Ravenna (16). This marble Spolia was of Roman origin, and so when transplanted into Aachen in northern Germany, recalled the historical tradition of Rome.

Despoliation gradually became a universal norm, especially in northern Europe after the Reformation. It was once a well-acknowledged practice to remove individual elements from a disused building and reuse them elsewhere. This would have included complete sections of the building such as an ornate bay window, perhaps a magnificently carved doorway or even a mosaic floor. In the period of the Stripping of the Altars and the accelerated implementation of Protestantism in the mid-sixteenth century, the abduction of building materials from abbeys or priories, plundered by private individuals for personal use within their own homes, was a fast, effective and relatively inexpensive way of creating a new fireplace, doorway or window. This really was pillaging; the religious buildings were plundered or ransacked and the loot or Spolia was absconded with. And thus, a stately home would have a marvellous bay window, which had been snatched from a local religious community. A fine example of this is Newstead Abbey, in Nottinghamshire, England, which was founded as a priory between 1163 and 1173. After the Dissolution, the Abbey was surrendered to Henry VIII in 1539 and acquired by Sir John Byron in 1540, an ancestor of the great poet, Lord Byron. The house incorporates many of the elements of the church, which have been adapted for domestic use. It could be argued that this actually saved much of this fine craftsmanship from a much worse fate; candlesticks and church plates were often melted down and sold off, altar tables were removed, rood screens defaced or torn down and chasubles unstitched, decorated church walls were whitewashed, the relics discarded and the paintings of saints were either burnt or hidden in parishioners' houses. Despoliation created a rich and diverse collection of country houses which were elevated by their association with the plundered architectural elements (see Figure 13.9).

Stone and Brooker, in their essay 'Spolia: Inappropriate Appropriations', argue that it is also a thoroughly Post-modern tactic, in that contemporary architects and designers will take existing objects and itinerant elements, and with deliberate incongruity place them within a new context (17). They argue that the

FIGURE 13.9 Newstead Abbey, Nottinghamshire, England, includes many elements of the local church when it was incorporated into the house.

Credit: Mechanical Curator Collection via Wikimedia Commons

post-modern Spolia can be divided into three categories: Ready-Mades, Persistent Meaning, and Continuity and Permanence. Ready-Mades describes those itinerant elements that are already complete and may even be new, they are then removed from their intended destination and placed within a new venue and thus imbued with a dual meaning, that of the original and that of the juxtaposed. Ready-made is a term that came into prominence when it was used to describe the conceptual art of Marcel Duchamp, who, somewhat controversially at the time, elevated mundane everyday elements into works of art. The Spider Lamp by Architects Tillner and Willinger is a contemporary addition to Helmut Richter's post-modern restaurant Kiang in Vienna. The bar itself is a radical collection of dynamically placed horizontal and vertical planes, while the expressive light fitting which is constructed from 16 classic black Anglepoise lamps hovers dangerously above the main table (see Figure 13.10).

Persistent Meaning describes projects that use fragments or parts of a much larger collection, which are reassembled in a new manner to create something original. An extraordinary and really quite extreme example of persistent meaning within the post-modern use of itinerant elements is the Museum in Gibellina Nuova in Sicily by Francesco Venezia. The small isolated town of Gibellina was

FIGURE 13.10 The Spider Lamp by Tillner and Willinger is ready-made, constructed from 16 Anglepoise lamps.

Credit: Tillner and Willinger

destroyed in an earthquake in 1968. Rather than attempt reconstruction, the complete population was moved almost ten miles to a more accessible position close to the highway to the capital city. The majority of the buildings are gratuitously new, organised in a modern grid; a far cry for the organic winding claustrophobia of the original place. The Museum, however, makes a direct reference to the original through the reuse of fragments of the San Lorenzo Palace. The elements of the north façade of the Palace were incorporated into the new building, and although the symmetry of the original building was to a certain extent observed, the exact position of the elements was not truly adhered to. So, the new building contains some of the characteristics of the old palace, and thus a memory of the destroyed town, but without mimicking it; pastiche was not employed. The fragments of the building are integrated into the walls of the Museum; they are displayed, suspended, exhibited as if the flaunted spoils of war. They are aesthetic reminders of the old town and ideological mementos of the bygone age.

Continuity and Permanence covers elements that have lost their original meaning and given a completely new purpose when they are reused. The Kuala Lumpur Performing Arts Centre (KLPAC) is situated is in a leafy suburb of Kuala Lumpur. The Centre is housed in a converted railway building, which was constructed during the British colonial era in Malaysia. The architects have appropriated the massive span of the space to insert a complete theatre. It was important for the theatre to look as if it was deliberately independent, and not part of the Colonial past of the original building, and yet still belonging to the tradition of the country. The theatre itself is placed deliberately off-centre, so breaking the symmetry and thus visually appearing to move away from the original structure. Spolia has been used to control the acoustics within the interior. Railway sleepers have been attached to one immense internal wall, while the opposite has drainpipes placed vertically against it. These bits and pieces of rescued fragments and parts serve a technological sound controlling purpose, and also act as a reminder of the lost identity of the building (see Figures 13.11, 13.12 and 13.13).

Conclusions

Just as in mediaeval times, when the rich would lead peripatetic lives, wandering from one grand home to the next, carrying with them a huge collection of furniture and trappings; it is possible to remove complete elements from a building and rearrange them elsewhere. It is the architecture that moves, that wanders across the landscape, and as it does, its meaning can change. Furniture can travel from place to place, wholesale elements can be used and reused. They can be exploited and manipulated, carried, transferred, transported, moved, circulated. Distinct parts of a building can be used and reused. It is not uncommon for elements of a building to be conveyed from one location and reused in another. An ornate doorway or fireplace is a valuable commodity, while whole screens, elaborate windows, even timber panelling can and have been transported to a new place.

FIGURE 13.11 Kuala Lumpur Performing Arts Centre is situated among the detritus of the old railway buildings.

Credit: Sally Stone

Spolia is an archaic term that describes the reclamation of existing archi-tectural elements to incorporate them into new buildings. It was once a well-acknowledged practice to remove individual elements from a disused building and reuse them elsewhere. This would have included complete sections of the building such as an ornate bay window, perhaps a magnificently carved doorway or even a mosaic floor.

FIGURE 13.12 Elements of the old building have been retained as memories of the previous existence.

Credit: Sally Stone

It is possible to remove a complete room from its original setting and place it within a new environment. The complete ornate panelled Shakespeare reading room meandered across the modernist plaza of Birmingham's Paradise Square, past the temple and through the eccentric circular voids of the post-modern collection of shifting planes to the very pinnacle of the top of the Library where it almost got lost at the end of the corridor. Semper argued that the true walls of a space are not the solid walls of construction, but the interior lining that covered these necessarily robust masonry buildings. He felt that this dressing-up of the interior space, not only conferred character upon the room, but it is also a custom as old as civilisation itself. The highly valuable disconnected lining could be transported from one location to another. Whole rooms have a distinct quality; a more direct relationship between the old and the new users and by virtue of their completeness, a great impact when relocated. Itinerant elements can be reused and manipulated, exploited and changed; an elaborate artefact may enhance a somewhat dowdy building, and confer a status that may not have previously existed. The element may lose its former meaning as the act of translation occurs when they are transported from one environment to another, but a new and fruitful relationship can be established.

FIGURE 13.13 The new facilitating elements of KPAC defiantly contrast with the existing structures.

Credit: Sally Stone

References

1. Satchell, M. (2015) On the Trail of King John Before (and After) the Signing of Magna Carta. Retrieved from www.cam.ac.uk/research/features/on-the-trail-of-king-john-before-and-after-the-signing-of-magna-carta.
2. The English word baggage comes from the old French baguer meaning to tie up, which evolved into the portable equipment of an army, including the plunder and loot. Interestingly the word Spolia also derives its name from the collection of the spoils of war. It is the practice of the winners of a battle plundering and then displaying the valuable goods of the losing side. It is also an expression used to describe a collage-like approach to remodelling of existing buildings.
3. Douglas, D. C. (1969) English Historical Documents Vol IV. Margate: Eyre & Spottiswoode.
4. Semper, G. (1851) The Four Elements of Architecture and Other Writings. Cambridge: Cambridge University Press.
5. Semper, G. (1851) The Four Elements of Architecture and Other Writings. Cambridge: Cambridge University Press.
6. Semper, G. (1851) The Four Elements of Architecture and Other Writings. Cambridge: Cambridge University Press.
7. Sega, C. (2005) "The Wall" from Constructing Architecture Materials Processes Structures: A Handbook. A. Deplazes (Ed.). Berlin, Germany: Birkhäuser, pp. 170–174.

8. Sega, C. (2005) "The Wall" from Constructing Architecture Materials Processes Structures: A Handbook. A. Deplazes (Ed.). Berlin, Germany: Birkhäuser, pp. 170–174.
9. Sega, C. (2005) "The Wall" from Constructing Architecture Materials Processes Structures: A Handbook. A. Deplazes (Ed.). Berlin, Germany: Birkhäuser, pp. 170–174.
10. Mercer, E. (1969) Furniture 700–1700. London: Weidenfeld and Nicolson, p. 116.
11. Mercer, E. (1969) Furniture 700–1700. London: Weidenfeld and Nicolson, p. 116.
12. Semper, G. (1851) The Four Elements of Architecture and Other Writings. Cambridge: Cambridge University Press.
13. Heidegger, M. (1971) "Building Dwelling Thinking" from Poetry, Language, Thought. New York: Harper & Row, pp. 143–162.
14. Derrida, Jaques (1966/1970) Structure, Sign, and Play. Macksey & Donato, p. 255.
15. Brenk, Beat (1987) "Spolia from Constantine to Charlemagne: Aesthetics Versus Ideology". Dumbarton Oaks Papers, Vol. 41, Studies on Art and Archeology in Honor of Ernst Kitzinger on His Seventy-Fifth Birthday. Dumbarton Oaks, Trustees for Harvard University, pp. 103–109.
16. Brenk, Beat (1987) "Spolia from Constantine to Charlemagne: Aesthetics Versus Ideology". Dumbarton Oaks Papers, Vol. 41, Studies on Art and Archeology in Honor of Ernst Kitzinger on His Seventy-Fifth Birthday. Dumbarton Oaks, Trustees for Harvard University, pp. 103–109.
17. Stone, S. and Brooker, G. (2011) "Spolia: Inappropriate Appropriations". Interior Tools Interior Tactics: Debates in Interior Theory and practice. Libri Publishing, pp. 223–233.

14

NEARNESS AND THINKING ABOUT DETAILS

Introduction

The individual details of an existing building can communicate the character of the original structure and thus the aspirations and needs of those that first built and occupied it, while the new elements of the adaptation facilitate the programmatic requirements of the contemporary users; thus, a symbiotic relationship is created within the strata of time and space. Old and new collide within a remodelled building, and the relationship that is established between them is dependent upon the manner in which the materials are brought together. The details or the individual features of the interior and the exterior of a building are the elements within the space that give it character and form identity. The details are the distinct components of the space, and it is the manipulation of these that becomes the expression of its use and of its users. It is through invention and ordering of the details that a space is given distinctiveness and thus is imbued with the power to represent a particular client, a brand or even a culture. It is often the surface finish of an object, element or the interior itself that communicates such an identity and character. The material quality of an interior is often the first point of contact for the user of the space and a well-crafted texture, or a thoughtful choice of components, will lend meaning to that interior. The choice and manner in which surfaces are organised is a response to the nature of the original space or building, the requirements of the client and of course the agenda of the designer.

It is interesting to note the etymology of the word 'detailed', which comes from the French for 'cut in pieces', thus the idea that any environment is constructed from many smaller parts, all of which contribute towards the greater whole. Marco Frascari in his seminal essay, 'The Tell-The-Tale Detail' (1), sums this up: 'In the details are the possibilities of innovation and invention, and it is through these that architects can give harmony to the most uncommon and difficult or disorderly environment generated by a culture.'

The manner in which a building is detailed, and the organisational system employed to arrange the details, will encourage the user of the space to behave in a particular manner. A handrail will invite someone to clasp it and its position will encourage them to glide easily between levels, or leap from the ground up the first few steps; a decorated opening will urge someone to look through it, the more grand the decoration, then the greater importance bestowed upon the view; while the grain of a floor finish will embolden someone to speed up, to act with haste and hustle, or maybe to slow down, to take their time, to ponder the nature of the space that they are situated within. This leads Juhani Pallasma in his book *The Eyes of the Skin* (2005) to describe: 'The door handle is the handshake of the building' (2).

6a Architects has designed a small shop for one of Britain's foremost fashion designers, Paul Smith. He is recognised for his creative aesthetic, which combines tradition and modernity; that is, the concept that the classical heritage can be appropriated and updated, but it is still recognisable. His work draws upon the quirky but not the frivolous; it is eccentric but not silly. This is the same approach that the architects took; they build upon the familiar lines and motifs found within traditional areas of London by using cast iron as the primary material for the new façade of the building. This is a material that is highly familiar, but maybe overlooked within the city streets, the railings, gratings, balconies, and lampposts. The ornamental language of this street furniture combined with the eighteenth century ground-level shop front was reinterpreted and then abstracted to form a sinuous pattern of interlocking circles. This ornamental design was then cast into a collection of panels that were slotted together to form a new solid iron façade. Another contextual allusion is the curved windows that project from the darkly textured iron, a direct reference to the curved glass of the nearby arcades. The textured façade is imbued with an intimacy; it invites passers-by to touch it, to feel the raised patterns of the surface. The material is traditional, but used in a highly contemporary manner, so that the building has the quality of always having been there, but also looking incredibly new. The façade is intriguing from a distance, but upon close examination, it contains the quality of nearness, of becoming greater, of giving more (see Figures 14.1, 14.2 and 14.3).

Nearness

It could be argued that within architecture and design, certain details contain this nearness. These details often belong to their region and in a way epitomise the local character and thus could not have been conceived of elsewhere. They are things of the region, therefore are not remote, but are close-up, immediate and near. Kenneth Frampton argues that one of the significant foundations of 'regionalist culture' is the independence of a region or city in terms of its culture, economy and politics (3). Some ten years later, Tzonis and Lefaivre elaborate upon this: 'What distinguishes the "regionalist" from the simply "regional" is that it incorporates regional elements into design as a means not only of adapting to local condition but also of criticising an architectural order that claims universal application' (4).

FIGURE 14.1 The cast iron façade of the Paul Smith Store, London, by 6a Architects, 2013, draws for inspiration upon the street furniture of the immediate location.

Credit: Sally Stone

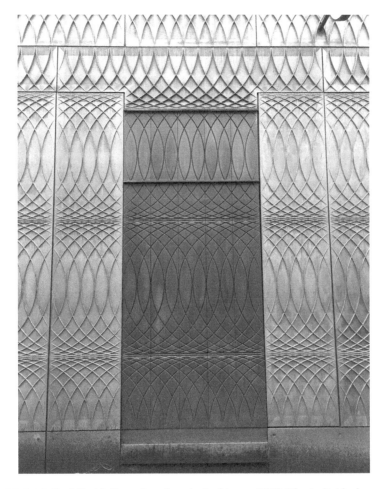

FIGURE 14.2 Paul Smith Store, London, 6a Architects, 2013. The individual panels are a contemporary interpretation of a traditional design.

Credit: Sally Stone

Possibly the greatest exponent of regional adaptation is, of course, Carlo Scarpa. His work could not have been produced anywhere other than the exact position of its implementation, so completely was it tied to place. Although he was a confirmed and authentic Modernist architect, he managed to combine the search for movement and the use of modern materials with a deep belonging to the region. Scarpa was born, lived, studied and worked in Venice; he was inspired by the city's constant and close-up relationship with climate and nature, in particular, the power of water. This is the constant concern in Venice: the height of the tide, the imminence of the Aqua Alta, the frequency of the rain, and then of course, how all of this is controlled and lived with. Water can cause chaos and disruption as much as it provides the means of

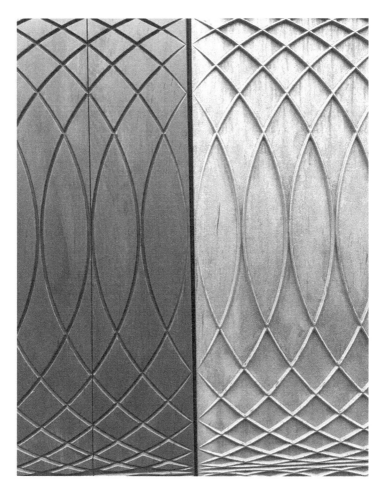

FIGURE 14.3 The ornamental language of the Paul Smith Store, London 6a Architects, 2013, directly references the eighteenth century cast iron balconies on the buildings in the surrounding neighbourhood.

Credit: Sally Stone

transport and communication, and therefore imbues the place with great beauty and the sense of time and decay, and thus also instils a certain nostalgia.

Scarpa regarded the process of detailed design not as something that would happen towards the end of a project, but as the prime generator for the architecture. He would examine the existing structure, investigate its nature, understand its character and then through a process of negotiation begin the activity of adaptation. Interestingly at a time when other Modernist architects were striving for smooth purity with unadulterated surfaces, Scarpa embraced texture, ornamentation and decoration. He believed that decoration had the ability to express the beauty of life and certainly he was against the definition of spaces represented by unadorned solidity and rudimentary formalisation (5). He did not focus on ornamentation in such the extreme manner of such architects as Antoni Gaudi, but he combined many of the aspects of Modernism, which he refined, re-evaluated and combined with his connection to the region to express his own ingenuity in Architecture. This is particularly noticeable in the designs for the Querini Stampalia Foundation in Venice. This adaptation of a Venetian Palazzo is an exquisite piece of manipulated space that links the canal at the front of the building with the rear garden by creating a flowing and almost fluid interior. The details are just as well considered; the ziggurat theme that Scarpa uses again and again in his work is used to create a fretwork marble box to contain the heating system, and the great steel gates that allow the water form the canal to flow into the building at high-tide appear to fluctuate with the movement of the water. But it is the recital hall that really shows how this delicate attention to detail could create a room seemingly in motion. The walls and the floor are clad in marble, and the great flags are arranged in an orthogonal pattern that appears to flow slightly diagonally across the room. The floor rises up the walls to create a datum at Aqua-Alta height and the entrance has just slipped away from the centre of the space. Within the room, the visitor is continually reminded of the proximity of the lagoon, of the connection that the city has with the sea and the sheer nearness of the water (see Figures 14.4 and 14.5).

Serial Vision

Gordon Cullen touched upon the importance of nearness in his seminal book, *Townscape*. Here he describes the great beauty of places that have evolved over time, that have grown and developed in tune with both the needs of the local population, but also with great regard for the vernacular materials, forms and traditions of the area. The relationships that are established within the collective buildings of the urban environment create places that are unique and exuberant. He developed a way of looking at and understanding a place based upon its revelation through walking, this he called 'Serial Vision' (6). This comprehension of a situation through a collection of views or experiences is something that he regarded as not just a way of understanding a place, but also as a design tool for the development and redevelopment of it. Serial Vision is a continuum of experiences that allows the visitor to really feel the nature and character of the environment they are visiting or inhabiting; whether this is inside, outside or possibly both. The experience consists of a series of quite abstract and generic terms, such as: thereness, undulation, closure, bluntness, intimacy, incident and narrows. It is within narrows that he uses the expression nearness: 'The crowding together of buildings forms a pressure, an unavoidable nearness of detail, which is in direct contrast to the wide piazza' (7).

Thus nearness has less to do with proximity and is much more associated with intimacy, which is directly linked with close acquaintance or connection. So nearness is about the character and the proximity of the object or material. Kenneth Frampton describes Alvaro Siza as a Regionalist architect explaining that he has

FIGURE 14.4 Querini Stampalia Foundation, Venice, Carlo Scarpa, 1963. The collection of subtle interventions facilitates the needs of the new users of the building using a language that is obviously contemporary, yet is not out of place within the ancient atmosphere of the city.

Credit: Sally Stone

FIGURE 14.5 Querini Stampalia Foundation, Venice, Carlo Scarpa, 1963. The building is so sympathetic to the nature of the place that as the tide rises, water is allowed to enter into the foyer, thus reinforcing the relationship between the lagoon, the city and the room.

Credit: Sally Stone

FIGURE 14.6 The Chiado area of Lisbon remodelled in 1988 by Alvaro Siza after the devastating fire. New connections between the city centre and the convent at the top of the hill were established.

Credit: Sally Stone

extraordinary sensitivity towards local materials, craft work and above all to the subtleties of local light (8). Alvaro Siza was commissioned to remodel the Chiado area of Lisbon after the devastating fire of 1988. The approach that the architect took was to strip away many centuries of accretions and accumulations to leave a pure collection of buildings and spaces. A simple route was then inserted into the space to create a much needed but hitherto difficult connection between the convent at the top of the hill and the main street at the bottom. The details are highly sympathetic to the area, they are simple but beautifully crafted, robust and again exhibit an almost timeless quality (see Figure 14.6).

Detailed Consideration

This same sense of nearness can be created within the remodelled building. The details of the new and the old can crowd together to create a sense of completeness, but also things far apart can be directly related to each other to form a composite whole. Detailed design is to a certain extent more than a close-up exploration, examination and manipulation of the material finishes. It is most importantly explored at the junction between things; at the point where the old meets the new, where one age touches another, or when two different aspects come into contact. This junction or joint can either be hidden, suppressed, almost negated, or it can be celebrated, it can be elaborated upon and given prime importance within the building. When Caruso St John was asked to design the new galleries at the Sir John Soane Museum in London, they settled upon an approach that complimented the highly innovative and influential building, rather than contrasted with it. Sir John Soane gradually converted three townhouses to contain a home for his family and an office for his practice over 30 years at the beginning of the nineteenth century. The collection of buildings were left to the nation and is now a museum dedicated to the legacy and collection of the man. His remodelling is ingenious and is regarded by many as the most significant domestic scale building ever constructed:

> We are interested in the emotional effect that buildings can have. We are interested in how buildings have been built in the past and how new constructions can achieve an equivalent formal and material presence. We are confused by the laissez faire state of contemporary architecture. In this environment of excess we have found ourselves attracted to the more intimate artistic ambitions of past architectural traditions. We feel more comfortable than we once did to follow these traditions quite closely. Anything that can contribute to the fragile continuities between the contemporary situation and past architectures is worth the effort. It is only by understanding and reflecting on the past that architecture can continue to be a relevant, social and artistic discipline.
>
> *9*

Caruso St John designed a small collection of exhibition cases and other furniture to facilitate a new small gallery, a shop and entrance. Their design exhibits the same lightness of touch, the same attention to detail and choice of sympathetic materials as Soane. The furniture has been designed to exactly inhabit the rooms, to fit snuggly within the space, so that it is almost as if it were always there, but the language, which at first glance appears to be from that earlier period, is obviously much more contemporary. Changes in the technological production of such materials as glass means that it is now possible to manufacture huge clean and pure elements, something that was almost impossible in Soane's time, so the scale and strength of the pieces gives it away. The junctions are minimal, almost akin to the minimalist sculptures of Richard Serra or Donald Judd. But the intentions are clear, not to fight with the building, but to compliment and complete it, to create an intimate exploration of the existing and the new.

Another project created at approximately this time by the same architects was a series of small facilitating interventions at the Tate Britain, London. The first phase included some remedial repair work and the installation of a sustainable environmental control system, plus the design of an exquisite spiral staircase. This intimate object solves the conundrum of the hitherto problematic link between the ground floor and the basement within the rotunda. It is a visual reminder that the gallery is a progressive

FIGURE 14.7 The new staircase in the Tate Britain, London, by Caruso St John Architects, 2013, creates a direct link between the ground floor and the basement.
Credit: Sally Stone

and forward-thinking establishment, while also creating a logical entrance sequence within what was previously a difficult space (see Figures 14.7, 14.8, 14.9 and 14.10).

The balustrade is decorated, and thus retains the memory of the nineteenth century origin of the gallery, and yet is also utterly contemporary. The new floor is made of terrazzo, and the pattern is derived from the original marble mosaic finish. The method of construction and the pattern are so obviously digitally conceived that they could only be from the twenty-first century. The very limited colour palette means that the staircase is strikingly arresting, but also comfortable; it has the qualities of always having been there, but seemingly very new at the same time. Thus the detailed design of the staircase affords within the visitor the sense of time

FIGURE 14.8 Digital modelling allowed the architects, Caruso St John, to create a delightful, detailed and complex ornamental pattern within the new staircase at the Tate Britain, London.

Credit: Sally Stone

and space, of intimacy with the immediate, but also a connection with the much larger completeness of the building.

Distancelessness versus Nearness

Bigness is the idea that what you see in the distance is the same as what you see up close. A building or interior has certain qualities when observed from far away,

FIGURE 14.9 The decorative pattern on the balustrade of the new circular staircase at the Tate Britain by Caruso St John Architects, 2013, is derived from the patterned mosaics of the original marble floor.

Credit: Sally Stone

and the character, nature and articulation of the building is completely apparent from a particular distance, one that allows the viewer to comprehend the complete building. This is then exactly the same impression that the viewer will observe when close to the building; there are no surprises, no further articulation and no elaboration of the junctions. The details are almost hidden, so that they are secondary to the impression of the whole; the complete is much greater than the individual parts. This approach is actually much more difficult to achieve than would first be thought of. The architect or designer must be able to manipulate the form and the materials so that the junctions and the convergence of materials is both smooth and appears inconsequential. Although Bigness is a term that emerged to describe a specific strand of late twentieth and early twenty-first century particularly Dutch

FIGURE 14.10 Detail of the historically sensitive and highly site specific cast Terrazzo balustrade of the helical staircase at the Tate Britain by Caruso St John Architects, 2013.

Credit: Sally Stone

architecture, Palladio could be regarded as a great exponent of the art. The magnificent sixteenth century church, Il Redentore, on the Giudecca in Venice, for example, was designed to be observed from across the Giudecca Canal. The pilasters on the triple façade are articulated so that the apparent layering of the three apparently separate elevations have been fused into a single composite face. The building is no more complex when observed from immediately next to the building, everything is just bigger; it is closer, but no more elaborate (see Figure 14.11).

Of course, it was the contemporary Dutch architects who took this idea much further. Rem Koolhaas explored the concept in the book, *Delirious New York*. He implied a latent 'Theory of BIGNESS' (10) based on the idea that beyond a certain size, the architectural gesture is the over-ridding generator of form, and that all of the other elements are subservient to that form. This includes the interior, which does not have to have any real connection with the exterior, it is merely contained by it. The China Central Television Headquarters in Beijing, designed by Rem Koolhaas' architecture firm, OMA, in 2004 in partnership with the engineering firm Arup is

FIGURE 14.11   The sixteenth century Redentore church, on the edge of the Giudecca Island, Venice, by Andrea Palladio, is intended to be viewed from across the wide expanse of the great canal.

Credit: Sally Stone

a massive building with an over-riding formal concept that overpowers all other aspects of the structure. Thus everything is equally near or far, close or remote.

Nearness is the opposite of this; the building becomes more complex, more articulated and thus has equal expression whether viewed from afar or close-up, it is just that the expression is different. The difference between this distantlessness and nearness is something that Heidegger grappled with. The remoteness created by distance is very levelling; it is something that creates sameness or cultural homogeneity. Everything is swept into a distance-less consistency. 'What is happening if, when we eliminate great distances, everything stands equally near and remote? What is this uniformity, within which everything is neither near nor remote – without distance, as it were?' (11). This is, to a certain extent, a precursor of the formal gesturing of Bigness.

Heidegger further complicated the discussion by arguing that just because something was close-up, that it was within reach, it did not necessarily confer nearness upon it. Nearness is much more connected with the psychological interaction between the object or thing and the person:

> However, the hasty elimination of all distances does not bring about nearness; for nearness does not consist in a small measure of distance. Something that stands closest to us in terms of distance – through images in film, through sound on the radio – can remain remote from us.
>
> *12*

The thing and its nearness interact. The thing encompasses nearness because its very nature is exposed, not because it is close-up. If the object, detail or thing contains honesty, that is, honesty of materials and function, then it also contains nearness. And it is this honesty of purpose that Heidegger was endeavouring to discuss. He uses the example of the unpretentious jug or pitcher, which was constructed to do a simple job in a clear and humble manner. The jug, which performs its task so well, contains Heidegger's nearness because it is determined upon its simple task (13).

Thus there is a direct connection between the idea of nearness and the user of the space; it is the physical experience of being that makes something or somewhere near. Embrechts, Manders and Somers argue 'that any architecture of nearness implies the dynamic involvement of the future inhabitants' (14). How something is detailed, how it feels, what it is like to touch, the texture, smell, the intimate connection that the user has with an object imbues it with that air of nearness.

References

1. Frascari, Marco (1984/1996) "The Tell-The-Tale Detail" from Theorizing a New Agenda for Architecture an Anthology of Architectural Theory 1965–1995. Kate Nesbitt (Ed.). New York: Princeton Architectural Press, p. 501.
2. Pallasma, Juhani (2005) The Eyes of the Skin. London: John Wiley and Sons, p. 56.
3. Frampton, Kenneth (1983/1996) "Prospects for a Critical Regionalism" from Theorizing a New Agenda for Architecture an Anthology of Architectural Theory 1965–1995. Kate Nesbitt (Ed.). New York: Princeton Architectural Press, p. 470.
4. Tzonis, A. and Lefaivre L. (1990) "Why Critical Regionalism Today?" from Theorizing a New Agenda for Architecture an Anthology of Architectural Theory 1965–1995. Kate Nesbitt (Ed.). New York: Princeton Architectural Press, p. 486.
5. Albertini, B. and Bagnoli, S. (1988) Scarpa Architecture in Details. trans. D. Mills. London: Architecture Design and Technology Press Limited, p. 30.
6. Cullen, Gordon (1961) The Concise Townscape. London: Routledge, p. 45.
7. Cullen, Gordon (1961) The Concise Townscape. London: Routledge, p. 45.
8. Frampton, Kenneth (1983/1996) "Prospects for a Critical Regionalism" from Theorizing a New Agenda for Architecture an Anthology of Architectural Theory 1965–1995. Kate Nesbitt (Ed.). New York: Princeton Architectural Press, p. 473.
9. Caruso, Adam (2004) Traditions. Amsterdam, Netherlands: OASE (Issue 65 'Ornamentation').

10. Koolhaas, R. (1994) Delirious New York; a Retroactive Manifesto for Manhattan. New York: Monacelli Press.
11. Heidegger, M. (1949/2009) "Bremen Lectures: Insights Into That Which Is" from The Heidegger Reader (ed. Figal) (trans J.Veith). Indiana University Press, p. 254.
12. Heidegger, M. (1949/2009) "Bremen Lectures: Insights Into That Which Is" from The Heidegger Reader (ed. Figal) (trans J.Veith). Indiana University Press, p. 254.
13. Heidegger, M. (1949/2009) "Bremen Lectures: Insights Into That Which Is" from The Heidegger Reader (ed. Figal) (trans J.Veith). Indiana University Press, p. 254.
14. Embrechts, Karen, Manders, Coby and Somers, Inge (2010) "Nearness" from Interiors Wor[l]ds. Luca B. Peressut, Imma Forino, Gennaro Posiglione and Roberto Rizzi (Eds). Umberto Allemandi & C. Torino, pp. 107–111.

FURTHER READING

Theory

Boyer, Christine (1994) The City of Collective Memory. Its Historical Imagery and Architectural Entertainments. Cambridge MA: MIT Press.

Colomina, Beatriz (1994) Privacy and Publicity, Modern Architecture as Mass Media. Cambridge MA: MIT Press.

Cullen, Gordon (1961) Townscape. London: Architectural Press.

de Sola-Morales Rubio, I. (1985) From Contrast to Analogy. Lotus International No. 46, p. 37.

Frampton, Kenneth (1983/1996) "Prospects for a Critical Regionalism" from Theorizing a New Agenda for Architecture an Anthology of Architectural Theory 1965–1995. Kate Nesbitt (Ed.). New York: Princeton Architectural Press.

Gregotti, Vittorio (1984) Architecture as Modification. Casabella 498–9, Jan/Feb.

Gregotti, Vittorio (1996) Inside Architecture. Cambridge MA: MIT Press.

Holl, Steven (1999) Anchoring. New York: Princeton Architectural Press.

Hollis, E. (2010) The Secret Lives of Buildings. London: Portobello Books.

Hollis, E. (2013) The Memory Palace: A Book of Lost Interiors. London: Portabello Books.

Krier, Rob (1993) Architectural Composition. New York: Rizzoli.

Leach, N. (Ed.) (1997) Rethinking Architecture. London: Routledge.

Leatherbarrow, David (2000) Uncommon Ground. Cambridge MA: MIT Press.

Leatherbarrow, David (1993) On The Life of Buildings in Time. Cambridge MA; London: MIT Press.

Meinig, D. and Jackson, J. (1979) The Interpretation of Ordinary Buildings: Geographical Essays. Oxford: Oxford University Press.

Marot, Sébastien (2003) Sub-Urbanism and the Art of Memory. London: AA Publications.

Richarz, C. Schulz, C. Friedemann, Z. (2007) Detail Practice: Energy Efficient Upgrades. Berkhäuser: Basel – Boston – Berlin.

Rossi, Aldo (1982) The Architecture of the City. Cambridge MA: MIT Press.

Rowe, Colin and Koetter, Fred (1984) Collage City. Cambridge MA: MIT Press.

Rowe, Colin and Slutzky, Robert (1997) Transparency. Berlin, Germany: Birkhäuser.

Schumacher, Thomas L. (1971/1996) "Contextualism: Urban Ideals and Deformations. Cassabella no. 359–360" from Theorizing a New Agenda for Architecture. Kate Nesbit (Ed.). New York: Princeton Architectural Press, pp. 79–86.

Silvetti, Jorge (1996) "Interactive Realms" from Modernism and History. Alexander von Hoffman (Ed.). Cambridge, MA: Harvard University Press.

Venturi, Robert and Brown, Denise Scott (1977) Complexity and Contradiction in Architecture. 2nd ed. London: The Architectural Press.

Venturi, Scott-Brown and Izenour. (1977) Learning from Las Vegas. Cambridge MA: MIT Press.

Vesely, Dalibor (2004) Architecture in the Age of Divided Representation. Cambridge MA: MIT Press.

von Hoffmann, A. (Ed.) (1997) Form, Modernism, and History: Essays in Honor of Eduard F. Seckler. Harvard University Press.

Avant Garde and Continuity

Corbusier, L, Loos, A and van de Beek, J. (1998) Raumplan Versus Plan Libre. New York: Rizzoli.

de Sola-Morales Rubio, I. (1985) From Contrast to Analogy. Italy: Lotus International No. 46.

Diamond, R. and Wang, W. (Eds) (1995) On Continuity. 9H No.9. New York: 9H Publications.

Grassi, Giorgio (1998) in Oppositions Reader. K. Michael Hays (Ed.). New York: Princeton Architectural Press.

Harries, Karsten (1998) The Ethical Function of Architecture. Cambridge MA: MIT Press.

Holl, Steven et al. (1998) Pamphlet Architecture 1–10. Princeton: Princeton Architectural Press.

Riegl, A. (1903/1996) "The Modern Cult of the Monument: Its Character and Its Origin" from Historical and Philosophical Issues in the Conservation of Cultural Heritage. N. Price (Ed.). Canada.

Yates, Francis (1992) The Art of Memory. New York: Random House.

Environment

Brunskill, R. W. (1971) Illustrated Handbook of Vernacular Architecture. London: Faber and Faber.

Carroon, J. (2010) Sustainable Preservation: Greening Existing Buildings. Hoboken NJ: Wiley.

Hoskins, W. G. (1955) The Making of the English Landscape. London: Hodder and Stoughton.

Mostafavi, Mohsen and Leatherbarrow, David (1993) On Weathering: The Life of Buildings in Time. Cambridge MA: MIT Press.

Mostafavi, Mohsen and Doherty, G. (2010) Ecological Urbanism. Zurich: Lars Müller Publishing.

Penoyre, John and Penoyre, Jane (1978) Houses in the Landscape. London: Faber and Faber.

Hawkes, Dean (2012) Architecture and Climate. Abingdon and New York: Routledge.

Lovelock, J. (2007) The Revenge of Gaia. London: Penguin.

McDonough, W. and Braungart, M. (2009) Cradle to Cradle: Rethinking the Way We Make Things. London: Vintage.

Penoyre, G. and Prasad, S. (2014) Retrofit for Purpose: Low Energy Renewal of Non-Domestic Buildings. London: RIBA Publishing.

Troi, A. and Bastian, Z. (2015) Energy Efficient Solutions for Historic Buildings: A Handbook. Basel: Birkhauser.

Building

Deplazes, Andrea (Ed.) (2005) Constructing Architecture: Materials Processes Structures: A Handbook. Basel: Birkhäuser.

Frampton, K. and Cava, J. (1995) Studies in Tectonic Culture: The Poetics of Construction in Nineteenth and Twentieth Century Architecture. Cambridge, Mass: MIT Press.

Habraken, N. J.; Teicher, Jonathan (Ed.) (1998) The Structure of the Ordinary. Cambridge MA: MIT Press.

Hartoonian, G. (1997) Ontology of Construction. Cambridge: Cambridge University Press.

Schittich, C. (2006) In Detail: Building Skins. Berlin: Birkhauser.

Detail and Ornamnt

Finessi, B. (1997) Enzo Mari: The Small as Method. Italy: Rassegna.

Frascari, Marco (1984) "The Tell-the-Tale Detail" by in Via 7: The Building of Architecture. Cambridge MA: MIT Press, pp. 23–37. Also in Kate Nesbitt (Ed.) (1996) Theorizing a New Agenda for Architecture an Anthology of Architectural Theory 1965–1995. New York: Princeton Architectural Press.

Cadwell, M. (2007) Strange Details. Writing Architecture. Cambridge MA: MIT Press.

Adaptation

Memory/ Memoria, a+t 17.2001.

Bloszies, C. (2012) Architectural Transformations: Old Buildings, New Designs. New York: Princeton Architectural Press.

Brooker, Graeme and Stone, Sally (2007) Form and Structure. Lausanne: AVA.

Brooker, Graeme and Stone, Sally (2008) Context and Environment. Lausanne: AVA .

Brooker, Graeme and Stone, Sally (2009) Elements and Objects. Lausanne: AVA.

Cantacuzino, S. (1975) New Uses for Old Buildings. London: The Architectural Press.

Cramer, Johannes and Breitling, Stefan (2007) Architecture in Existing Fabric. Basel: Birkäuser.

Kirtich, John and Eakin, Garret (1993) Interior Architecture. New York: Van Nostrand Reinhold.

Littlefield, David and Lewis, Saskia (2007) Architectural Voices. Chichester: Wiley.

Machado, R. (1976) "Old Buildings as Palimpsest" from Progressive Architecture. 57 (11) pp. 46–49. Stamford: Reinhold Publishing.

Petzet, Muck and Heilmeyer, Florian (2012) Reduce Reuse Recycle. Hatje Cantz (Ed.).

Robert, Philippe (1989) Adaptations: New Uses for Old Buildings. New York: Princeton Architectural Press.

Schittich, Christian (Ed.) (2003) Building in Existing Fabric. Munich: Birkhäuser Edition Detail.

Scott, Fred (2007) On Altering Architecture. Abingdon: Routledge.

Stone, Sally and Brooker, Graeme (2004) Rereadings. London: RIBA.

Stone, Sally and Brooker, Graeme (2013) From Organisation to Decoration: A Routledge Reader of Interiors. Abingdon: Routledge.

Stone, Sally and Brooker, Graeme (2018) Rereadings. Volume 2. London: RIBA.

Wong, Liliane (2017) Adaptive Reuse: Extending the Lives of Buildings. Basel: Birkhäuser.

Inside

Benjamin, Walter (1999) The Arcades Project. Cambridge, Mass: Belknap/Harvard.

Brooker, Graeme and Stone, Sally (2009) What is Interior Design. Mies: Rotovision.

Evans, Robin (1997) Translation from Drawing to Building and Other Essays. London: AA Publications.

Geist, J. F. (1985) Arcades. Cambridge MA: MIT Press.

O'Donnell, Caroline (2015) Niche Tactics. New York: Routledge.

Pimlott, Mark (2007) Without and Within. Rotterdam: Episode.

Pollak, Sabine (2003) "Culture of Living" from Roberto Rizzi (Ed.) Civilization of Living: The Evolution of European Domestic Interiors. Milan: Edizioni Lybra Immagine.

Praz, Mario (1982) An Illustrated History of Interior Decoration. London: Thames and Hudson.

Rice, Charles (2007) The Emergence of the Interior. Abingdon: Routledge.

Schittich, Christian (Ed.) (2002) Interior Spaces. Basel: Birkhäuser Edition Detail.

Sparke, Penny (2008) The Modern Interior. London: Reaktion Books.

Thornton, Peter (1993) Authentic Décor: The Domestic Interior 1620–1920. London: Weidenfeld and Nicolson.

Wharton, Edith and Codman, Jr, Ogden (1898) The Historical Tradition, The Decoration of Houses BT Batsford. London: B T Batsford.

Outside

Aben, Rob (1999) Saskia de Wit. The Enclosed Garden. Rotterdam: 010 Publishers.

Canniffe, Eamonn (2006) Urban Ethic. Abingdon: Routledge.

Canniffe, Eamonn (2008) The Politics of the Piazza. Abingdon: Routledge.

Crane, N. (2016) The Making of the British Landscape. London: Weidenfield & Nicolson.

Gehl, Jan (1936/2006) Life Between the Buildings: Using Public Space. 6th ed. Copenhagen: Danish Architectural Press.

Gehl, Jan (2013) How to Study Public Life. Washington, Covelo, London: Island Press.

Jacobs, Jane (1961) The Death and Life of Great American Cities. New York: Random House.

Kostof, Spiro (1991) The City Shaped. London: Thames & Hudson.

Lynch, Kevin (1960) The Image of the City. Cambridge MA: MIT Press.

Rowe, Peter G. (1999) Civic Realism. Cambridge MA: MIT Press.

Welter, V. and Lawson, J. (2000) The City after Patrick Geddes. Oxford: Peter Lang.

Conservation and Heritage

Glendinning, M. (2013) The Conservation Movement A History of Architectural Preservation Antiquity to Modernity. London: Routledge.

Hems, Alison and Blockley, Marion (Eds) (2006) Heritage Interpretation. Abingdon: Routledge.

Jokilehto, J. (1999) A History of Architectural Conservation. London: Routledge.

Morris, W. and Webb, P. (1877) "The SPAB Manifesto". [online] The Society for the Protection of Ancient Buildings: www.spab.org.uk/about-us/spab-manifesto, accessed 23 December 2017.

Pevsner, N. (1980) "Ruskin and Violett-le-Duc" from Eugène Emmanuel Violett-le-Duc. P. Farrant, et al. London: Academy Editions.

Schofield, J. (2016) St Paul's Cathedral: Archaeology and History. Oxford: Oxbow Books.
Strike, James (1994) Architecture in Conservation. Abingdon: Routledge.
Welter, V. (2002) Biopolis: Patrick Geddes and the City of Life. Cambridge MA: MIT Press.
Woodward, Christopher (2002) In Ruins. London: Vintage.

Use

Duffy, Frank (1997) The New Office. London: Conran Octopus.
Duffy, Frank (2008) Working and the City. London: Black Dog.
Myerson, J. (2008) After Modernism: The Contemporary Office Environment. Manchester: Manchester University Press.
Turkel, S. (2011) Alone Together. New York: Basic Books.

Places

Goy, R. (1997) Venice: The City and its Architecture. London: Phaidon Press Limited.
Haslan, Dave (1999) Manchester England The Story of the Pop Cult City. London: Fourth Estate.
Morris, Jan (1974) Venice. London: Faber and Faber.
Parkinson-Bailey, John (2000) Manchester: An Architectural History. Manchester: Manchester University Press.

Architects and Buildings

Aurelli, P. V. (2012) Form and Resistance: A Conversation with Caruso St John. Madrid: El Croquis, p. 166.
Crinson, Mark (Ed.) (2009) James Stirling: Early and Unpublished Writings on Architecture. Abingdon: Routledge.
de Carlo, Giancarlo (1992) Benedict Zucchi. Oxford: Butterworth Architecture.
de Carlo, Giancarlo (2004) "Tortuosity" from Domus. 866, January, pp. 24–25.
Kahn, L. (1986) What Will Be Has Always Been. New York: Rizzoli.
Kleihues, J. P. (1989) The Museum Projects. New York: Rizzoli.
Moore, Rowan and Ryan, Raymund (2000) Building the Tate Modern. Tate Galley Publishing.
O'Donnell, Tuomey (2014) Space for Architecture, The Work of O'Donnell + Tuomey. Artifice books on architecture.
Siza, Álvaro (1994) Alvaro Siza: Works and Projects 1954–1992. Barcelona: Gustavo Gili.
Siza, Álvaro (2014) The Function of Beauty. Carlos Castanheira. London and New York: Phaidon Press.
Siza, A. L., Frampton, K. and Ddc. (2000) Álvaro Siza: Complete Works. London: Phaidon.
Ursprung, P. (2002) Herzog & de Meuron: Natural History. Montreal: Lars Muller Publishers.

Spatial Agency

Aston, Helen and White, Stefan (2011) Not Content: Projects for a Shared City. Devon: Book Publishing.
Awat, Nishat, Schneider, Tatjana and Till, Jeremy (2011) Spatial Agency: Other Ways of Doing Architecture. Abingdon: Routledge.
Jones, Peter Blundell, Pettescu, Doina and Till, Jeremy (2005) Architecture and Participation. Abingdon: Taylor & Francis.

Art

Benjamin, Andrew (1993) Installation Art. Art and Design Profile no 30. Academy Art and the Tectonic. Art and Design. Academy.

de Olivira, Nicolas, Oxley, Nicola and Petry, Michael (1994) Installation Art. Abingdon: Thames and Hudson.

Irwin, R. (1985) Being and Circumstance – Notes Towards a Conditional Art. Culver City: Lapis.

Lee, Pamela M. (1999) Objects to be Destroyed: The Work of Gordon Matta-Clarke. Cambridge MA: MIT Press.

Rendell, J. (2010) Site-Writing. London: I B Tauris.

Robbins, Mark (1992) Angles of Incidence. New York: Princeton Architectural Press.

History

Cappezutto, Rita (April 2002) Confronting the Architecture of Evil. *Domus*, p. 90.

Crouch, Dora P. (1984) History of Architecture. New York: McGraw Hill.

Dennis, Michael (1986) Court and Garden. Cambridge MA: MIT Press.

Jenkins, Keith (1991) Rethinking History. London and New York: Routledge.

Jones, Peter Blundell and Canniffe, Eamonn (2007) Modern Architecture Through Case Studies 1945–1990. Architectural Press.

Klotz, Heinrich (1998) The History of Postmodern Architecture. Cambridge MA: MIT Press.

Rybczynski, Witold (1987) Home: A Short History of an Idea. Harmondsworth: Penguin.

Other Stuff

Arendt, H. (1958) The Human Condition. Chicago: University of Chicago Press, §2.

Benjamin, Walter (1955/1992) The Work of Art in the Age of Mechanical Reproduction in Illuminations. New York: Fontana Press.

Connell, John and Gibson, Chris (2003) Sound Tracks Popular Music, Identity and Place. London and New York: Routledge.

Eco, U. (1989) The Open Work. Cambridge: Harvard University Press.

Evans, Robin (1995) The Projective Cast. Cambridge MA: MIT Press.

Firebrace, William (2001) Things Worth Seeing: A Guide to the City of W. London: Black Dog Publishing.

Foucault, M. (1977) Discipline and Punish. New York: Vintage.

Hopper, Dennis (2001) A System of Moments. Germany: Hatje Cantz Verlag.

Hyde, Rory (2013) Future Practice: Conversations from the Edge of Architecture. Oxon: Taylor & Francis.

Mitchell, William (1995) City of Bits: Space Place and the Infobahn. Rotterdam: Nai101 Publishers.

Svabo, C. and Shanks, M. (2015) "Experience as Excursion: A Note towards a Metaphysics of Design Thinking" from Experience Design: Concepts and Case Studies. P. Benz (Ed.) London: Bloomsbury.

Vidler, Anthony (2008) Histories of the Immediate Present: Inventing Architectural Modernism. Cambridge MA: MIT Press.

Vidler, Anthony (1992) The Architectural Uncanny. Cambridge MA: MIT Press.

INDEX